The New Keynesian Economics

The New Keynesian Economics

Unemployment, Search and Contracting

Jeff Frank

Lecturer in Economics
University of Essex

WHEATSHEAF BOOKS

First published in Great Britain in 1986 by
WHEATSHEAF BOOKS LTD
A MEMBER OF THE HARVESTER PRESS GROUP
Publisher: John Spiers
Director of Publications: Edward Elgar
16 Ship Street, Brighton, Sussex

British Library Cataloguing in Publication Data

Frank, Jeff
   The new Keynesian economics : unemployment,
   search and contracting.
   1. Macroeconomics
   I. Title
   339   HB172.5

   ISBN 0–7108–0239–0
   ISBN 0–7108–0244–7 Pbk

Typeset in Times by Photo·graphics, Honiton, Devon

**Printed and bound in Great Britain by
Biddles Ltd, Guildford and King's Lynn**

THE HARVESTER GROUP
The Harvester Group comprises Harvester Press Ltd (chiefly publishing literature, fiction, philosophy, psychology, and science and trade books); Harvester Press Microform Publications Ltd (publishing in microform previously unpublished archives, scarce printed sources, and indexes to these collections); Wheatsheaf Books Ltd (chiefly publishing in economics, international politics, sociology, women's studies and related social sciences); Certain Records Ltd and John Spiers Music Ltd (music publishing).

To my Parents

I am beginning to catch sight of what I might call the 'deep-lying subject' of my book. It is—it will be—no doubt, the rivalry between the real world and the representation of it which we make to ourselves. The manner in which the world of appearances imposes itself upon us, and the manner in which we try to impose on the outside world our own interpretation—this is the drama of our lives. The resistance of facts invites us to transport our ideal construction into the realm of dreams ...

André Gide, *The Counterfeiters*,
trans. Dorothy Bussy
[New York, Alfred A. Knopf, 1927, p. 189]

Contents

Figures

Tables

Foreword

This is a book about economic theory and is written in the form of abstract models, using technical notation and formulations. Yet, if it is to be any good at all, it must seek to address the true issues in macroeconomics: the demoralisation caused by unemployment, among new graduates from the universities and among miners; the continuing poverty of individuals and groups in the US and the UK, despite the selective affluence; and most importantly, perhaps, the general 'mean-spiritedness' that pervades a stagnant economy as inflation induces property speculation rather than productive investment, as the lack of growth and the lessening of opportunity causes a self-centred economic orientation of individuals trying to protect their own standard of living in a non-expanding environment.

Preface

This book is intended as a self-contained study of macroeconomic theory, beginning with the traditional models and progressing into recent search and contracting analyses and their macroeconomic implications. It is written to be accessible to the undergraduate student, by leaving out unnecessarily complex mathematics, but not by avoiding difficult conceptual problems. While the book is presented as a unified whole, developing what I hope is a coherent view of macroeconomics, the two parts are rather different. The first part derives from my second-year lecture notes, and it is intended that the second-year student who reads no further in the book would nonetheless gain some understanding of macroeconomics that he would not find in the standard texts. The second part can be read to gain a basic comprehension of search and contracting as isolated models, but the more interesting elements have to do with the attempts at clarifying the relationships between the various models and in presenting, as the fundamental thesis of the book, the case for contracting in explaining macroeconomic fluctuations.

There is a very definite viewpoint throughout the book and we have attempted to state it in the title. The world seems undeniably Keynesian in a number of ways. It does not seem an adequate description of the economy to presume that there is a natural rate of unemployment that only varies, for example, when trade unions become more or less unsuitably aggressive. Rather, the unemployment rate varies with the economic environment and it varies with government policy. Economies settle into patterns of growth that may be unfavourable in comparison with past experience or with other countries. Restrictive monetary policies, at least for some time period measured in years, cause recessions and high unemployment. There is no presumption that the market system works, in the absence of government intervention, to achieve even economic efficiency, much less other social goals. The viewpoint in this book is Keynesian in that it accepts these empirical realities as the basic issues for theoretical analysis.

Yet we cannot theoretically accept the Keynesian model as it stands. The combination of aggregate demand theory and the Phillips curve, traditional post-war Keynesian economics, addresses the right questions and is not immediately inconsistent with empirical reality. The problem is that there are too many unanswered questions, and the answers are necessary before the traditional policies can safely be adopted. These questions invariably take on the form: 'What are the long-run effects?' Whether the issue is expansionary fiscal or monetary policy, or incomes policies, traditional Keynesian analysis simply does not tell us enough about what will happen over time. The reason for this is that fifty years after the publication of the *General Theory*, there is still no adequate theoretical underpinning for the model explaining the mechanisms by which it operates.

These weaknesses have provided both a theoretical and a policy motivation for a 'new' but 'Keynesian' approach to macroeconomics, a return to the traditional tools of economic theory— optimisation decisions on the part of individuals, supply and demand curves derived from these decisions, and concepts of equilibrium to aggregate into a market outcome—in an attempt to see whether a true Keynesian generalisation of neoclassical equilibrium theory can be found. For this exercise, it is time that macroeconomics moved beyond the adversarial approach, accepting the reasonable contributions from monetarists but recalling the empirical problems of unemployment that define the field of analysis. Neoclassical economists are right in insisting that a theory categorise as an equilibrium only situations where individual agents cannot do better by changing their behaviour, including their information-processing behaviour. Yet they are clearly wrong in rejecting the search for a generalised equilibrium model that incorporates the possibility of aggregate demand market failures. A theme of this book is that contracting, in conjunction with the recent trade coordination analyses in the literature, starts to provide such a model.

The existence of this book is due to encouragement from Edward Elgar representing the publisher. My work in macroeconomics goes back to my PhD dissertation written under the supervision of James Tobin. My appreciation goes to Professor Tobin, who has been perhaps the main standard-bearer for the Keynesian tradition in the United States. Besides his helpful comments on the manuscript, I also appreciate numerous useful suggestions by Gary Biglaiser, Andrew Oswald and Simon Price. None of these individuals, of course, are implicated in the viewpoints expressed in the book. I also thank my current third-year macro students, the first to use this book. Finally, I owe a special debt to the congeniality of the Essex department during the years 1981–83, and thank my colleagues and students of the time.

1 Introduction

1.1 THE NATURE OF THE PROBLEM

It is perhaps particularly appropriate in a book on economic theory to begin by considering the nature of the policy problems the theory is to address, and to examine, if only casually, some data from actual economies, presented in Tables 1.1 and 1.2. We suggest, from the data, that macroeconomic policy problems can usefully be classified by duration:

1. Recessions characterised by falls in real gross national product (GNP), rises in the unemployment rate, and falls in the inflation rate, occur throughout the period in Table 1.1 but are of generally short duration. The unemployment rate rises, in the US data, only in the years 1954, 1957–58, 1961, 1963, 1970–71, 1974–75, and 1980–82.
2. Over significant periods the performance of an economy seems to be worse than over other periods, as in the comparison of the period 1974–81 with 1960–73 in Table 1.2 (real GNP growth in the US, 2.7 *vs* 4.1, and in the UK, 0.9 *vs* 3.1).
3. Over rather extended periods an economy might seem to perform poorly in comparison to other countries, as in a comparison of UK *versus* US economic performance in Table 1.2 (with a base at 1960 of 100, the index of industrial production in the US in 1981 stood at 228 *vs* 141 for the UK, and consumer prices at 307 *vs* 600 for the UK).

Of course, interpretation of data depends upon the theoretical construction one has in mind. A Keynesian economist might, for

1

Table 1.1: *GNP growth, inflation, and unemployment rates in the USA and UK (%)*

	Real GNP growth		Inflation		Unemployment Rate	
	USA	UK	USA	UK	USA	UK
1950	8.7	3.1	1.0	2.9	5.3	1.4
1951	8.3	3.0	7.9	9.0	3.3	1.1
1952	3.7	−0.5	2.2	9.4	3.0	1.5
1953	3.8	4.1	0.8	3.1	2.9	1.5
1954	−1.2	4.2	0.5	1.7	5.5	1.2
1955	6.7	3.7	−0.4	4.6	4.4	1.0
1956	2.1	1.0	1.5	5.0	4.1	1.0
1957	1.8	1.8	3.6	3.6	4.3	1.3
1958	−0.4	0.3	2.7	3.2	6.8	1.8
1959	6.0	4.6	0.8	0.6	5.5	1.9
1960	2.2	5.5	1.6	1.1	5.5	1.5
1961	2.6	2.3	1.0	3.3	6.7	1.4
1962	5.8	1.1	1.1	4.2	5.5	1.8
1963	4.0	3.9	1.2	2.0	5.7	2.1
1964	5.3	5.5	1.3	3.2	5.2	1.6
1965	6.0	2.5	1.7	4.8	4.5	1.3
1966	6.0	1.9	2.9	3.9	3.8	1.4
1967	2.7	2.2	2.9	2.4	3.8	2.1
1968	4.6	4.0	4.2	4.8	3.6	2.3
1969	2.8	2.1	5.4	5.4	3.5	2.2
1970	−0.2	2.2	5.9	6.3	4.9	2.4
1971	3.4	1.9	4.3	9.4	5.9	3.1
1972	5.7	3.3	3.3	7.3	5.6	3.4
1973	5.8	4.1	6.2	9.1	4.9	2.4
1974	−0.6	−1.9	11.0	16.0	5.6	2.3
1975	−1.2	−1.0	9.1	24.2	8.5	3.6
1976	5.4	2.6	5.8	16.5	7.7	4.9
1977	5.5	2.4	6.5	16.7	7.1	5.2
1978	5.0	3.8	7.7	8.3	6.1	5.2
1979	2.8	1.9	11.3	13.4	5.8	4.9
1980	−0.4	−2.1	13.5	18.0	7.1	6.3
1981	1.9	−2.2	10.4	11.9	7.6	9.8
1982	−1.8	——	6.1	——	9.7	——

Sources: Calculations from data in: *Economic Report of the President, 1983* and *Economic Trends, Annual Supplement, 1983*. 'GNP' figure for the UK is actually gross domestic product. Inflation refers to the US Consumer Price Index and UK Retail Price Index. Measures of the variables are not necessarily comparable across the two countries.

Table 1.2: *Comparison of growth rates, industrial production, and prices*

	USA	Japan	France	Germany	Italy	UK
Growth rates in real GNP (%):						
1960–73 annual average	4.1	10.4	5.8	4.7	5.2	3.1
1974–81 annual average	2.7	4.4	2.5	2.2	2.1	0.9
Industrial production in 1981 based upon 1960=100	228	557	224	204	275	141
Consumer prices in 1981 based upon 1960=100	307	434	427	225	638	600

Source: Calculations from *Economic Report of the President, 1983*.

example, explain the differential performance over the period 1974–81, compared to 1960–73, by reference to the two major recessions in the later period. Long-term behaviour might be simply the graphing together of many short-term events, and it might be best to concentrate upon short-term analysis based upon aggregate demand theory. In contrast, a monetarist looking at the data might observe that the recessions are short and can largely be ignored. The longer-run determinants of inflation, unemployment, and growth might then be examined in an equilibrium theory not substantially differing from that used in microeconomics, or in a neoclassical growth theory that traces out the behaviour of a simplified equilibrium over time.

But it might be helpful if we look at the economy through untrained eyes and use common sense in an untutored analysis. Severe short-term breaks in the trend of growth do occur, and it seems reasonable to associate these with restrictive monetary policies, high interest rates, loss of consumer or business confidence, a high value of the currency in foreign exchange leading to a loss of export markets, and similar factors. The general performance of economies during the 1974–81 period cannot easily be disassociated from the 'oil crisis'. But if one wants to explain, for example, the generally unimpressive performance of the post-war British economy, one naturally turns to longer-run factors of education, the welfare state and the tax structure necessary to fund it, the factors determining investment in productive capital, the role of trade unions, and even sociological factors including the class structure.

While the ideal macroeconomic theory would encompass all these factors in a unified whole, that does not currently exist, and the textbook approach of separating the short-term and long-term analyses might be a useful intermediate step to a complete theory. We might be Keynesians in the short-run, looking primarily at monetary and fiscal policy, and neoclassical in terms of analysing longer-run factors. In terms of policy, we could take a Keynesian approach to stabilisation policy and a monetarist approach to long-run policies of tax structure and public goods provision.

Even if one is willing to maintain that dichotomy, however, one quickly runs into a major problem—neither the Keynesian theory of recessions nor the neoclassical monetarist theory of the long-run equilibrium, is adequate. The problems are both in theory and in policy. In theory there is no clear basis for Keynesian short-run phenomena, and textbooks usually address this by supposing that, in the short-run, either 'expectational errors are continually committed' or 'prices are fixed'. But what precisely is the mechanism underlying the expectation errors (so that we can keep it in mind in formulating policy)? For example, do the policy actions themselves change expectations? Alternatively, what does it mean that prices are rigid (much less, what is the cause of this phenomenon) in a period of inflation when they are constantly rising? In a properly dichotomised approach, the Keynesian theory would become a detailed study of transitions, from one equilibrium to another; but, to do that, it would have to explain the speed of the transition and consider whether the path of the transition affects the ultimate endpoint. If slow adjustment of expectations or prices is the basis for a transitional Keynesian phase, we need a theory describing the basis of the slow adjustment—how expectations and prices adjust over time. This will then tell us, for example, whether a government policy can operate rapidly enough to be stabilising.

It will tell us whether the government should be trying to mitigate or prevent recessions, or whether these are self-correcting in a short enough time to be ignored from the policy perspective.

Monetarist theory, on the other hand, fails to be an adequate long-term description of the economy since the practitioners direct the analysis to demonstrate the optimality of the market system. The political biases cause undue attention to be devoted to the role of unemployment compensation and trade unions in unemployment, and do not allow detailed study of the role of investment, financial and (non-union) labour market imperfections, and other factors that might require a more liberal role for government intervention. Microeconomic general equilibrium theory shows that a number of assumptions, clearly not met in a real economy, are necessary to demonstrate the efficiency of the market system. Yet macroeconomic general equilibrium neoclassical theory, with what is basically the same model, takes the efficiency presumption for granted.

It is now time to explain what we mean by a 'new Keynesian economics', keeping in mind the above reservations we have towards both the traditional Keynesian and monetarist approaches. In terms of methodology, it is too soon to discard the traditional economics approach that the way to examine economic behaviour is to consider the optimal strategies of individual agents, given their environment, and to aggregate this behaviour into market behaviour by the means of supply and demand curves and equilibrium conditions. If a theory (and we have in mind primarily the Keynesian model) fails to have this underlying microeconomic foundation of analysis, that theory is not sufficiently completed to be acceptable. On the other hand, a theory should be in accord with empirical observation, and on this basis the neoclassical model is unacceptable.

We are then seeking a model not only with, like the Keynesian model, empirical validity but also, like the neoclassical model, a firm foundation in optimisation behaviour. The primary focus of our search in this book will be upon the labour market, following the emphasis of the literature over the last two decades. Surprisingly, perhaps, we are able to come to a much more optimistic conclusion about the potential for a proper Keynesian model than many recent commentaries.

1.2　THE DEVELOPMENT OF MACROECONOMIC THEORY

The most convenient way to give an overview of the contents of this book is to follow the chronological development of macroeconomic theory. The process by which theories arise is important in understanding them. The two major schools in macroeconomics have, like political parties, continued through several generations of members, modifying over time in response to outside events (the currently pressing policy problems) and to a dynamic that is both internal and responsive to the challenges set by the other. The viewpoints of a Keynesian or monetarist today cannot be understood without reference to this past, any more than one can understand Democratic Party policies in the US without recalling the New Deal.

The role of policy problems in determining the direction of theory can be noted from the date of the *General Theory*, 1936. It comes as no surprise that the major theory of involuntary unemployment arose from the depressed periods of the 1920s and 1930s. Similarly, the Phillips curve relating inflation and unemployment was a product of the 1950s, when inflation appeared—unusually, in a not particularly expansionary economy (Table 1.1; US inflation rose to 3.6 per cent in 1957, a year when real GNP growth was only 1.8 per cent). The new monetarism gained ground in academic circles in the double-digit inflation of the 1970s. Nor, given the adversarial relationship of the schools, should it be surprising that the one responds to the other, that the rethinking of Keynesian models, by Keynesians, follows the resurgence of monetarism.

Traditional Monetarist and Keynesian Models

Prior to the 1920s there was not so much a theory of macroeconomics (to be understood as the economics of unemployment and inflation) but rather a theory of prices and interest rates, and a cataloguing of business cycles. The price level was ultimately determined by the money supply since real output was taken to be fixed by the availability of the fully employed productive resources in the economy. This follows the quantity theory of money that the price level (for given output) is proportional to the money supply, and (from this) that the growth in money supply equals the rate of inflation. Further, under the gold standard, monetary expansion was necessarily limited by the supplies of gold, preventing an indefinite inflation. Interest rates, in real terms (after adjusting for any inflation) were determined by the productivity of capital. Other practitioners graphed business-cycle behaviour and applied names to the apparent cycles of various durations.

All this is not very much different from the models of current monetarist (or neoclassical—we will generally use these as synonyms in the book) macroeconomists, taking into account the different groups within the school. The basic monetarism of Irving Fisher in the early part of this century is essentially the monetarism presented today by Milton Friedman. More extreme followers, who do not believe that the monetary authorities can follow a non-inflationary growth rule for money, suggest a return to the gold standard. And business-cycle analysis has been recently resurrected by Robert Lucas, a proponent of what might be considered the 'new monetarism'.

The original monetarism not only had no explanation for unemployment but in general did not even discuss it. Indeed, even Keynes, in his *Treatise on Money*, discussed prices and the distribution of income (in a form of the Cambridge school model, now more commonly associated with Kalecki, Robinson, Sraffa, and others), but failed to consider changes in output and employment. The challenge to this complacency arose in the 1920s in the UK, when unemployment rates remained substantially above pre-war levels. Pigou responded to this challenge with a theory of search unemployment, where unemployment arises as workers shift between jobs, moving to jobs where their productivity is higher. But what was happening in the 1920s? Were job opportunities shifting about more? Pigou had the sense to realise that this could not be the whole story and proposed a further answer. After the war, trade unions became more powerful and demanded higher wages; governments, feeling a debt to war veterans, acquiesced in the process. Workers simply priced themselves out of jobs. Both of these stories are directly reflected in the current monetarism. The alternative explanation was provided by Keynes in the *General Theory*. The new hypothesis was that there was an insufficient demand for the output of firms so that workers, no matter how low their wages, could not profitably be employed— the output could not be sold. An equilibrium would arise where production and employment was determined by the demand for goods. But if firms cannot sell their output, why don't they lower their prices, and if workers cannot sell their labour, why don't they lower their wage? Indeed, in the Great Depression, prices and wages did fall. But, while a given firm or worker can probably increase his sales by lowering his price and gaining sales from his competitors, it is not obvious that this process would lead to sales in the aggregate being expanded. Each firm may simply fail in its efforts to attract additional business since its competitors are lowering prices just as rapidly.

Much of the discussion after the publication of the *General Theory* was over precisely this issue: if all wages and prices fell, would that restore sales and employment or would the same depressed level of transactions simply occur at lower prices? The theoretical answer became clear: various real-balance effects should restore aggregate demand as prices fall. The idea is that individuals might hold a certain amount of nominal wealth (i.e. measured in dollars or pounds); as prices fall, the real value of that wealth increases and should lead the holders to increase their demand for consumption goods in accord with their greater wealth. But then one must isolate the assets where this effect holds. As an example, suppose that one individual in the economy has loaned a certain sum, in nominal terms, to another. Then, when prices fall, the real value of that debt has increased, making the borrower worse off (since his wages have fallen, it is more difficult to repay) and making the lender better off (the repaid dollars or pounds buy more goods than before). The net effect is approximately zero. Most assets have two sides in this sense, and the real-balance effect described becomes approximately zero. The exception is holdings of currency—individuals holding money are better off with no compensating loss to another individual in the economy. This real-balance effect, however, would seem to be rather weak at best and might perhaps take decades to restore a return to full employment.

This then leads to one perspective on the difference between Keynesian and monetarist analyses: if a fall in aggregate demand leads to a recession, is the recession self-correcting and, if so, what is the time scale involved? From the experience of the Depression, the evidence was taken to support the Keynesian viewpoint that in the absence of government intervention, a recession could be very prolonged. The debate switched to the desirability of various interventionist policies. In particular, as framed by Hick's IS-LM analysis, the issue became whether monetary or fiscal policy was more effective in combating a recession. Hicks suggested that monetarism might be depicted by a vertical LM curve and Keynesianism by a horizontal LM curve, and from this formulation, monetarism meant that only monetary policy could affect output, and Keynesianism that only fiscal policy. These descriptions of monetarism *versus* Keynesianism represented an unfortunate misstatement of both positions that even today remains in many textbooks. In fact, monetarism is precisely the view that money cannot affect real output (except for a short transitional period), and most Keynesians realise the importance of monetary policy.

The proper question dividing the two schools on policy issues eventually became posed in a series of articles by Friedman and Tobin: 'How much does a change in the money supply get reflected in price changes and how much in quantity (output and employment) changes?' This 'missing equation' determines whether monetary (and, for similar reasons, fiscal) policy affects output in the economy and is a viable tool in stabilising output and employment, or whether monetary policy should strictly be used to control inflation. In that debate, Tobin claimed that the 'missing equation' did in fact exist; that it was the Phillips curve. This construction appeared in the late 1950s along with numerous other studies induced by the unprecedented levels of peacetime inflation. Phillips empirically examined the relationship between inflation and unemployment, and concluded that an inverse relationship existed—when unemployment was low, inflation was high. Low unemployment could be associated with an excess demand for labour and hence to rising wages and prices. While the other explanations of the 1950s inflation (e.g. Galbraith's model of administered prices and Holzman's model of group competition for income shares in the economy) have been largely forgotten, the Phillips curve became fully integrated into the Keynesian framework.

Adding the Phillips curve to the basic aggregate demand, Keynesian apparatus in some ways completes the model. If output and unemployment remain unchanged over time, the quantity theory of money operates so that the rate of inflation will equal the growth in the money supply. But from the Phillips curve, a given rate of inflation (and thus growth in the money supply) determines the unemployment rate. The higher the growth in money, the higher inflation and lower unemployment.

But can the Phillips curve be used in this way? In particular, will the change in monetary policy (a shift to a higher growth rate) move the economy along the Phillips curve or will it shift the curve? Empirically, the Phillips curve ran into problems in the later 1960s and early 1970s—points were observed with high inflation for moderate rates of unemployment (e.g. the US figures of 11 per cent inflation and 5.6 per cent unemployment in 1974). While part of the explanation may be due to oil price shocks and other unusual changes in the economic environment, this still entails that the Phillips curve does not tell the entire story about the relationship between prices and quantities. Theoretically, another serious problem arises. The Phillips curve describes a relationship between nominal wage (the wage measured in dollars or pounds) adjustment and the excess demand for labour as measured by the unemployment rate. But surely, if there is low unemployment indicating a high excess demand for labour, wages should rise relative to the rate of inflation; that is, the real wage should rise. But the rising wages should feed into prices, causing these to rise ever more rapidly. If there is low unemployment, one might expect an acceleration of inflation as wages are set to exceed price rises but feed into increasing price inflation. In a simple example, if prices are rising at 5 per cent a year and the Phillips curve dictates that, because of excess demand for labour, wages rise at 6 per cent, this will feed into a new price inflation rate of 6 per cent, and (since the labour market situation is unchanged) wages might start rising at 7 per cent, and so on, in an accelerationist cycle. The only stable level of unemployment would be the 'natural rate', the rate where there is no particular excess demand for labour and therefore no spiral caused by firms seeking to bid up wages in excess of prices.

This argument became incorporated in the textbooks as the distinction between 'short run' and 'long run' Phillips curves. The short-run curve was based upon price-inflation expectations at any given moment, but as this inflation rises, this becomes incorporated into expectations, and the short-run Phillips curve moves upwards. The only curve showing points indefinitely feasible was he vertical line at the natural rate of unemployment. Unemployment rates below this could be sustained in the short run, but only because of a lag in expectations about the inflation rate. The monetarist *versus* Keynesian question was then rephrased: 'Is the long-run Phillips curve vertical?' Keynesians insisted that, even in the long run there was a viable trade-off between inflation and unemployment. Monetarists insisted that there was not, and an intermediate position allowed that a trade-off might exist for long enough to be usable, although not indefinitely.

In this form, the policy issues can be clarified. If one can trade off unemployment for inflation over both the short and long run, one chooses a policy leading to the best balance between the two. If both the short- and long-run Phillips curves are vertical (or the short run is very short indeed), then one accepts the natural rate of unemployment and minimises inflation. But suppose that the short-run curve is a viable trade-off over an extended period of time—then one must decide whether to choose an unsustainably low rate of unemployment today at the cost of a higher inflation rate tomorrow (when unemployment will return to the natural rate); this calculation requires, however, some knowledge of the length of duration for which the short-run curve is pertinent (i.e. the transition period).

But before we accept this statement as the policy menu and the agenda for determining which approach is best, note that these are not all the theoretical alternatives. The short- and long-run Phillips curves could both be vertical in the sense that there is no trade-off between inflation and unemployment (or it could be a positive relationship rather than the inverse one), yet other factors could still operate to shift the natural rate around. There could be a short-run trade-off in the context of a long-run curve, vertical but dependent upon other factors. These and other possibilities must be raised as a caution before accepting the vertical-or-not distinction between Keynesian and monetarist models.

The UV and Search Approaches to the Labour Market

The Phillips curve acquired an important place in the body of Keynesian economics, yet its theoretical foundation was admittedly weak. But if Keynesian economics required a closer examination of the labour market, to rationalise the Phillips curve, so did monetarist approaches. To be plausible, a monetarist model must include some determination of the unemployment rate, and must also explain why severe deviations from the usual rate sometimes occur. In the later 1960s and early 1970s, both Keynesian and monetarist developments of labour-market microfoundations appeared in the literature. We will refer to these as the UV-curve approach and the search approach, respectively. The two are closely related since they are addressing the same weakness in the traditional theories—the labour market was set up with supply and demand curves for labour, and the equilibrium provided some determination of employment levels. But the Phillips curve, in particular, pointed out the need for a theory of unemployment rather than a theory of employment levels. This required a shift from the static supply-and-demand approach in employment to a dynamic analysis. This exercise might be viewed as analogous to the use of the quantity theory either as a static theory of the price level (the price level is proportional to the money supply) or as a dynamic theory of inflation (the growth in the price level, the rate of inflation, equals the growth in the money supply). The dynamic theory of unemployment, however, has a somewhat more complicated relationship to the static theory of employment.

Let us begin with the UV approach. To support the Phillips curve, we want to show some relationship between the unemployment rate and excess demand in the labour market, and therefore between the unemployment rate and the pressure on wages that lead to inflation. The UV approach views the labour market as a dynamic matching process in which there are unemployed workers (U) seeking out the available vacancies (V). Over time, some of the unemployed acquire jobs and leave the unemployment register. Meanwhile, however, other workers lose their jobs (or retire), and these workers, plus new entrants into the labour force, augment the ranks of the unemployed. For these factors to balance out, so that the number of unemployed remains the same over time, the number of new job acquisitions by the unemployed must equal the job losses by the employed. Suppose for simplicity that there is a given number of job losses each period so that, to maintain employment and unemployment at their current levels, new hires must equal that amount. From the matching process, the number of new hires depends upon the number of vacancies available and the number of unemployed looking for them. For ach level of U there is some level of V such that the new hires chieve the requisite number—if V is less than that, vacancies are lifficult to locate, and insufficient hires occur, while if V is greater, xcessive hires occur, both possibilities changing the number of inemployed. Similarly, if U is lower, so there are fewer workers ooking for jobs, the level of hirings is maintained only if there are a greater number of vacancies, making them easier to find. This eads to a whole curve of UV combinations that maintain hiring at he requisite level to keep U constant over time.

To turn the UV curve into a Phillips curve, we suppose that the lifference between V and U represents an excess demand for abour and therefore leads to a pressure for rising wages. Any level of U along the UV curve is associated with a particular level of V ind, from the discussion above, a low U is associated with a high √, and therefore high wage-inflation, and a high U with a low V, ind therefore low wage-inflation.

This does not complete the exercise, however, since we are in he framework of unemployment levels rather than rates, as in the Phillips curve. We could make this translation if we supposed that here was a fixed labour supply (so that U divided by this would be he unemployment rate). But this still leaves a problem: what letermines the point achieved on the UV curve and thus the issociated point on the Phillips curve? This is just a rephrasing of he original Keynesian problem of what determines the level of employment, and for an answer one could again recite 'aggregate lemand' but with no more or less justification than in the static ramework. The dynamic UV-curve approach adds new features not found in the original static Keynesian labour market, but it loesn't address the fundamental question of the consistency of the Keynesian model.

While the UV-curve approach takes the number of vacancies as given and assumes that any worker locating a vacancy accepts that ob, while others are involuntarily laid off, the dynamic theory of inemployment used to augment the monetarist approach is very lifferent. In the search models, it is wages at different firms that are given, with firms offering jobs to all applicants. Unemployment is maintained only because some of the job-seekers decline jobs because they view the wage as insufficient. The UV approach then has applicants denied jobs because there are insufficient vacancies—a job-rationing that is Keynesian in spirit—while the search approach allows wages to ration jobs, and hence the resulting unemployment is often considered as voluntary.

Unemployment is maintained in the search model because applicants sometimes refuse jobs, but they do this rationally. They refuse a job if they think they can locate one with a higher wage in a reasonable period of time. For a given distribution of wages in the economy, each unemployed searcher calculates the minimum wage he will accept (in preference to continued search for a higher-paying job), and then (on average) it takes a determinable period of time before a job, with that minimum wage or better, is locatable. As in the UV-curve approach, this duration then determines the U that maintains unemployment at its current level, balancing the inflows into jobs against the job-losses due to for example, retirements (where we assume that the labour force is stationary in size and new entrants equal the number of retirees).

For a given distribution of wages in the economy, the search model produces a resulting unemployment rate—the 'natural rate'. But this is not complete as stated, since a full model would include a determination of the wage distribution. The completion here is to associate the wages on offer at the different firms with the marginal productivities of labour at the firms—thus one firm offers a higher wage because labour is more productive there. In effect, this is adding a labour supply formulation to complete the model in a neoclassical-monetarist way, much as we added aggregate demand in the UV approach to complete that model in a Keynesian manner. Further, this associates the 'natural rate' determined by the search model with the earlier 'natural rate' in the Phillips curve—it is the point where supply equals demand in the labour market, and there is no pressure for any wage changing.

There are two distinct features above that contrast the UV and the search approaches, and since these distinctions will arise again along with a third that we will now mention, in the contracting literature, it will be useful to clarify them. The very nature of the UV model is that job-rationing occurs; if the unemployed do not directly obtain jobs, it is because there is no available vacancy, and they must continue to search out a vacancy. In the search model an applicant to a firm is always offered a job, but he may choose to decline it because of the wage. Thus one model rations jobs by vacancy-availability, the other by wage-setting. But the second difference comes in the completion: the UV model supposes that the number of vacancies is created by aggregate demand, so a lower level of aggregate demand leads to an outcome with fewer vacancies and more unemployed; the search model is completed when firms do not wish to change their wage rates, because supply and demand is balanced. Thus a Keynesian or monetarist outcome in terms of equilibrium depends on this closure, which is not fundamental to the models—a UV model could be constructed with supply–demand equilibrium, giving a unique 'natural rate' but still with job-rationing by vacancy-availability. The method of job-rationing and the outcome are different issues. But here our third point comes up, and it is easiest to comprehend in the search model. We suggested that firms set wages to equate supply and demand. But in fact, if a firm sets the wage, it is likely to set the monopsony wage, not the competitive supply equals demand wage. Yet we know that monopsony generally leads to an inefficient outcome with an equilibrium with low transactions. Thus nothing to this point has spoken to the issue of the efficiency or the desirability of the outcomes in either the UV or the search model.

Rather than consider these issues in more depth at this point, we turn to another problem with the search story. At the beginning of this section we noted that a monetarist story of the labour market must include some discussion of why unemployment might temporarily be well in excess of the natural rate. The search literature contains an answer to this. Recall that unemployed applicants would decline a job if they thought the wage was low relative to what they might obtain by continued search at other firms. Now suppose that a sudden, unexpected inflation (deflation) occurs; then all wages can be taken to have risen (fallen), but workers might not have adjusted their expectations to the change. Then, in an inflation (deflation), they start receiving higher (lower) offers than expected and end up accepting (rejecting) more offers than is normal, and more than they would have if their expectations had properly adjusted. In the short run, until expectations adjust, the unemployment rate differs from the natural rate.

But for how long can workers make these expectational errors? An immediate answer would be that this process must be very short indeed since it does require a questionable amount of ignorance by workers. Workers must not be able to observe any current wage-index or (since price-inflation will presumably be associated with the wage-inflation) observe the general level of prices in the stores. But rather than discounting the validity of this model on these simple grounds, the new monetarists adopt what seems a contrived logic. They suppose that workers can be fooled in this manner but have a rationality of expectations that is even more profound. While workers cannot observe the current rate of inflation, they can use economic models to predict the future rate.

The principle of rational expectations is that agents rationally process information in forming expectations. This can be made concrete by an example. Suppose we had an individual who believed in monetarist economics, including the quantity theory of money. If he learns that the money supply growth rate for next period will be 5 per cent, he uses the model to predict that next period's inflation will be 5 per cent. Then, assuming the quantity theory is a correct description of the economy, and the growth in money supply occurs at 5 per cent, the agent will not be fooled by inflation and will make correct decisions about job-acceptance. In the context of our earlier comments, workers do not have to observe the current wage-inflation but merely know the growth in money supply. But suppose they do not know this with certainty, the 5 per cent figure being an average. Then, if actual growth is a bit higher than this, inflation will be a bit higher than expected, and (not being able to observe actual inflation) workers will accept jobs they would not accept if better informed. It is at this point in the argument that the 'policy ineffectiveness' result is pertinent. Suppose the monetary authorities want to take advantage of this uncertainty to sustain a low-unemployment outcome into the future, so they constantly have the money supply grow at a rate in excess of expectations. But then agents in the economy will predict this attempted effort, incorporate it into their expectations, and the excess growth policy will be ineffective. We return to the earlier accelerationist views about the Phillips curve and how the only sustainable point is at the natural rate of unemployment.

But all this is rather excessive artillery and, further, is misdirected if intended to attack Keynesian formulations. It is a legitimate, if unnecessarily complex, argument against using as a basis for activist policy the expectational-errors, search, story of how the unemployment rate might diverge from the natural rate. The much simpler assumption that workers can observe the general inflation rate is sufficient to make the argument. But the

rational-expectations policy-ineffectiveness argument applies only
to the expectational-errors story, which (as we have noted already)
is a monetarist story; the argument has nothing to say about other,
Keynesian models. This is not to say that rational expectations is
not a legitimate and important point—my viewpoint is that any
model should be consistent with rational expectations. But nothing
in the usual arguments demonstrates any logical, inherent inconsistency between rational expectations and Keynesian models.

Contracting

Although the UV and search models did explore the labour
market in greater depth, added needed dynamics, and introduced
the basis for a major role for information into the traditional
models, the underlying distinguishing features and shortcomings
of the Keynesian and neoclassical approaches remain. The Keynesian model has involuntary lay-offs and is consistent with high
unemployment, but the fundamental problem remains: why don't
wages and prices fall to increase vacancies and to lower unemployment? The search model has only voluntary unemployment and a
rather implausible explanation—the expectations-error approach
—for non-natural-rate unemployment. Why can't workers observe
the general rate of inflation?

Within the Keynesian school, however, there had always been
the notion that perhaps wage and price rigidities could explain
Keynesian phenomena—'prices are sticky'. Certainly if one
assumed that nominal wages and prices were fixed, one could
easily sustain the Keynesian aggregate demand mechanism; recalling our earlier discussion, there is no real-balance effect to restore
full employment equilibrium. Yet Keynesians, like Keynes, were
resistant to adopting this as the basis of the theory. The fixed-price
literature, associated with Barro and Grossman, gained popularity
in the 1970s, but the fundamental problem remained—there was
no basis for it, either in empirical observation (prices fell in the
Depression) or in theory. Why wouldn't an agent, faced with an
insufficient demand for his product or labour, lower the price?

For this reason there was great enthusiasm when the contracting
model, originated by Azariadis and Baily, suggested that wage
rigidity could be shown to be optimal behaviour on the part of
firms, and that this wage rigidity was associated with involuntary
lay-offs of workers. On the face of it, a firm that kept wages up and

laid off workers in an unfavourable situation would seem to be operating in a suboptimal manner. Why not lower its wage offer as in the search approach and let the excess workers quit, thus saving on the wage bill paid to the remaining workers? The 'implicit'—or, more accurately, 'optimal'—contracting models made the following point: if I go to work for your firm today, I expect to remain there for some period of time, and I am concerned not just with the wage you pay today but with the wage you will pay tomorrow and with any risk I have of being laid off. Any commitments the firm can make about its future policies make it easier to recruit today, and the firm can therefore recruit at lower initial wages. In the simple contracting model a strong result emerges: the firm should guarantee a fixed wage into the future and, insofar as unfavourable events dictate a lowering of the workforce size, it should commit itself to the lay-off strategy to be used to implement the reductions. It is not in the firm's long-term interest to lower wages when the unfavourable events occur, because that will make it costly to recruit workers in the future.

This seemed like the beginning of a solution to the Keynesian puzzle, but problems arose as the literature began a closer examination of the model. The problem was that although the model generated a fixed wage, it also entailed separate lay-off rules that did not follow the usual marginal product and wage equalisation. Indeed, if workers had no alternative occupation if laid off, and gained no leisure value or unemployment benefits, the optimal contract required full employment as long as the marginal product of labour was positive, however small. In any case, the model either generated the same natural rate as the search models, of (if workers were risk-averse) less unemployment. All that was changed in fact, relative to the search models, was the mechanism which resulted in unemployment—here it is involuntary—and not the macroeconomic properties of the model. Part of the problem was that the analysis was all in real terms; in particular, the rigid wages were real wages. If all firms, in response to an aggregate demand fall, were to lower nominal prices and wages, the neoclassical real-balance effect would again restore full employment.

At this point, both the search and contracting literatures turned largely to microeconomic-efficiency questions. In suitably defined equilibria, both sorts of models determine natural rates of unemployment deriving from the information and uncertainty problems in the economy. But these long-term unemployment rates may not have desirable efficiency properties. Recall from our discussion of search markets that the model is usually closed by assuming that firms set their wage rates, but (as we noted there) this would seem to be a monopsony specification. Formalising this, the literature has derived the result that search equilibrium leads to too little unemployment relative to the efficient outcome. In contrast, recent contracting models have led to results of excessively high unemployment. These results are important since they show, in models that are fully acceptable by the criterion of individual optimising behaviour, that there may be an essentially microeconomic role for government intervention, using tax and benefits policies to restore efficiency to the labour market. For example, the monopsony search model provides a role for government unemployment benefits, not just for income distribution reasons, but actually for reasons of economic efficiency.

From a macroeconomic perspective, however, the results in the literature were disappointing. The new classical school, using the search model, had only the somewhat implausible expectations-error approach to explaining periods of high unemployment. The only contracting model which seemed to address the issue of high-unemployment periods was the staggered-contracts model. Later in this book, we will argue that that model, which provides a role for nominal rigidities in the contracting process, actually replicates the expectational-errors approach rather than providing a proper Keynesian theory.

As macroeconomists have become pessimistic about the potentiality of contracting to solve the Keynesian riddle, a new literature has developed—the trade coordination literature. This literature has revolved around the following sort of parable. In a trading economy, one produces to trade with other agents. Now suppose, for whatever reason, one expects other agents to produce very little, so that there will be few trading opportunities—then one will not produce very much. This is really just a repetition of the original Keynesian argument: if there is low aggregate demand, there is low demand for each firm's production, and it will cut employment and output. To go beyond the simple Keynesian aggregate demand story and provide the microeconomic foundations for the model, one has to address the fundamental Keynesian problem: why do agents cut production to the point where, at a low level of aggregate demand, there is no incentive to lower prices? For this, there must be some imperfection in the system. The literature has suggested, for example, search inefficiencies or increasing returns to scale in the production technology. In the final chapter of the book, on equilibrium recessions, we will present a new approach based on contracting that seems to provide at least a rudimentary answer to the problem of constructing a firmly founded Keynesian theory.

1.3   THE PLAN OF THE BOOK

This book has several purposes that are, hopefully, not contradictory. On the one hand, there is an expository purpose, to present accessibly the material in the literature. Part I, covering the traditional macroeconomic models, is largely concerned with this objective. It can be read on its own—particularly suitable, perhaps, for second-year economics students—but is also included as providing a basis for later discussions in the book about the fundamental features of Keynesian macromodels. It presents the traditional Keynesian and neoclassical models, carefully examining the optimisation bases and the equilibrium conditions, and then in Chapter 5 considering the extent to which the traditional literature can address the issue of price or quantity adjustment that distinguishes the neoclassical and Keynesian positions.

Part II seeks to make accessible the search and, particularly, the contracting models. This was in some ways, however, a difficult task since the relations between these two models (and their variants) and what they actually have to say about both microeconomic and macroeconomic issues has perhaps not been well understood within the profession. Thus we have tried in Part II to go beyond exposition of a set of models into relating them, at the cost of making it more difficult for the reader to simply refer to a particular model of interest and read an isolated exposition in the text. I would be surprised, for example, if the reader could turn to Chapter 7 on contracting without first reading Chapter 6 on search.

But there is another purpose, the major theme of the book, that has only come out clearly in the final version of the manuscript—to present the case for contracting. We argue that contracting arises naturally in the labour market due to imperfections that would otherwise be present, that this contracting provides the basis for understanding why unemployment occurs through involuntary lay-offs rather than voluntary departures as wages are reduced, and finally and most importantly, that contracting in conjunction with a monopolistically competitive formulation of the economy provides the basis of a Keynesian theory fully based upon rational microeconomic agents. This last model is presented in Chapter 10, and I have tried to present it in a somewhat more self-contained manner than some of the other chapters to allow practitioners to read it in isolation.

This theme explains the organisation of Part II of the book. We present the efficient search model in Chapter 6, and its application to the rational expectations (expectations error) new classical school; in Chapter 7 we consider the efficient contracting model and show how in effect it replicates the results in the search model except in the mechanism of job separations (involuntary lay-offs). We then turn to inefficiencies arising in the labour market. In Chapter 8 we show that search markets degenerate into a monopsonistic outcome, and that contracting arises naturally and voluntarily on the part of firms seeking to recruit workers. This is in effect the first half of the case for contracting—it will naturally supplant unorganised search in the labour market. The next step, in Chapter 9, is to consider why the fully efficient contracts might not arise, using the asymmetric information contracting literature. At this point it is convenient to consider the staggered contracts approach, since if that has any microeconomic legitimacy it is through the asymmetric-information process. In any case, we find that it simply replicates the expectational-errors approach and is not of particular interest from a Keynesian macroeconomic viewpoint. Chapter 10 presents our alternative macromodel, using the asymmetric-information approach in conjunction with a monopolistically competitive formulation of the economy to show the possibility of equilibrium recessions caused by aggregate demand factors.

Part I
The Traditional Models

Introduction

We begin by considering the traditional models of macroeconomics, the monetarist-neoclassical (recall that throughout the book we will use monetarist and neoclassical as synonyms) and the Keynesian approaches. This is done from first principles to clarify precisely how the models differ in assumptions and implications, and to indicate the extensive common ground between the theories. The importance of having a clear vision of the fundamentals of macroeconomics, in moving forward into newer approaches, cannot be overemphasised. The definition of the issues in these basic approaches, and the models developed to illustrate them, are not relics of the past but are vital foundations to the future development of macroeconomic theory. The relevant formulations, however, are not the simplified models that too often appear in the texts, such as the aggregate supply–demand apparatus or the emphasis upon a mechanical IS–LM apparatus, but are the specifications of market behaviour, in the individual markets, that get roughly aggregated into these 'macroeconomic tools'.

Macroeconomics is conducted on an aggregated basis, and this tends to be viewed as a primary feature of the analysis. However, it should be kept in mind that the level of aggregation is chosen to obtain the simplest possible model retaining the features necessary to answer the given issues, and is not a virtue or a vice in its own right. Thus in macroeconomics we often pretend that all workers or firms are essentially identical and analyse the behaviour of a 'representative' agent. Similarly, we consider highly aggregated markets; for example, the market for output goods. The point is that for examining certain questions, a highly simplified aggregated model is sufficient; when it fails to answer the question, a more disaggregated construction is often necessary. If we want to know about the general level of production in the economy, it is probably sufficient to develop a model with just one output good, but if we want to know about the relative production of apples and oranges, it is clearly necessary to specify both markets.

In the models in this Part, we will generally assume that we can work with identical firms and workers, although from time to time we move away from this 'representative agent' approach. We will also consider an economy with only four markets: labour, output, bonds, and money. This gives us a simpler framework than the careful specification of individual agents and goods in microeconomic general equilibrium theory, but any results we get should be applicable to the full specification. The reason for this is that we will use precisely the tools of analysis that one uses in microeconomics: supply and demand curves obtained from individual agent's optimisation problems, and equilibrium conditions to solve for the market result. All the 'macroeconomic' tools, such as the IS–LM framework, are consistent with this and gain their validity as representations of the microeconomic market-equilibrium conditions.

This is not to say that Keynesian economics is consistent with general equilibrium neoclassical microeconomics. The difference has to do with equilibrium conditions. General equilibrium theory has agents taking prices as given and assuming that they can transact (either buy or sell) as much as they want at the market prices. The equilibrium prices are then postulated as those that clear markets, with supply and demand being equal in each market. Stories are told about the Walrasian auctioneer or the invisible hand, but in terms of the theory the equilibrium condition is imposed as an assumption. Keynesian models impose different equilibrium conditions; in particular, they do not generally assume market-clearing. This does change the optimisation problems faced by individuals, since now they cannot, in their plans, assume that they can transact as much as they want at the market prices, but it does not change the fundamental fact that agents are still optimising (deciding what to do), which is then aggregated into supply and demand curves which are then subjected to non-market-clearing equilibrium conditions.

On the grounds discussed above, Keynesian economics meets the test of being consistent with microeconomics; it has microeconomic foundations (indeed, many of the contributions in the *General Theory* take on the form of improving the microeconomic analysis of, for example, monetary and investment theory). The inconsistency lies not with the microeconomic methodology in general equilibrium theory but with another model which in fact has never really been fully specified—a model where part of the decisions made by agents is price-setting behaviour. Keynesian economics fails the test of microeconomic principles that agents have no incentive to change their prices, a test that is meaningless in the Walrasian auctioneer world of general equilibrium theory. This is a legitimate argument against Keynesian theory, since agents in the empirical economy clearly do set their prices, and this is a problem that we will continually phrase throughout this book. That it is a bit odd as an argument on the part of those who happily assume the Walrasian auctioneer is another matter, but it can be understood given the feeling that the legitimacy of Walrasian (neoclassical) equilibrium conditions derives from their meeting this criterion, that the Walrasian story is shorthand for lots of small agents setting prices.

The agenda for this part of the book is to go through the four major markets and to set out the individual optimisation decisions and equilibrium conditions that lead to the neoclassical-monetarist and Keynesian specifications of equilibrium. In Chapter 5 we go somewhat beyond the basic Keynesian model to consider the Phillips curve and the UV aproach, but for reasons to be discussed there these are in some sense necessary to complete the Keynesian model.

2 The Labour Market

Most of the points distinguishing the neoclassical and Keynesian approaches can be examined within the labour market. For this reason it is the natural place to begin our analysis; indeed, the labour market seems to have a centrality to the issues, in this sense, and it will be the area of concentration of the entire book.

We begin with the neoclassical approach, constructing a simple labour market with demand derived from firm optimisation behaviour and supply determined from a disutility of labour model. The resulting equilibrium, in the neoclassical model, not only determines the quantity of labour employed and the real-wage rate but also determines output in the economy. Further, this equilibrium displays the usual economic efficiency results in that it maximises an appropriately defined net social benefit. We consider Pigou's argument, which has resurfaced in current debates, that an excessively high real wage leads to unemployment.

The neoclassical construction is based upon the notion that a firm, at the going market price for its good, can sell whatever quantity it desires—a typical feature of competitive markets. A simple Keynesian approach is to suppose that instead the firm is limited in the quantity it can sell at the market price—it is sales-constrained. This sales-ration might be determined from the simple multiplier model. We consider the implications of this construction for the labour market, and how an equilibrium might be specified. This is a very different equilibrium than the neoclassical one, and incorporates the essential difference in Keynesian analysis.

2.1 THE NEOCLASSICAL MODEL

The basis of a neoclassical (a term for traditional economics which in the macroeconomic context becomes equivalent to monetarism) model is the determination of supply and demand curves and the location of their intersection, which is called 'equilibrium'. In the labour market the demand comes from firms which utilise the labour in the production of commodities. The supply of labour derives from decisions from potential workers as to whether, at the offered wage, it is preferable to work or to enjoy leisure.

The Demand for Labour

Firms utilise factor services, labour and capital, to produce output which is then sold. Firms maximise profits, the difference between revenues and costs, by choosing the appropriate scale of production and the particular technique of production. In this section we will use a short-run production function where the amount of capital (machines) at the firm is fixed, thus determining the technique of production, and the firm chooses its level of production by hiring more or fewer workers. Markets are taken to be competitive (which is the distinguishing neoclassical assumption), which means that a given firm takes the price of its output P and the wage rate W as given by the market—the firm can sell as much output as it chooses to produce and hire as many workers as it desires at these market prices. P and W are in 'nominal' terms; that is, they are measured in pounds or dollars. (This is contrasted with 'real' values later in the discussion.) In examining a particular agent's behaviour (in this case, an arbitrarily chosen firm), the prices are given (or 'exogenous'); the market will later be taken to set prices to bring the actions of individual optimising agents into accord in an equilibrium, but this can be examined only after considering the individual behaviour.

A firm will maximise profits:

$$\Pi = PQ(N) - WN$$

where N is the level of employment and $Q(N)$ is the production function stating the level of output produced at each level of employment. The production function is normally taken to have the concave shape drawn in Figure 2.1a. The meaning of this particular curvature is seen by looking at marginal products of labour (*MPL*), the increment in output when each additional worker is employed. As drawn, the curve displays what is called the law of diminishing marginal productivity—each additional worker adds to output, but at a diminishing rate. This law (or, more properly, assumption) can be justified by supposing that if only one worker is hired, he gets to use the best machine in the factory, so his productivity is high, but if another were to be hired, he would be assigned to the next best machine, where his productivity would not be as great. Note that the diminishing *MPL*s have nothing to do with the characteristics of the particular worker but rather with the stretching of the given capital stock across the workers. Since P and W are given by the market, once the firm knows its production function $Q(N)$ it can then calculate profitability at each possible level of employment and choose the level of employment and (from the production function) output that achieves the highest profits. For this exercise the assumption of diminishing marginal productivity is vital since it allows for a unique employment level that maximises profits.

A way for the firm to solve the mathematical problem of maximising profits is to begin at 0 workers and ask whether it pays to keep hiring additional workers. An additional worker produces his marginal product, *MPL*, which can be sold at the market price P, producing a revenue of $P \cdot MPL$, called the marginal value product of labour, *MVPL*. His labour services cost W, so if $P \cdot MPL$ exceeds W, it is profitable to hire him. This then is the rule for optimal hiring. Another way of stating the rule is to divide through by P, giving the condition for profitable employment as *MPL* exceeds w, where we define the 'real wage' $w = W/P$. The real wage is the 'commodity wage' or in effect the number of units of output the worker receives as compensation for his labour (with the nominal wage W, the worker can buy w units of the output at the market price P). From this we note that the firm only cares, in its decisions, about the real wage and not about the absolute levels of W and P; the latter determine the level of profitability (in nominal terms) but do not affect the strategy used to maximise profits.

This rule for hiring can straightforwardly be used to construct the labour demand curve with respect to the real wage. First we derive the $MPL(N)$ curve, showing the MPL as a function of employment. Some care is needed here, primarily in terms of whether we allow the firm to hire partial workers or just integer numbers $N = 0,1,2,3, \dots$. Working from the latter assumption, we can define $\overline{MPL}(1)$ as $Q(1) - Q(0)$, $\overline{MPL}(2) = Q(2) - Q(1)$, and so on, defining only MPLs of integer values and using the bars to denote that this definition is being used. It will be somewhat easier for the later analysis, however, if we allow partial workers to be hired; this leads to a smooth $MPL(N)$ curve defined over all possible N. Figure 2.1a shows the relationship of these two MPL constructions. An intuitive way of viewing this is to observe that the $\overline{MPL}(1)$ defined as $Q(1) - Q(0)$ is the average of the MPLs of that first worker's part-time efforts (by the law of diminishing marginal productivity, he is taken to produce more during the first half of his work-day than the second).

We now observe that the $MPL(N)$ curve is in effect the labour demand curve. We have the rule for hiring, that the firm hires all workers whose MPL exceeds the real wage w. But now, in the $MPL(N)$ diagram, take the market real wage w, and read over to the $MPL(N)$ curve, and then down to the horizontal axis. This marks the worker whose $MPL = w$, and by the law of diminishing marginal productivity all the previous workers have an MPL in excess of w and should be hired. Thus the $MPL(N)$ curve can be used precisely as the demand curve.

Since the $MPL(N)$ curve is the labour demand curve, we can use features of the $MPL(N)$ curve whenever we have a labour demand curve; one feature in particular is of interest—the area under the $MPL(N)$ curve is $Q(N)$, the output produced. Recall that the MPL of a worker is just what his hiring adds to output. Then if we sum up the MPLs of the workers, we have the total increase in production relative to no workers, or total production. The way to sum up the MPLs is to take the area under the curve. (For those not familiar with this result from the calculus, return to the $\overline{MPL}$ construction in Figure 2.1a. Turn the $\overline{MPL}$ points into areas as shown by multiplying by one, and then sum over the workers.)

Finally, note that the labour demand curve also entails a division

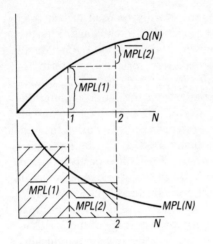

Figure 2.1a: *Production function Q(N) and resulting MPL(N) curve*

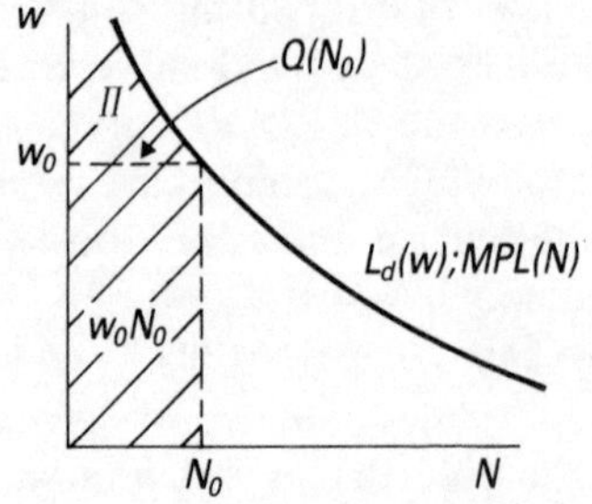

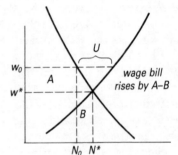

Figure 2.1b: *Labour demand curve, firm's response to w_0 and resulting division of product between wage bill ($w_0 N_0$) and profits*

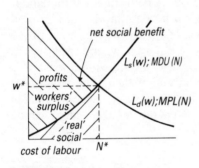

Figure 2.1c: *Neoclassical equilibrium maximises net social benefit (output less lost leisure value of labour)*

Figure 2.1d: *A higher wage may increase the total real wage bill although at the cost of employment and output, and the creation of unemployment U*

Figure 2.1: *Features of the neoclassical equilibrium in the labour market*

of this output between labour and profits. A market w induces the firm to hire along the $MPL(N)$ labour demand curve. That w, multiplied by the resultant N, is the total wage bill of the firm measured in terms of the firm's output (i.e. in real or commodity terms). The residual of total output less the real-wage bill remains with the firm as profits, although it should be noted that this measure includes the cost of any capital utilised by the firm. This is shown, for wage w_0, in Figure 2.1b.

The above discussion allows us to derive the labour demand curve pertinent to a particular firm. To find the total demand for labour in the market, however, we have to add up over all the firms. This can be done, as in microeconomics, by observing that if firm A's labour demand, at a wage of 5, is 2, and firm B's is 4, then the total demand over the two firms is 6; from this, one takes the individual firm labour demand curves and sums them 'horizontally' to find the market labour demand curve. In macroeconomics, however, while there is no reason in principle not to follow the microeconomic procedure, it is usually simpler to adopt the 'representative agent' assumption. There are two (equivalent) variants on this: (1) assume that all firms are essentially identical, and (2) assume that there is just one large firm, but that it does not use any monopoly power. By assuming that firms are identical, we avoid a complication that can be seen, for example, from our use of real wages above. Recall that we had a rule for hiring that the *MVP* exceed *W*, or, dividing by *P*, that the *MPL* exceed *w*. If we had different firms, producing different products sold at different prices, we would be dividing by different *P* values, and each firm would have (for the market *W*) different *w*'s. This complication, distinguishing the price of apples and oranges, is not important for the current discussion, and the representative-firm approach allows us to avoid it. It is important to remember, however, that the representative-firm assumption we shall use (adopting the heuristically simpler version of a single firm) is merely a simplifying assumption and does not in any essential way distinguish macroeconomics from microeconomics.

The Supply of Labour

We will adopt a very simple Marshallian approach to the supply of labour. (This is, incidentally, a case where the assumption of the representative agent is not sufficient for analysis.) Different potential workers in the economy have differing disutilities of labour, to be understood as the value of foregone leisure. The disutility is measured as the amount of commodity compensation the individual requires to make him indifferent to work as opposed to leisure. If we number the individuals in the economy in order of increasing disutility of labour (so that individual 1 requires the least commodity compensation to work), we observe that for any particular disutility value x, workers 1 through some number N (dependent upon x) have a disutility below that amount. We can then draw a curve graphing the number N appropriate to each x. This is denoted as the marginal disutility of labour, $MDU(N)$, curve since (reading it the other way around) it shows, for each N value, the disutility of labour of the Nth, or marginal, worker.

Since the $MDU(N)$ measures the amount of commodity compensation that the Nth worker needs to induce him to work, this curve is the labour-supply curve. It shows, for a given real wage w, how many individuals have disutilities of work below that level and hence are willing to supply labour. The curve $MDU(N)$ is upward-sloping from the construction since we have ordered the workers in terms of increasing disutility of work—more heuristically, a higher wage induces those potential workers with a higher disutility to enter the workforce.

We now apply the argument used with the $MPL(N)$ curve and observe that the area under the $MDU(N)$ curve represents the total disutility of labour incurred by the N workers, summing up the individual disutility of each. But consider what happens at a particular market wage w. From the labour-supply—$MDU(N)$—curve we determine the number of workers seeking employment at that wage, and under competitive assumptions all those will be employed. This gives us a total wage bill received by workers as wN, in real terms. Subtracting off the total disutility of the workers, viewed as a true cost of working, there is a workers' surplus—compensation (to all but the marginal, Nth, worker) in excess of disutility. This surplus is entirely analogous to the surplus obtained by firms in the previous section (i.e. profits). These surpluses together represent in some sense the benefits conferred by the existence of the market.

Equilibrium

Neoclassical equilibrium is based upon determining a market real wage w^* such that the number of people desiring jobs at that wage is the same number as firms wish to hire at that wage. The wage w^* and the resulting employment N^* describes the equilibrium.

The neoclassical equilibrium is found, in the usual way, at the intersection of the supply and demand curves. Recall the identity between labour demand and the $MPL(N)$ curve, and labour supply and the $MDU(N)$ curve, and introduce the more usual notation $L_d(w), L_s(w)$ for labour demand and supply depending upon the wage rate. Both representation forms are legitimate depending upon whether one looks at, for example, the labour demand curve as telling the number of workers demanded at a given wage or the wage that induces the firm to demand that number of workers. We can write algebraically the equivalent conditions for equilibrium:

$$L_d(w^*) = L_s(w^*) = N^*$$

$$MPL(N^*) = MDU(N^*) = w^*$$

The neoclassical equilibrium is shown in Figure 2.1c. A feature of this equilibrium is that it entails certain profits and workers' surplus as shown in the figure, and a total surplus from summing these two.

The neoclassical equilibrium arises since firms and workers decide their strategies, contingent upon the eventual market price, but in the assurance that at the market price they will be able to buy or sell as much as they desire. This assurance is validated since the market price is 'set' to bring the actions of all the agents into accord, clearing the market. Conservative economists make much of this 'volunteerism' of the market economy as if the fact that no agent is forced into a transaction is sufficient to ensure the desirability of the outcome. Even in efficiency terms, however, the market must meet other criteria to be judged desirable.

A natural basis for judging a market's performance, in the context of our discussion to this point, is to examine the total surplus produced by the market in profits and in workers' surplus. These represent the gains to firms and workers in the aggregate from the existence of the market. If a different outcome, for example, would raise workers' surplus but leave profits unchanged, it would clearly be better. Since economists do not generally judge the distribution of income, we can adopt the criterion that the market outcome is desirable if it maximises net social benefit defined as the sum of profits and workers' surplus.

We now want to see whether there is another outcome that leads to a higher net social benefit than the neoclassical equilibrium. To examine this, suppose that there is a dictator with total power (thus violating the volunteerism of the neoclassical model) to set w and N and choose who works, even if the wage is below the individual's disutility of labour (so that the individual does not want to work) or if the wage exceeds the MPL (so that the firm does not want to hire the worker). Can the dictator find another outcome with higher net social benefit than the neoclassical equilibrium? The first thing to observe is that the wage set is irrelevant to this issue; it only affects the distribution of the total surplus between the firms (as profits) and the workers (as workers' surplus). The net social benefit at an employment of N, as the difference between total output and total disutility of work, is found by summing over the N workers the difference between the MPL and the disutility of work of each; that is, it is the difference between total output and the total disutility of work, as in Figure 2.1c. If the dictator wants to choose N to maximise net social benefit, he begins by employing workers with the lowest disutilities and continues until the MDU becomes equal to the MPL; this last worker just adds to output what he is foregoing in leisure value. But this condition, that maximises net social benefit, is the same condition as achieved in the neoclassical equilibrium, and that is the basis for claims about the efficiency or desirability of that equilibrium. It is important to note that a higher level of employment, as much as a lower, would be undesirable. An additional worker beyond N, if he was coerced into working by the dictator, would add less to production than he lost in leisure value, thus lowering the total surplus in the economy. This is important in considering policies that raise employment—if employment is already at N^*, such an increase is not desirable even if the policy could be effective in achieving it.

But when the neoclassical equilibrium achieves the efficient employment level N^*, it also does more than that—it determines w^*, the division of the surplus between firms and workers. The resulting distribution of income might be considered to be undesirable, and a government might seek on that basis to effect a higher wage. Within the market context, however, a government (or possibly trade unions) can raise the wage, but this will change employment and output as well. A wage set at $w_0 > w^*$ causes firms to demand fewer workers than N^*. It also causes unemployment through the rationing of jobs since the higher wage induces more workers to enter the labour force. This is the familiar argument used against minimum wages and trade unions, that workers are 'priced out of jobs'. Of course, these results hold only since the government imposing the minimum wage, or the trade union raising wages above competitive levels, are taken not to have the power to enforce that employment levels be maintained at N^*. Even so the wage policy might have a desirable effect on income distribution that outweighs the efficiency loss. This depends upon the elasticity of the labour demand curve; if it is inelastic, so that a rise in the wage of a certain percentage leads to a smaller percentage fall in employment, the wage bill will rise, profits bearing the cost of the policy. These effects are shown in Figure 2.1d.

The idea of workers pricing themselves out of jobs arose as one of Pigou's (1933) explanations for the high unemployment of the inter-war period. He argued that trade unions (with the acceptance of the government, which felt a particular responsibility for the welfare of war veterans) established a real wage above equilibrium, causing excess unemployment. Pigou's other major observation about unemployment, even at the neoclassical equilibrium, has similarly become a part of modern monetarist beliefs. The simple labour supply–demand model, at equilibrium, has no unemployment, but in an actual economy there will be 'transitional' unemployment as some sectors in the economy expand and others contract. This shifting of job opportunities leads to a shifting of workers, but this takes time and leads to a frictional unemployment. In this approach, equilibrium is again defined by:

$$L_d(w^*) = L_s(w^*)$$

but this will no longer equal employment. Rather, labour demand is composed of jobs that are filled, N, and those vacancies that remain, V: $L_d = N + V$. Labour supply consists of those having jobs and those that are unemployed but seeking out the vacancies: $L_s = N + U$. Equilibrium then entails that $N + V = N + U$, or $V = U$. In this equilibrium there are a number of unemployed seeking out new jobs but an equal number of jobs waiting to be found. Depending upon the institutional efficiency of the economy in matching the unemployed into the available jobs, this equality of U and V may be achieved at higher or lower levels. This frictional unemployment, for further analysis, really requires one to go beyond the single representative firm approach, and we will consider this in greater depth in our discussions of UV analysis and search theory.

Conclusions

The neoclassical equilibrium in the labour market solves for the real wage, employment, and level of output. These are indeed most of the variables of interest in macroeconomics, and this demonstrates the apparent centrality of the labour market to macroeconomic analysis. The equilibrium has desirable properties in maximising net social benefit, although it may lead to an unfortunate income distribution. A 'disequilibrium' real wage, set at too high a level, may improve income distribution but at the cost of lowering employment and output, and creating unemployment. The neoclassical model can be extended to include transitional unemployment by the introduction of unemployment and vacancy analysis.

We have not yet considered one of the usual exercises in presentations of neoclassical equilibrium—comparative statics—and a brief discussion might be useful. Comparative statics is concerned with how equilibrium shifts as either the demand or supply curve shifts. Two examples are particularly pertinent to the labour market. Demographic changes might increase labour supply; this rightwards shift of the curve would lower the equilibrium real wage but increase employment and output. The capital stock in the economy might increase, raising the marginal productivity of workers and thus labour demand, raising the equilibrium wage, employment, and output.

2.2   THE KEYNESIAN MODEL

The fundamental Keynesian observation is that the neoclassical model assumes that firms operate in an environment where, at the market prices P and W, they can sell as much output as desired and hire as much labour. Observation indicates, however, that in fact firms cannot sell an unlimited output at the market price. A way of formalising this is to suppose that firms, in addition to receiving

rices from the market, also receive 'sales-rations' of the max-
num amount that they can sell. In this section we consider the
npact of this change in environment upon the firm's behaviour
nd the resulting labour market implications, as well as the simple
ultiplier approach to the determination of output in a sales-
ationed market.

Before constructing this Keynesian version of the labour mar-
et, however, it will be useful to discuss further the 'Keynesian
bservation'. We are remaining in a world where the market,
hrough some mechanism, determines prices, and only adding the
ossibility that it determines sales-rations as well. To claim that
his is empirically validated, as a framework, requires that we
bserve firms that have no price-setting power and also, at the
oing price, are limited in their sales by market demand. This is
ery different from a monopolistically competitive world where,
or example, General Motors or British Leyland would like to sell
nore cars at the going price but are limited by the size of the
narket, since GM and BL in effect determine the demand by the
rice they choose to set. It may be that this year they can maintain
ales only by substantial price-cutting, but that is not evidence for
he Keynesian observation. We will return to this issue later in the
ook, since the economy by casual observation consists of price-
etting firms, and we will want to know if the Keynesian model is
obust with respect to that reformulation.

The Effect of Output Sales-Rations on the Labour Market

he existence of output sales-rations directly affects labour de-
nand. As in the earlier discussion, the firm seeks to maximise
rofits, by choosing employment and the resulting output, subject
o the market parameters P and W. But now the firm is also
ubject to the constraint that it cannot sell more than $\hat{Q}$, as we will
enote the level of the sales-ration. The firm could produce more
han that, but since it can't be sold, there is no point in doing so
ven if production was costless. (There is the possibility of building
p inventories, but we will ignore that complication.) The firm's
ptimal strategy can be characterised most easily by utilising the
arlier $MPL(N)$ curve in defining an 'effective' marginal product
urve which drops to zero at the level of employment $\hat{N}$ such that
$\hat{Q}$ is just produced. This effective marginal product curve takes
ccount of the zero value of production beyond $\hat{Q}$ and represents

the new demand for labour curve. For any w in excess of the w_{max} marked on the diagram in Figure 2.2a, the firm hires along the earlier $MPL(N)$ curve. But for a wage below this level, the firm continues to hire the number of workers, $\hat{N}$, whose output can just be sold. Note that a higher sales-ration would replicate the $MPL(N)$ curve to a greater employment level and then would become vertical.

There is no particular reason to change our earlier labour-supply formulation, and we can therefore combine this with the new labour demand curve in seeking to define an equilibrium for the labour market. For a given sales-ration level, the two curves are shown in Figure 2.2a. We have drawn this supposing that $\hat{Q} < Q^*$; not surprisingly, as we discuss below, the sales-ration is otherwise irrelevant and the only sensible equilibrium is Q^*. A natural way of proceeding in the current case might be to define equilibrium as the point of intersection of the curves, shown as $w_{min}, \hat{N}$. A problem with this, however, is that we have no unemployment; rather, the real wage has fallen, discouraging workers from labour-force participation to the point where the number wanting to work, at the low wage, equals the number of jobs. This is an important issue—even if there are sales-rations that limit employment, why should this result in actual involuntary unemployment through a rationing of jobs rather than in a lower wage? The falling of the wage to w_{min} admittedly does not create any more jobs, but it effectively rations them without involuntary unemployment.

If we do not want to adopt this definition of equilibrium, however, we have other alternatives. For all market wages between w_{min} and w_{max} the firm wishes to hire $\hat{N}$ workers, and there is a labour supply exceeding or equalling that amount. This whole range might be viewed as potential Keynesian equilibria since we have no particular reason to choose one over the other. Corresponding to each of the relevant wages there is an associated unemployment level, reaching a maximum at w_{max}, shown in Figure 2.2a as U_{max}, and a minimum at w_{min}, zero. In the sequel we will simply consider all these as possibilities. Note that the earlier neoclassical wage w^* is included within the range, and if one believes that the sales-rations are due to a recession but that the real wage does not adjust at all, one might think w^* the

appropriate wage to choose; observation from the diagram indicates that there is some involuntary unemployment at w^*.

A feature to note at this point is the comparative statics of
equilibrium with respect to an increase in the sales-ration. Should
$\hat{Q}$ rise, the resulting equilibrium entails a higher $\hat{N}$, but (because of
the potential range of wages consistent with this) the change in the
real wage and in unemployment is unclear. Of course, this holds
only when the sales-ration is less than Q^*; as it approaches Q^*, the
range of possible wages, to sustain the Keynesian output and
employment, shrinks to just w^* and we return to the neoclassical
equilibrium. If the sales-ration were to rise beyond Q^*, there is no
equilibrium at $\hat{Q}$ since there is no wage such that the firm wishes to
hire $\hat{N}$ workers, and there is at least that number willing to work. It
is for this reason that Q^* is referred to as the full-employment
output and N^* as full employment—a Keynesian equilibrium must
entail a lower output and employment.

The approach here shows how the labour market can sustain a
sales-rationed level of output; in the following section we will
consider what determines that level. But first it is important to
note that our story is not entirely the one presented in the *General
Theory*. Keynes' proposed mechanism did not have firms facing
individual sales-rations but rather supposed that the market established the wage w_{max} to induce firms to hire just that labour that
would produce the amount that could be sold in the aggregate.
The underlying story would be something like this: a fall in
aggregate demand causes output prices to fall more rapidly than
wages until the increasing real wage reduces employment and
production, along the $MPL(N)$ curve, to stabilise prices. The
theoretical problem with this story is that there is no rationale for
why wages don't continue to fall to eliminate the unemployment,
although the sales-rations approach does not necessarily have a
better answer to this objection. The more serious problem, in the
literature at the time, was that the empirical analysis did not seem
to support the idea that the wage tended to be at the w_{max}
appropriate to the various levels of production observed over
time. That is, if w remained at the w_{max} levels, changing this as
output changed, wages should move counter-cyclically, falling
when output rose in an expansion and rising when output fell in a
recession. Yet the evidence was that wages moved pro-cyclically.

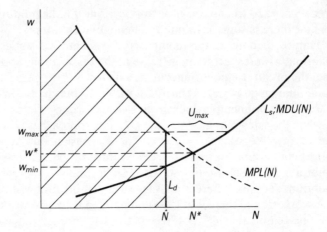

Figure 2.2a: *Keynesian sales-ration solution in the labour market, where the shaded area is $\hat{Q}$*

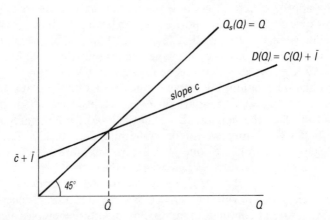

Figure 2.2b: *Keynesian cross diagram showing determination of equilibrium output*

Figure 2.2: *Features of the Keynesian equilibrium in the labour market and the simple multiplier process*

This is a major part of the motivation presented by Barro and Grossman (1971) in support of their sales-rationed model.

*Note that the notation of using * for neoclassical equilibria and ^ for Keynesian equilibria will be retained throughout the book.*

Determination of Output by Simple Multiplier Theory

Unlike the neoclassical equilibrium, where the labour-market equilibrium also determines the output level, the sales-ration approach requires that $\hat{Q}$ come from outside the labour market where it then in effect dictates the equilibrium. The simplest approach to determining output is to examine simple multiplier theory which is meant to represent an equilibrium in the goods market.

In the absence of government, the demand for goods can be taken to be composed of consumption-good demand and investment-good demand. Consumption demand arises as individuals in the economy (either workers or the owners of firms) receive income Y and then spend some part of this on goods. We write the consumption demand as dependent upon the income level, $C(Y)$, and define the marginal propensity to consume (MPC) as the derivative $C'(Y)$, the additional consumption expenditure as income rises by one unit. The proportion of additional income spent on consumption, the MPC, is not unreasonably assumed to be between 0 and 1. The remainder of individuals' income, $Y - C(Y)$, is taken to go into savings. The investment demand for goods comes from firms wishing to expand their capital stock by buying new machines, and in the simple multiplier model this is taken to be exogenous, perhaps determined by 'entrepreneurs' animal spirits', at some level $\bar{I}$. The total demand for goods can then be written:

$$D(Y) = C(Y) + \bar{I}$$

where the demand depends upon income.

Now turn to the supply of goods. If firms produce Q as the amount of goods, this not only represents the supply of goods but also the income in the economy. Recalling our earlier discussion of the labour market, the production goes to some agent, either the worker (as wages) or the owners of the firm (as profits). This allows us to substitute Q for Y in our demand for goods equation, and then to set $D(Q) = Q$ as an equilibrium when the demand equals the supply of goods. Writing $\hat{Q}$ as the Keynesian equilibrium that solves this equation:

$$\hat{Q} = C(\hat{Q}) + \bar{I}$$

For further analysis, it is easiest to adopt a linearity assumption, with $C(Y) = \bar{c} + cY$, where c is the earlier MPC. Then:

$$\hat{Q} = \bar{c} + c\hat{Q} + \bar{I}$$

and:

$$\hat{Q} = (\bar{c} + \bar{I})/(1 - c) = k(\bar{c} + \bar{I})$$

where $k = 1/(1 - c)$ is the simple Keynesian multiplier. Graphically, one has the 'Keynesian cross' diagram shown in Figure 2.2b. The equilibrium output is the multiplier times the exogenous (not dependent upon the income level) components of demand, $\bar{c}$ and $\bar{I}$. An increase in either of these would increase equilibrium output.

A common exercise with multiplier models is to add a government sector. A simple government using fiscal policies of taxation in the amount T and buying goods in the amount G (any difference being the government surplus/deficit) would affect the demand for goods in two ways: the tax T lowers private sector disposable income to $Q - T$, but the expenditure G raises demand for goods by that amount. We can write out the new demand function for goods at any output level Q:

$$D(Q) = C(Q - T) + \bar{I} + G$$

and, under linearity of the consumption function, solve for the goods-market equilibrium:

$$\hat{Q} = (\bar{c} + \bar{I} - cT + G)/(1 - c)$$

This gives us a new multiplier formula, and we can observe that an increase in G (keeping T unchanged, so that the deficit rises) increases equilibrium output, a rise in T lowers output and 'balanced-budget multiplier' exists where G and T rise equally, increasing (in this formulation) national output by an amount exactly equal to the increase in G and T. Numerous other multiplier formulations can be derived from this basic approach by adding, for example, taxation dependent upon income, or a foreign trade sector.

Conclusions

In the Keynesian approach with a sales-ration on firms, the equilibrium is characterised by the level of employment that just produces the sales-rationed level of output, provided that this is less than the neoclassical equilibrium output. The wage lies mewhere between the levels we have denoted w_{max} and w_{min}; here it lies within that range determines the level of involuntary employment. The sales-ration level can be determined from the ultiplier process.

The traditional Keynesian fiscal-policy activism arises from the ultiplier formula—if equilibrium output is below the full-ployment level Q^*, an expansionary fiscal policy will raise utput and the associated employment level. The case for using eynesian fiscal activism, in the absence of high costs associated ith the policy itself, is precisely the argument that the neoclassic-equilibrium had desirable features; that is, it maximises net cial benefit. For an expansionary fiscal policy to be adopted, wever, it is important that the cause of unemployment and low utput be inadequate aggregate demand for goods. In our discus-on of the neoclassical model we raised the possibility that too gh a real wage, set perhaps by monopoly unions, might lead ms to lower employment and output. In that case, the fiscal licy would be ineffective (and would presumably impose such sts as inflation that we do not yet have the framework to alyse). Yet a major empirical problem arises that is unfortunate-generally applicable to macroeconomic models. Consider the oclassical model with the excessively high wage, and the Keyne-an sales-ration model where the wage happens to be at the upper rt of the possible range. Observation of the wage and employ-ent levels, even if one has some past observations to judge them , cannot distinguish between the two situations—either the high age could be causing the low employment, or a sales-ration and w employment could be allowing the high wage. In one case the gh wage is the cause of the problem, and in the other it is merely symptom; yet the two cases are observationally indistinguish-le. It is for this reason that policy determinations are difficult in acroeconomics, and the methodology that argues that competing odels should be judged on the empirical evidence is not neces-rily helpful.

3 The Loanable Funds Market

The neoclassical equilibrium in the labour market determined th
major variables of macroeconomic interest: employment, outpu
and the real wage (the last important in gauging the distribution c
income in the economy). One of the remaining major tasks is t
determine the rate of interest and the resulting division of th
national product into consumption and investment, with th
implications that has for the future growth of the economy. W
will do that in the current section by solving for equilibrium in th
loanable funds market. The other major issues, the determinatio
of the price level and the rate of inflation, will be considered in th
following chapter on the money market.

In the Keynesian model, the level of investment has a mor
fundamental role than in the neoclassical model. Its impacts ar
not just on the future, through the additional capital equipmer
available to the economy, but are on the level of output toda)
This is seen in the simple multiplier model where national outpu
depends upon investment and its role in aggregate demand. Th
problem with that analysis, however, was that the level of inves
ment was taken to be exogenous, somehow predetermined. Give
the role of investment in that model, however, it is important t
understand the factors determining its magnitude, and this agai
takes us to the loanable funds market.

Given that we stated at the beginning that we would consider a
economy with four markets—output goods, labour, money, an
bonds—the loanable funds market is something of an artifici;
market. It is taken to be the market where savings (the supply c
loanable funds) meets the investment demand for loanable funds
The commodity being traded is loans, and the relevant price is th

interest rate on those loans. However, as should be seen from the initial section below, this market is really just the obverse side of the goods market, and in finding an equilibrium in this market we are really solving for an equilibrium in the goods market.

3.1 THE RELATION OF THE LOANABLE FUNDS MARKET TO THE GOODS MARKET

We begin by restating the earlier goods market clearing condition in investment and savings terms. A heuristic statement of a neoclassical equilibrium in the loanable funds market is provided, and we can see how a disequilibrium in this market leads to the Keynesian problem of insufficient demand for goods. The distinction between neoclassical and Keynesian equilibria in the loanable funds market is then clarified. Note that in our investment and savings notation I and S below, we will be referring to real rather than nominal values.

Restatement of the Goods Market-Clearing Condition

In our discussion of the simple multiplier model, we wrote the goods market-clearing condition as equality between the demand for goods, at the equilibrium level of production, and that level of production. With exogenous investment demand for goods:

$$\hat{Q} = C(\hat{Q}) + \bar{I}$$

Subtracting consumption from both sides:

$$\hat{Q} - C(\hat{Q}) = \bar{I}$$

But the left-hand side is income less consumption, or savings:

$$S(\hat{Q}) = \bar{I}$$

This is the loanable funds formulation of the goods market-clearing condition, with saving being the supply of loanable funds and investment the demand by firms for those funds. That investment is taken to be the same as the demand for loans might seem unusual, but it is really only an accounting identity. Our assumptions had all the income from production going to individuals as either wages or profits; this requires the firm to borrow

for investment purposes, with retained earnings being an implicit
loan from the owners of the firm.

The loanable funds equilibrium condition given is of course
merely a restatement of the earlier goods-market equilibrium
condition, but it is one that is useful for understanding why
Keynesian inadequate goods-demand problems ever arise. Before
addressing this question, however, we first note that the earlier
Keynesian cross diagram can easily be redrawn in the new format,
as in Figure 3.1a.

The Natural Rate of Interest

While the goods market-clearing equation first arose in our
discussion in the context of the Keynesian model, the idea that the
goods market should clear in any macroeconomic equilibrium is
surely not objectionable, and indeed is part of the neoclassical
model. The problem with the simple multiplier formulation,
however, is that consumption and investment (now restated as
saving and investment) levels were not derived from agents'
optimisation behaviour. It was just assumed that investment was
exogenous and that consumption followed some pattern with
respect to income. It would seem more reasonable that these
should depend upon the costs involved—essentially the interest
rate. Firms are less likely to invest if the cost of financing the
investment, the interest rate they will have to pay, should rise.
Similarly, households, in deciding how to divide their income
between consumption and saving, should consider the return to
saving (the interest on their savings).

At this point we shall adopt fairly arbitrary functional forms to
take account of the dependence of investment and savings upon
the interest rate; much of the remainder of this chapter will
analyse the dependence in greater depth. We will assume that
investment depends upon the interest rate, writing $I(r)$ to show
this dependence, and further that the relationship is inverse—a
higher r entails a lower I—as summarised in the derivative $I'(r)$
being negative. For saving, it is reasonable to suppose that this
depends upon income, as in the simple model of the previous
chapter, but also upon the interest rate; this is written: $S(r,Y)$.
Here S should be positively related to r and to Y—this is stated in
the form that the partial derivatives of S with respect to r and to Y
are positive.

Further analysis differs depending upon whether we adopt the neoclassical or the Keynesian approach to the labour market. From the neoclassical equilibrium in that market, output in the economy will be at Q^*, and this goes as income to some individual; thus $Y = Q^*$. Then we have a demand for loanable funds $I(r)$ and a supply $S(r,Q^*)$—since income is fixed at Q^*, the only factor affecting savings is the interest rate determining how much individuals save from their given incomes. We draw these supply and demand curves in Figure 3.1b and readily locate an equilibrium at their intersection r^*, $I^* = S^*$. This equilibrium interest rate r^* is often called the natural rate of interest following the terminology in Wicksell (1946).

It is important to note that the neoclassical solution entails, from the equivalence of the loanable funds and goods market-clearing conditions in the previous subsection, clearance of the goods market at the production level Q^*. The solution is not just a neoclassical equilibrium but a Keynesian equilibrium! The argument is not that the neoclassical point cannot be a Keynesian equilibrium, but rather that numerous other points can also be Keynesian equilibria. Suppose in particular that the interest rate is not at r^* but is somehow established above that level at the $\hat{r}$ in Figure 3.1b. The loanable funds market (and therefore the goods market) can still clear if output, equalling household income, adjusts so that:

$$S(\hat{r},\hat{Q}) = I(\hat{r})$$

As output falls from Q^* to $\hat{Q}$, saving falls to bring it into equality with the lower level of investment that occurs at the high interest rate $\hat{r}$ (relative to investment at r^*). This equilibrium is shown in Figure 3.1b. In this sense (which is often called Wicksellian), the low-output Keynesian equilibrium arises since the high interest rate causes investment to fall, and output falls to accommodate this. Although we here describe the effect of the falling output to lower saving to equilibrate the loanable funds market, one can think of the process as following the earlier multiplier formula. The $\hat{Q}$ value can then be taken back to the labour market as a sales-ration to complete the Keynesian equilibrium. Of course, there are unlimited potential values of $\hat{r} > r^*$, and therefore associated Keynesian equilibria.

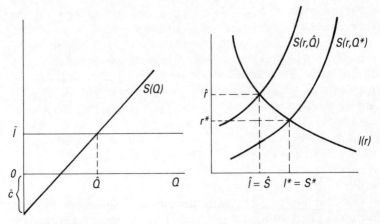

Figure 3.1a: *Loanable funds representation of simple multiplier model*

Figure 3.1b: *Neoclassical and Keynesian equilibria in the loanable funds market*

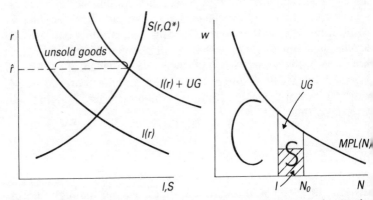

Figure 3.1c: *Immediate effects of high interest rate in loanable funds market before Keynesian adjustment*

Figure 3.1d: *Diagram showing the unsold goods problem in labour market*

Figure 3.1: *Features of neoclassical and Keynesian equilibria in the loanable funds market*

Keynesian Disequilibrium and the Stability of Equilibrium

The above discussion associates a low-output Keynesian equilibrium (distinguishing this from the neoclassical equilibrium, which also meets the criteria for a Keynesian equilibrium) with too high an interest rate (relative to r^*); the economy responds with an output adjustment to equilibrate the loanable funds and goods markets, at the high interest rate. The neoclassicals would argue that theirs is the only possible equilibrium, since if the interest rate was initially too high, it would do the adjusting. This is really an issue about adjustment processes, where the particular process may determine the outcome.

To examine this, consider an initial situation where production in the economy is at Q^* but the interest rate is at some $\hat{r} > r^*$. This is not an equilibrium in the loanable funds or goods markets since the savings generated exceeds investment. Something will have to adjust: either the interest rate will fall (restoring neoclassical equilibrium) or output will fall. To try to judge which will happen, we can consider the dynamics of the situation. Return temporarily to the goods-market formulation and write the excess supply of goods as the difference between production and demand:

$$UG = Q^* - [C(\hat{r},Q^*) + I(\hat{r})] = S(\hat{r},Q^*) - I(\hat{r})$$

where we have used the definition of savings as the difference between income (equalling output) and consumption and have shown the natural extension of the consumption function to include dependence not just on income but on the interest rate. The gap between saving and investment represents an excess supply of goods that cannot be sold on the market, as shown in Figure 3.1c.

In our formulation to this point, we have assumed that the firm paid out the full amount of output to workers and owners of the firm, so that this is the income received; as noted earlier, if the firm wanted to invest, it would then borrow the funds. But a problem arises in the unsold-goods case we are considering. In this situation the firm is building up inventories at the rate UG, and the eventual Keynesian response is to cut production to eliminate this inventory build-up. But consider what happens in the short run, before the firm has any chance to lower production. The firm is selling only $Q^* - UG$ goods but is paying out an income of Q^*—the firm must finance its inventory accumulation. The alternatives are to continue to pay out Q^* to workers and shareholders, and borrow UG on the loanable funds market, or to cut dividend payments to shareholders by UG, lowering their income. In either case there is an immediate effect on the loanable funds market since the first raises the demand and the second lowers the supply from savings.

Whichever strategy the firm follows, the short-run outcome is the same, but it is most easily seen for the case where firms borrow the amount UG to finance the unintended inventory accumulation so the supply of loanable funds (S) is unchanged but the demand rises by UG. As is shown in Figure 3.1c, the new demand curve, $I(r) + UG$, intersects the savings curve at $\hat{r}$; that is, the loanable funds market clears even though the interest rate is too high and output has not changed from Q^*. This is neither a neoclassical nor a Keynesian equilibrium in the market, but the market has cleared nonetheless. To understand this occurrence the literature introduced the terms 'intended' and 'unintended' investment. (The terms, *ex ante* and *ex post* are sometimes used to represent the same concepts.) The idea is that, in the neoclassical and Keynesian equilibria, the loanable funds market clears when agents are not surprised, when there is no unintended inventory accumulation; however, even if those conditions for equilibrium are not met, the loanable funds market clears *ex post*.

This temporary clearance of the market as firms finance unintended inventory accumulation is certainly not an equilibrium. Firms are not going to produce the unsold goods indefinitely. The importance of the point is that it suggests that, starting from the situation of the high interest rate $\hat{r}$ and neoclassical production levels Q^*, there is no reason to expect interest rates to fall to restore the natural rate r^*. The demand for loanable funds is augmented by the need to finance the inventories, and this will keep interest rates high. The adjustment process is more likely to be the Keynesian one, where firms respond to the inventory build-up by cutting employment and production.

The underlying issue here is 'the stability of equilibrium'. An equilibrium is of interest to us because we expect the economy, in general, to be at that point; if there is some disturbance, we expect the economy to return to that point. Both the neoclassical and the Keynesian equilibria in the loanable funds market are legitimate. The stability argument presented is that, starting from a given interest rate, it is more likely that output will adjust to the Keynesian equilibrium appropriate to that interest rate, than that the interest rate will fall to the neoclassical full employment equilibrium. Of course, we have considered the loanable funds market in isolation, and there may be other factors that lend greater stability to the neoclassical equilibrium.

Conclusions

The discussion in this section indicates the centrality of the loanable funds market to the Keynesian argument. A simple diagram to relate the current algebra to our earlier discussion about the labour market is presented in Figure 3.1d. At employment N_0, an amount equal to the area under the curve is produced and distributed to households as income—C returns as a demand for goods, leaving S as a residual. If the investment demand I is less than S, a gap of unsold goods UG appears. When this is financed in the loanable funds market, $I + UG$ equals S, causing an *ex post* clearing of the market. Firms are then taken to adjust employment and output to stop the unintended inventory accumulation.

The problem of unsold goods is presumed not to arise in the neoclassical model, since the interest rate is taken to adjust to r^*, clearing the loanable funds market and the goods market at full employment output Q^*. It is important to note that the argument is about the interest rate adjusting to clear the market, since many textbook presentations refer to something called 'Say's Law': 'supply creates its own demand'. Associating the neoclassical approach with Say's Law is, however, as unfair as associating Keynesian economics with the simple multiplier model. The neoclassical argument is that, if there is an insufficient demand for goods, the interest rate falls, restoring investment demand and lowering savings, thus increasing consumption demand.

3.2 THE HOUSEHOLD CONSUMPTION–SAVING DECISION

The discussion in section 3.1 arbitrarily adopted functional forms for saving and investment. In this section we examine the basis for the saving function $S(r,Y)$ by developing the household optimisation problem that determines saving and consumption. To do this we need to formulate first the relevant budget line facing the household and then the preferences of the household expressed in indifference curves in order to determine the optimal solution. From this, we consider the dependence of saving upon the interest rate, and then upon the level of income. The final subsection considers two applications of the model to macroeconomic issues.

The Budget Line

The budget line facing the household shows the various choices that are available. We consider a household that receives income over two periods—the household must choose its consumption in each of the two periods with savings being the residual (in the first period) of income less consumption. We will work in real terms (the household is concerned with its actual commodity consumption, not the nominal value of that), so the household will choose: c_1 and c_2, with $s = y_1 - c_1$, where y_1 is real income in the first period. Saving only occurs in the first period given the two-period existence of the household; it can be negative, representing a loan to be repaid in the second period.

While we will want to draw the budget line in real consumption terms, it is useful to consider how this derives from the actual nominal values of income. The relevant variables are:

Y_1 Y_2 nominal income in each period
P_1 P_2 price of goods in each period
i nominal interest rate

The nominal interest rate is the percentage rate actually observable in the economy, and we assume perfect capital markets in the sense that households can borrow or lend at the same rate i. The nominal income figures can be transformed into real values by dividing through by the price level:

$$y_1 = Y_1/P_1 \quad y_2 = Y_2/P_2$$

but defining a real interest rate is somewhat more complicated and will be considered below.

The budget line shows the combinations of real consumption in each period available to the household, subject to the parameters of its income and the interest rate. One possibility is immediately available: the household can spend all its first-period income in the first period and all its second-period income in the second period, neither borrowing nor lending: $c_1 = y_1$, $c_2 = y_2$, $s = 0$. Other possibilities on the budget line arise as the household saves or borrows, transferring consumption from the first period to the second, or *vice versa*. We construct the budget line by considering the rate at which households can transfer consumption in this way, which will give a natural definition of the real interest rate.

Suppose that the household cuts current real consumption by one unit of goods, releasing P_1 in nominal terms to be saved. This would draw interest at the nominal rate i, so in the second period the household would obtain (in addition to its second-period income): $(1 + i)P_1$, in nominal terms. This can then be spent on second-period goods at the price P_2, buying the following number of units:

$$(1 + i)P_1/P_2 = (1 + i) [(P_1 - P_2)/P_2 + 1]$$

Substituting $\pi = (P_2 - P_1)/P_2$:

$$= (1 + i) (1 - \pi) = 1 + i - \pi - i\pi$$

The term $i\pi$ can be ignored as the product of two small fractions, and introducing $r = i - \pi$, we can substitute:

$$= 1 + r$$

By this algebra, giving up one unit of goods today gains $(1 + r)$ units of goods tomorrow. The real rate of interest r is the growth in the actual number of goods obtained by saving over the number that could be consumed today. To interpret its definition as $(i - \pi)$, observe that π is a measure of inflation, so r is the nominal rate of interest, the growth in monetary value of the funds saved, less the rate of inflation (the decline in their purchasing power).

This rate of transformation of first-period goods into second-period goods, by saving (or, in reverse, by borrowing), is the slope of the budget line; since we already know one point on the line $(c_1 = y_1, c_2 = y_2)$, we can draw the line as in Figure 3.2a. To derive an algebraic expression for the line, observe that consumption in the second period is determined by income in the second period plus any saving from the first period, and the real return on that saving:

$$c_2 = y_2 + (1 + r)s = y_2 + (1 + r) (y_1 - c_1)$$
$$c_2 + (1 + r)c_1 = y_2 + (1 + r)y_1$$
$$c_1 + [c_2/(1 + r)] = y_1 + [y_2/(1 + r)]$$

In this last form, the present discounted value of consumption equals the present discounted value of income, all in real terms. The end-points of the budget line can be found from this in the usual way, by setting c_1 and c_2 respectively to zero, and solving for the other—this allows the labelling of the lengths shown in Figure 3.2a.

Household Preferences with Respect to Consumption over Time

The reason for transforming the problem into real variables is that it is the quantity, not the price, of consumption that enters into the household's utility. In the usual way, one expresses the household's preferences in the form of indifference curves over quantity bundles of the goods; in this case, period-1 consumption and period-2 consumption. These curves are drawn in Figure 3.2b, where the chosen shape of the curves (they do not intersect the axes) ensures that the household will eventually choose a point (a consumption bundle) with positive consumption in both periods. The shape is often described as following the law of diminishing marginal rates of substitution (*MRS*). By this we mean that the absolute value of the slope (the *MRS*) of each indifference curve diminishes as we move down the curve towards the c_1 axis. The *MRS* is the rate at which the household can trade consumption across the two periods and remain just as well off—the diminishing *MRS* means that, starting from a position with a high consumption of c_1, the household is willing to trade a large amount of c_1 for a relatively small amount of c_2.

It is useful to define the 'rate of time preference' of the household at a particular consumption bundle as:

$$\rho = MRS - 1$$

This ρ is the bonus in second-period consumption (over current consumption foregone) necessary to maintain the utility level of the household. Note that both the *MRS* and ρ depend upon the starting point, and we write $MRS(c_1, c_2)$ and $\rho(c_1, c_2)$ to show this dependence. From the diminishing *MRS*, ρ becomes smaller as we move down the indifference curve and eventually will become zero and negative. This occurs when the household starts out with such a large amount of c_1 that it is willing to trade for c_2 even if it gets less than one unit in return for each unit of c_1 foregone. Actual trades that a household makes, of course, will occur at the market price incorporated in the budget line; the indifference curves merely mark the willingness to trade.

The Optimal Choice of Consumption and Saving

The optimal choice for the household, given the budget line and preferences as formulated above, is found at the point on the budget line that reaches the highest indifference curve (furthest to the north-east). This occurs (given the straight budget line and the drawn shape of the indifference curves) at a unique point of tangency, where the budget line and an indifference curve (where it intersects the budget line) have the same slope. Since the slope of the indifference curve is by definition the marginal rate of substitution, and that of the budget line $(1 + r)$, the condition for optimality is:

$$MRS(c_1, c_2) = 1 + r$$

or:

$$\rho(c_1, c_2) = r$$

and the household chooses its pattern of consumption over time such that the rate of time preference equals the market interest rate. An optimal choice $\tilde{c}_1, \tilde{c}_2$ and the resulting $\tilde{s}$ are shown in Figure 3.2b.

It is important to note that, for given preferences, the household's consumption point depends only upon the position of the budget line showing the choices open to the household. The budget line, in turn, is described fully by the household's present discounted value of income (its wealth) and the market interest rate at which the household can borrow and lend. But while consumption in the two periods depends only upon these two factors, saving depends as well upon the pattern of the income stream. For given wealth, if two households have identical preferences but one receives all its income in the first period and the other in the second, it follows that they will both follow the same consumption pattern, requiring that the first household saves but the second borrows.

Dependence of Savings upon the Interest Rate

To derive the supply curve for loanable funds (savings), we need to consider how each household's optimal saving changes as the parameters of the problem change—when r changes or when the y values change. To find the market supply curve, we must then sum over the individual households. As before, we will assume that the

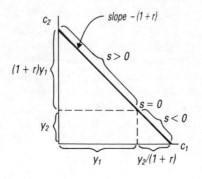

Figure 3.2a: *The budget line and savings*

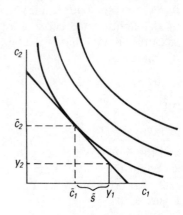

Figure 3.2b: *The tangency condition for consumption choice and resulting saving*

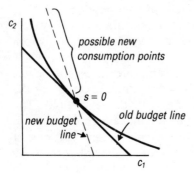

Figure 3.2c: *When savings are initially zero, an increase in r raises s*

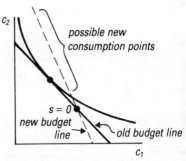

Figure 3.2d: *When savings are initially positive, an increase in r may lower s*

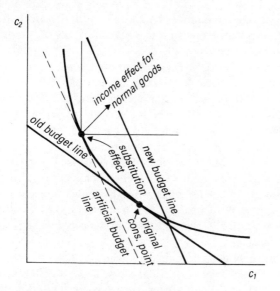

Figure 3.2e: *Income and substitution effects of an increase in r when s is initially positive*

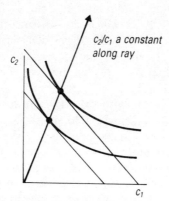

Figure 3.2f: *Homothetic preferences*

representative-agent approach is valid, and therefore that the market savings curve takes on the characteristics of a representative individual's curve.

We begin by considering the role of the interest rate r; a change in r changes the budget line facing the household. However, one point on the old budget line is unaffected and still available to the household—the point where the household was neither borrowing nor lending, since it was neither paying nor receiving interest. This positions the new budget line, which can be fully described by observing that the absolute value of the slope is $(1 + r)$, which has now increased (decreased) with r. When r changes, the budget line pivots around the zero savings point, as shown in Figure 3.2c for an increase in r. With a change in r, a number of new consumption bundles are available, but a number previously available are now no longer possible.

To find out how saving changes when r changes, we need to specify the initial level of saving; we will get a different answer depending upon this. The easiest case is when the old budget line had been such that the optimal $s = 0$, as in Figure 3.2c. Observation of that figure shows that the pivoting of the budget line due to a higher interest rate opens up better possibilities (part of the new budget line lies above the indifference curve obtained under the old budget line), all of which are characterised by a higher consumption in period 2 and a lower consumption in period 1. Since the income stream has not been changed, this means that saving has risen from zero to some positive amount ($s = y_1 - c_1$ rises with the fall in c_1).

We do not get this definite answer when the initial choice had been other than $s = 0$. Figure 3.2d shows the case where initial savings were positive, and the interest rate rises. Observation of the diagram shows that the new budget line contains better points than the old, but some of these display an increase in c_1 and some a fall. The actual point chosen will depend upon the pattern of the other indifference curves, but without specifying the preference structure fully we cannot tell whether the household saves more or less. This result should not surprise us since it is the typical result of household optimisation behaviour—there are income and substitution effects, which may be of competing signs, and depending upon which dominates, the change in demand may be of either direction. The usual procedure is to decompose the total change in demand (the move from the old to the new consumption point) into the substitution effect (move along the old indifference curve to find tangency with an 'artificial' budget line having the slope of the new budget line, but with different intercepts), which in the current case definitely entails a fall in c_1 and therefore a rise in saving, and the income effect (moving from the artificial budget line to the new budget line). If both 'goods'—that is, consumption in each period—are 'normal', the income effect in this case is to increase both c_1 and c_2, thus lowering saving. There are then two competing effects, and saving can either rise if the substitution effect dominates, or fall if the income effect dominates. The income and substitution effects are shown in Figure 3.2e.

The income effect in this case arises since, if the household was initially saving, the higher interest rate means that if saving was unchanged, the household would consume more in the second period but exactly the same in the first—it is sensible that the household will want to shift some of this 'windfall' back into first-period consumption by cutting its saving. Alternatively stated, the household can transfer as much consumption into the second period with less saving due to the higher return on the saving. The substitution effect measures the impact of the greater incentive to save since the return has increased on saving. The only thing unusual in this case, relative to standard examples of household behaviour, is that the competing-effect case occurs when the goods are normal rather than one being inferior. Note that in the zero-initial-saving case we gained a definite result because the income effect was absent; if s remained at 0, the higher interest rate does not affect consumption at all.

As we have noted, inconclusive results are common to household behaviour problems and are never seen as a roadblock to drawing household demand òr supply curves based upon the sign of the substitution effect; that is, we would typically suppose that savings depends positively on the interest rate, even though our theory does not guarantee this.

Dependence of Saving upon Income
We now consider changes in saving when income varies, holding the interest rate constant. A distinction is made between permanent income changes when income in both periods rises, and temporary changes when only first period income rises. For this

analysis it is easiest to work with a special case where the indifference curves take on a 'homothetic' form. By this we mean, loosely speaking, that the indifference curves are parallel to each other; more precisely, for each ray we might draw from the origin, each indifference curve has the same slope where it intersects the ray. This case, shown in Figure 3.2f, has considerable heuristic value, although it does mean that our analysis is not directly applicable to the general case of arbitrary indifference curves.

Recall that a change in the present discounted value of the income stream, for given r, shifts the budget line to a new parallel position. If the budget line was initially tangent to an indifference curve at some point, the parallel shift in the budget line, under homothetic preferences, will lead to a tangency with another indifference curve at a point on the same ray from the origin as the original consumption point. The feature of a given ray is that c_2/c_1 is a constant equalling the slope of the ray. Thus the new consumption point maintains the same proportion of consumption in the two periods, so c_1 and c_2 both rise or fall by the same percentage as the budget line shifts. Further, from the budget constraint:

$$c_1 + [c_2/(1 + r)] = y_1 + [y_2/(1 + r)] = y$$

where we introduce the notation y for the present discounted value of the income stream, it follows that, if y rises (falls) by a certain percentage, both c_1 and c_2 rise (fall) by exactly that percentage. This holds true only in the homothetic case, and it greatly simplifies the problem.

Now consider two cases: (i) y_1 and y_2 rise by the same percentage, and (ii) y_1 rises but y_2 is unchanged. In case (i), the present discounted value of income, y, will rise by the same percentage as its components, and from the discussion above, c_1 and c_2 also rise by that percentage. But then $s = y_1 - c_1$ rises in absolute value by that percentage. (Note that, if s was initially negative, it becomes a larger negative amount; we will however concentrate upon the case where s is initially non-negative.) In case (ii), when y_1 rises by a certain percentage, y will rise by a lesser percentage, and c_1 and c_2 grow by this smaller amount. But then, since c_1 grows by less than y_1, s must increase (this holds whether the initial s was positive or negative). Case (ii), where the income effect is transitory, displays a definitely positive increase in savings (for the homothetic preferences), and a greater increase than in case (i), where the income increase is permanent.

In general, since we will be looking at sustained equilibria, the first case would seem to be most pertinent—in the Keynesian approach we consider how a sustained higher or lower output of goods might equilibrate the loanable funds market. From the discussion, an increase in output and income is likely to increase saving, although not necessarily by the strict proportionality of the homothetic example. The second case does make the point that the entire income path over the future is relevant to consumption and saving decisions today.

Two Applications of the Consumption over Time Model

We consider two applications of the model: (a) the issue of taxation versus borrowing by the government (in effect, whether the government deficit matters) and (b) the impact of social security programmes on saving in the economy.

(a) The Ricardian Equivalence Principle: Suppose that we introduce a government which expends G (in real terms) in the first period, and that this can be financed by taxing our representative household g, in the first period, or by borrowing g from the household in the first period. (Since our household is representative, g multiplied by the number of such households in the economy should equal G.) If the government chooses to borrow rather than tax, in the first period, it must tax in the second period to repay the debt: it must tax in the amount $(1 + r)g$. Does it make any difference which strategy the government follows?

Observe that either policy, taxes today of g or taxes tomorrow of $(1 + r)g$, leaves the household with the same budget line since the present discounted value of income, net of taxes, is the same. But then the household's consumption in each period is not affected by the alternative policies (although it is less than would be the case if there was no taxation in either period). Given the pre-tax income y_1, the household saves $y_1 - g - c_1$, under the first policy, and $y_1 - c_1$ under the second, but this increase in savings by g is precisely what the government borrows—the supply of loanable funds, from savings, for the private sector is unchanged. This leads some economists (notably Barro, 1974) to conclude that the government deficit (for given government expenditure) doesn't matter, since it leaves the private sector loanable funds market unchanged, and therefore the equilibrium interest rate need not change.

The usual rejoinder to this argument is that the two-period model given may not be appropriate to the issue. In particular, suppose that our household exists for only two periods, and other households are formed after that time. The effect of a government deficit may be to transfer the burden of taxation from the current household to these later generations. Then the current household, under the government deficit case, will consume more and save less (net of the government borrowing) than under the taxation case, and this should lead to higher interest rates.

(b) The Effect of Social Security on Savings: Consider a special case of the two-period model, called the life-cycle model, where the household only receives income in the first period, while members are working, and saves to provide income in the second, retirement period. Now suppose that the government introduces a social security system where the government raises taxes from current workers (households in their first period) to finance pensions for the retired (households in their second period). A household in its first period will now reduce its savings, since it knows that it will receive its social security pension. This argument has been used to suggest that social security is responsible for the falling saving rate in the US in particular.

Conclusions

The model we have developed for household saving behaviour suggests that savings, in real terms, should depend upon the real interest rate and on the real income stream; further, there is some reason to believe that a higher r or a permanent increase in income will increase s. A transitory increase in income is likely to increase s by even more than a permanent increase. This analysis legitimises, to some extent, the initial form we stipulated for the savings function, $S(r,Y)$.

3.3 THE INVESTMENT DECISION BY FIRMS

We turn now to the demand for loanable funds arising from the need by firms to finance their investment in new capital equipment. In keeping with macroeconomic terminology, investment will refer only to this acquisition of physical capital and not to the acquisition of financial assets. We begin with a discussion of a neoclassical model of investment and then consider what modifications are appropriate for a Keynesian environment.

The Present Discounted-Value Approach to Capital Acquisition

We will first set up the firm's actual optimisation problem, in nominal terms, and then show how this is translated into real terms. The firm is deciding whether or not to buy a machine that costs P_k. If the firm buys the machine, it anticipates that the purchase will increase its earnings in future years by the amounts: $R_1, R_2, R_3, \ldots$ (while the machine is bought at time 0, it cannot be utilised until time 1). The problem is to compare these receipts in the future with the expenditure of P_k today. This is handled by the present-discounted-value (PDV) technique which takes account of the fact that receipts in future years are not worth as much as the same receipts today, since current receipts can be placed in the bank to draw interest.

To calculate the PDV of the stream of receipts, we ask what sum the firm could borrow today and repay with the stream of receipts. The amount R_1 received a year from now will repay a loan of $R_1/(1 + i)$ taken out today; the amount R_2 received two years from now would repay a loan of $R_2/(1 + i)^2$. Similar discounting applies to later periods and we write:

$$PDV = R_1/(1 + i) + R_2/(1 + i)^2 + R_3/(1 + i)^3 + \ldots$$

Since the PDV can be interpreted as the sum that can be borrowed and repaid with the stream of receipts, it represents the maximum P_k (for given Rs and i) that the firm would be willing to pay for the machine, given that the firm must then take out a loan in the amount P_k.

In the discussion to this point, we have allowed the Rs to vary over time but have maintained a stationary (over time) i. If the interest rate differed in each period, we could write:

$$PDV = R_1/(1 + i_1) + R_2/(1 + i_1)(1 + i_2) + \ldots$$

as a natural extension of the earlier formulation. In fact, we will generally work with the case where not only i but also R (suitably adjusted) is stationary.

To develop the model more fully, it is necessary to explore what determines the earnings gains R from purchasing a machine. The new machine basically increases the productivity of workers—in the labour-market diagram, the $MPL(N)$ curve is shifted out, as shown in Figure 3.3a. The actual earnings gain, however, takes account of two factors: for the given employment, output is higher; but, in addition, the firm hires more workers and gains a surplus on all but the last worker hired. The resulting profits gain (recalling that we are not subtracting the cost of finance, so these are not 'true' profits) is shown in the diagram. Note that this gain, which we will call the marginal productivity of capital (MPK), depends upon the real wage in that, if w had been lower, there would have been more workers whose productivity increased. In the sequel we will consider whether the firm should purchase 1,2,3 ... new machines, requiring that we define MPK not just for the first new machine but for subsequent purchases. We suppose that the second machine shifts the $MPL(N)$ curve out by a smaller amount than the first, so that the MPK of the second machine is less; we write $MPK(K)$ as the function relating the MPK to the machine's number, and this displays a diminishing marginal product of capital corresponding to our earlier law of diminishing MPL. Note that our MPK differs from the more general formulation, common in microeconomics, where one writes $MPK(K,N)$ to show dependence upon employment as well; we have solved out this dependence by stipulating a given real wage.

Since our labour-market diagram is in real terms, the MPK is in real terms and must be multiplied by P to give a nominal value for R. This R is stationary over time if (i) the real wage is stationary over time so the MPK of a given machine does not change, (ii) there is no depreciation of the machine over time, and (iii) there is no change in the price of output P. If the price changes over time, we have $R_1 = P_1 \cdot MPK$, $R_2 = P_2 \cdot MPK$, and so on. We will for the time being maintain stationarity in w and assume no depreciation, but will assume that there is a constant rate of inflation π into the future. Thus:

$$P_1 = P_0(1 + \pi), P_2 = P_1(1 + \pi) = P_0(1 + \pi)^2, \ldots$$

We can write the PDV of the earnings gains from buying a machine at time 0, with the machine beginning to be utilised at time 1:

$$PDV = P_0 MPK \left[(1 + \pi)/(1 + i) + (1 + \pi)^2/(1 + i)^2 + ... \right]$$

This takes on the form of a geometric series, and we observe the mathematical result that, for $c < 1$, $1 + c + c^2 + c^3 + ... = 1/(1 - c)$, and from that, $c + c^2 + c^3 + ... = c/(1 - c)$. Applying this to the current case, with $c = (1 + \pi)/(1 + i)$:

$$PDV = P_0 MPK \left[(1 + \pi)/(i - \pi) \right] = P_1 MPK/r$$

recalling the real interest rate r.

The condition for buying a machine is then: MPK/r exceeds P_k/P_1, where the latter is interpreted as the real cost of the machine. (That we divide the price of the machine by P_1 rather than P_0 is not particularly important and will be ignored in the rest of the discussion.) As in our other optimisation problems, it is the real values of the variables that becomes pertinent.

We can use the optimisation condition derived to define a demand curve for machines. Starting from an initial condition where the firm owns no machines, we have the $MPK(K)$ curve defining the earnings gains from potentially purchased machines. We graph $MPK(K)/r$ in Figure 3.3b, and can then see where this intersects the horizontal line at P_k/P_1 to determine how many machines should be bought—$MPK(K)/r$ is then the demand curve for machines, relative to their price. A change in r shifts the $MPK(K)/r$ curve, and therefore changes the demand.

Of course, our major interest is not in examining how the demand for machines depends upon their price, relative to the price of output—this is a question about the relative price of goods which is more pertinent to microeconomics—but rather we want to consider how demand changes with r. We therefore show how to construct a demand curve with respect to r. We know that the firm is indifferent to buying a particular machine if:

$$MPK(K)/r = P_k/P_1$$

where K is the number of that particular machine. For each machine there is some r such that this indifference condition is met—define that r as the 'marginal efficiency of capital' (*MEK*) of that machine. We graph this as a new curve in Figure 3.3c. But the $MEK(K)$ curve is the demand curve for machines with respect to r since, for a given market r, the firm will buy all the machines whose MEK exceeds r. The demand curve is downward-sloping, with a higher r lowering demand.

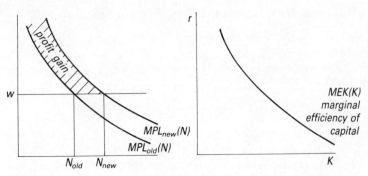

Figure 3.3a: *Gain from purchasing new machine*

Figure 3.3c: *Marginal efficiency of capital demand curve*

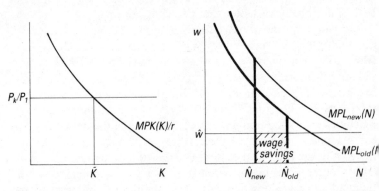

Figure 3.3b: *Optimal capital choice*

Figure 3.3d: *Gain from purchasing new machine under sales-ration*

Figure 3.3: *The firm's investment decision*

The Relationship of Investment to the Capital Stock

The reader will note that we were very careful in the preceding subsection to refer to the purchase of machines, or capital acquisition, rather than investment. The reason for this is that, under our stationarity assumptions (w and r unchanging over time, the $MPK(K)$ schedule given, and no depreciation), the firm should buy at time 0 the number of machines given by the $MEK(K)$ curve, but has no reason to continue to buy machines at future dates. The $MEK(K)$ curve is a demand for capital, not for investment. There

are two ways to use the model as an investment model, without
fully developing a growth model: (a) add depreciation to the
model or (b) introduce adjustment costs. The more satisfactory
approach might be to formulate a growth setting, with technological improvements perhaps providing a basis for growth over
time in the capital stock and in output, but this would require a
re-working of the entire macroeconomic model.

(a) Depreciation of Capital: Suppose that machines depreciate
at the rate δ each period; the machine becomes physically less
productive by that factor each period and, to maintain productivity
at the initial level, the firm would have to buy δ of a machine each
period. Increasing the capital stock by one machine then entails an
initial purchase, at price P_{k0}, an additional purchase of δ of a
machine at time 1 at cost $P_{k1} = P_{k0} (1 + \pi)$, and so on, where we
incorporate inflation in the price of machines at the same rate as at
output. The *PDV* of the eventual cost of a machine is calculated:

$$PDV = P_{k0} + [(1 + \pi)/(1 + i)]\delta P_{k0}$$
$$+ [(1 + \pi)/(1 + i)]^2 \delta P_{k0} + ...$$

Using the formula for geometric series:

$$= P_{k0} + (\delta/r) P_{k1}$$

The rule for buying the machine is that this must be less than the
PDV of the revenues from the machine; as in the preceding
subsection, we derive an *MEK(K)* curve as the demand curve for
machines. The new curve is related to the old curve but, from the
algebra, is below it due to the cost of the depreciation.

Once again we can use our *MEK(K)* curve to find, for a given r,
the optimal number of machines for the firm to hold. But now, if
the firm buys all those machines at time 0, it must continue to buy
machines each period in the future, in the amount δK to cover the
depreciation. Multiplying the *MEK(K)* curve by δ, we derive an
'investment' curve showing the purchases each period in the
future, assuming that the firm has initially acquired the optimal
capital stock.

(b) Adjustment Costs and Investment: The other way of
stretching out capital acquisition over time into a continuing
investment process is through adjustment costs. In this approach,

if K^+ is the ultimately desired capital stock and K the current capital stock, the firm adjusts slowly:

$$I = \alpha \, (K^+ - K)$$

purchasing in the current period some fraction α of the total additional capital it would like to acquire. The rationale for this slow adjustment can take two forms: (i) the price of machines might depend upon how many are bought at one time, a second machine bought at a given time being more expensive than the first, or (ii) it may be costly to integrate a large number of new machines into a factory at one time in that the ongoing production process might be disturbed. Since (i) violates the observation that quantity discounts usually lower the price on the second unit rather than raise it, (ii) is usually adopted as the explanation for slow adjustment.

The adjustment-cost approach is not a complete explanation for investment over time in that it can explain investment as a response to a shift in the desired stock of capital, but this investment will continually taper off following the formula for adjustment (as K approaches K^+, I goes to zero). One possibility is to set up a model where firms in the economy are constantly being formed and others are declining—the new firms are expanding and investing, while the declining firms are allowing their capital to depreciate. This begins to get us into growth theory however, and is not necessary for the basic macro model.

The Dependence of Investment upon Output

The discussion to this point suggests an investment function of the form $I(r)$, where I is expressed as a number of new machines, and investment is an inverse function of r derived from the capital demand function described earlier (p.67). We now want to consider how the introduction of Keynesian sales-rations might affect the analysis.

Suppose that our firm, currently owning K machines, faces a sales-ration $\hat{Q}$, and is employing just that number $\hat{N}$ of workers needed to produce $\hat{Q}$, shown as $\hat{N}_{old}$ in Figure 3.3d. The purchase of a new machine leads to a fall in employment since fewer workers are now needed to produce $\hat{Q}$. In contrast to the non-sales-ration case, where the gain from the new machine was in the increased productivity of current workers, and the hiring of new workers, the entire gain here is obtained by making workers redundant, saving their wages—the shaded area in the diagram. The number of workers made redundant can be found by locating a new level of employment, $\hat{N}_{new}$ in the diagram, such that the two bold-bordered areas are equal; at this point the new output is the same as the old.

Under the sales-rations, there is a new rule for the firm deciding whether to buy a machine: does the *PDV* of the labour-cost savings exceed the cost of the machine? Note that r continues to enter, since a higher r lowers the *PDV* of the savings and therefore makes the purchase less desirable. But the level of the sales-ration also enters. Suppose that a lower sales-ration is in existence, so that the initial employment (before the purchase of the machine) is less than before. Purchasing the machine increases the productivity of these, fewer workers, and therefore the gain in output would be less than before; this gain is then reflected in the redundancy of a smaller number of workers, and the wage savings are less, making the machine less desirable. A lower sales-ration would then seem to operate negatively on investment.

In a Keynesian environment, then, we would write $I(r,Q)$, where investment is inversely related to r but positively related to Q, and national output is entered to represent the sales-rations operating on individual firms. In addition to this change of form of the investment function we also note that investment plays a different role in the neoclassical and Keynesian models—in the neoclassical model, increased investment at a particular firm raises the productivity of labour and, for a given w, increases the demand for labour; in the sales-ration environment, capital is a substitute for labour, and investment at a firm entails a lower demand for labour. This does not take account, however, of the aggregate demand effect of investment: increased investment demand in the economy, through the multiplier (or more properly, through the loanable funds market equilibrium), raises the level of national output and the sales-rations, and in this indirect way tends to increase employment. Thus, while workers at a particular firm might oppose investment, recognising that it may cost jobs at the firm, labour as a whole might favour the investment since it expands output and employment in the economy.

Conclusions

We will adopt the general form for the investment function $I(r,Q)$ for the later analysis. Although this was derived in the Keynesian context (insofar as I depends upon Q and not just r), it encompasses the neoclassical case by fixing Q at Q^*. We will use the investment function, in conjunction with the earlier savings function, to solve for an equilibrium in the loanable funds market.

Some care is needed in the analysis in distinguishing between a shorter- and longer-run equilibrium. By this we do not mean the typical textbook distinction of the short run as some time frame in which expectational errors and wage rigidities hold, nor do we mean our earlier distinction between *ex ante* and *ex post* clearing of the loanable funds market; rather, we want to distinguish between a 'growing' and a 'stationary' equilibrium. At any time there is a capital stock in the economy, and some level of investment just covers the depreciation of that capital stock—if investment exceeds this, the capital stock is growing. This entails that the investment function will change over time (to reflect that any new machines are in addition to a larger initial stock of machines, and thus have lower MPKs), and, perhaps even more significantly, the $MPL(N)$ curve will be shifting out over time as the new machines increase labour productivity. The usual approach in macroeconomics is to take one period at a time. Thus, at any given time, there is a current capital stock that provides a basis for evaluating new investment and that positions the $MPL(N)$ curve. We can then analyse what happens in the current period, use the resulting investment level to adjust our capital stock for the next period, analyse what happens in that period, and so on. The alternative is to look for a longer-run stationary equilibrium where the capital stock has eventually grown to the point where the new investment just replaces depreciation. This second approach gets us into growth theory and will not be covered in the current book.

A second issue is related to this. If the economy is not continually replicating its outcomes in a stationary equilibrium, either because of growth or because of Keynesian aggregate demand shocks of some sort or another, firms will have some difficulty in predicting what will happen in the future. But the whole model of investment requires firms to have expectations about the future: in the neoclassical model, about future real wages and interest rates; in the Keynesian model, about future real wages, interest rates, and sales-rations. (Incidentally, a similar problem applies to the savings model, where consumers must have expectations about their future income to determine how much to save today.) The projections of the future are extremely important, and Keynes argued that perhaps the major determinant of the level of investment was the state of 'animal spirits of entrepreneurs'. The volatility of investment through this mechanism is vital in the Keynesian model in explaining recessions and booms, and to some extent suggests a model of self-fulfilling expectations. If firms expect a recession to occur in the future, and as a result lower their investment today, this may well precipitate the recession. The neoclassical counter-argument is to invoke 'rational expectations' where firms expect full employment all the time, allowing an easier calculation of expectations that, again, are self-fulfilling. The idea of expectationally self-fulfilling Keynesian equilibria is an interesting area for future research, and we will return to this in Chapter 10 towards the end of the book. In our current analysis, however, we will largely take the expectations as given, rather than solving for them in a rational-expectations framework.

Although the causal model for expectations, outside of the simple neoclassical rational expectations model, is not well developed, Tobin has suggested how the current state of expectations might be observed in the economy as a basis for a theory of investment. The market price of a firm's shares in the stock-market reflects the market's evaluation of the future profitability of the firm, of the future wages, interest rates, and sales-rations the firm will face, as well as the market's assessment of the firm's ability to successfully cope with the environment. If the firm uses this information in its investment decisions, or if the market on balance correctly predicts the future, the market-valuation approach can be used to predict investment. When market valuation rises, this indicates that the market anticipates a higher return to the firm's capital and should therefore induce further investment. Tobin's model, following this principle, defines q as the ratio of the market evaluation of a current unit of capital (installed at the firm) to the purchase cost of a new machine; as q rises, the value of the machine to a firm exceeds its cost, and investment should rise.

One final point is necessary for the later analysis. Our $I(r,Q)$

curve, as derived, is measured in terms of the number of machines the firm desires to buy. This is not necessarily the same as being measured in terms of general output goods, as Q and S are measured, since we have allowed the price of machines, P_k, to differ from the price of output goods. For the remainder of our analysis, however, we will suppose that in fact machines can be treated as if they were units of output in the sense that I will be taken to be measured in general output units, and therefore comparable to Q and S.

The Implicit-Rental Approach to Investment

The *PDV* technique for evaluating an investment is only accurate for certain cases: a sufficient condition is that the relevant environmental variables (in the cases considered above, r, w, $P_k/P_1, \hat{Q}$) remain constant over time. In this case, if it ever pays to buy the machine, it pays to buy it today. If, however, the variables change over time, the *PDV* of buying the machine today may exceed the purchase cost, but it may still be more profitable to wait and purchase the machine at some future time. The correct technique, in general, is the implicit-rental approach. In this section we develop that approach, primarily for completeness (and because it is of some interest in its own right); for our later analysis, the *PDV* technique will be sufficient.

To develop the implicit-rental approach, consider a two-period model where the nominal interest rate i is constant over time, but the other nominal variables are time-specific: $P_{k0}, P_{k1}, P_{k2}, R_1, R_2$, and we return to the initial formulation with Rs rather than output prices and *MPK*s. There are four potential possibilities for the firm with respect to the acquisition of this machine:

1. The firm can buy the machine at time 0 and hold it throughout the two periods, selling it at the end for P_{k2} (note that the problem now ends at time 2, so there must be some terminal allocation of the capital, which is taken not to depreciate).
2. The firm might never buy the machine.
3. The firm might wait, buying the machine at time 1 for P_{k1}, using it to produce in period 2, and then selling it for P_{k2}.
4. The firm might reverse its investment, buying the machine at time 0, using it to produce in period 1, and then selling it for P_{k1}.

The new possibilities to consider are (3) and (4).

The solution to this problem is determined by asking whether it pays to hold the capital in any given period. In a period t in which the firm has the machine, it gains R_t less the cost of the capital given by the price, $P_{k,t-1}$, the finance cost on the loan taken out to buy the machine, $iP_{k,t-1}$, less the amount recovered by selling the machine, P_{kt}. It is profitable to hold the machine in a given period t if:

$$R_t - (1 + i)P_{k,t-1} + P_{kt} \geq 0$$

Manipulating this:

$$R_t \geq [i - (P_{kt} - P_{k,t-1})/P_{k,t-1}] \, P_{k,t-1}$$

where the right-hand side is called the implicit rental on capital, the interest cost less any capital gains on the machine. Note that if machines display the same inflation as in the rest of the economy, the implicit rental can be written $r_t P_{k,t-1}$, and it is the carrying cost given by the real interest rate. While we have not explicitly incorporated depreciation, it is intuitive that it enters into an implicit rental as: $(r_t + \delta)P_{k,t-1}$. The firm should hold the machine in any period if the earnings exceed the implicit rental.

We now want to compare the answers from the implicit-rental approach with those in the *PDV* calculation. There are two cases to consider:

1. Stationarity of the environment. To consider this case, write $R_t = P_t MPK$; the implicit rental condition for holding the machine is then that MPK/r exceeds $P_{k,t-1}/P_t$; this is precisely the *PDV* condition derived earlier for the case where the relevant variables were stationary over time.
2. Non-stationarity. Suppose that the R_1 and R_2 values are given (but not the same), and we calculate the *PDV* of these; if the *PDV* exceeds the price of the machine, the earlier rule was to purchase the machine at time 0. However, it may be the case that R_1 is small (or even negative), and the firm could do better by waiting and buying the machine at time 1 for use in period 2. The implicit-rental approach rule, since it calculates the gain for each period, would tell the firm to wait in its purchase.

Since most of our analysis considers stationary equilibria, the *PDV* approach will generally be adequate for our purposes. The implicit-rental approach does have the advantage of providing an intuitive basis for calculation of the net return to any asset in a period, and is usually preferable as an approach.

3.4   THE *IS* CURVE

Our detailed examination of savings and investment behaviour leaves us with two functions: $S(r,Y)$, where Y equals Q in the absence of taxation, and $I(r,Q)$. All our variables are in real terms from the derivations used for the functions. Savings depends positively on the real interest rate and on income, while investment depends negatively on the real interest rate and, in a sales-ration environment, positively upon the level of the sales-ration represented by national output. As we have discussed, savings represents a supply of loanable funds and investment a demand for loanable funds (to finance the purchase of machines), and the clearing of the loanable funds market entails clearing of the goods market. In the current section, we show how the outcomes that clear the loanable funds market can be summarised in the *IS* curve introduced by Hicks (1937).

Derivation of the *IS* Curve
We have graphed the S and I functions in Figure 3.4a, where a higher subscript on Q denotes a higher level, with the full-employment neoclassical equilibrium output Q^* being the maximal obtainable in a market system. Since both S and I depend upon Q as well as upon r, graphing of a curve with respect to r requires specification of a particular Q; changing Q shifts the curve.

In Figure 3.4a the neoclassical solution for the loanable funds market can be determined by looking for the intersection of the $S(r,Q^*)$ and $I(r,Q^*)$ curves, thus solving for the natural rate of interest r^* discussed in section 3.1, and the associated level of investment. This is one market-clearing solution.

For the Keynesian approach, we proceed in a similar way, by looking for the intersection of the $S(r,Q)$ and $I(r,Q)$ curves at each particular level of Q up to Q^*; all these combinations of r and Q clear the loanable funds and goods markets, and are graphed as

he *IS* curve on Figure 3.4b. Provided that the dependence of *I*
ipon *Q* is relatively weak (the *S* curve shifts more than the *I* curve
is *Q* changes), the *IS* curve is downward-sloping.

The *IS* curve shows all the market-clearing combinations of *r*
ind *Q*, including the neoclassical equilibrium r^*,Q^*. Neoclassical
:conomists would not object to the *IS* curve in principle but would
:laim that the curve is irrelevant in that only r^*,Q^* will ever be
>bserved. The Keynesian argument is that the other points are in
act sustainable as some sort of equilibrium: a high *r* leads to a low
Q to clear the loanable funds market, and this low *Q* is sustained in
he labour market, perhaps by sales-rations.

Relation to the Keynesian Multiplier Model

We now want to relate the *IS* loanable funds (and goods)
narket-clearing locus to the earlier multiplier model, first in the
ibsence of government. The simple form of that model had
:onsumption (and, since $S = Y - C$, saving) depending only upon
ncome and not upon the interest rate; investment was taken to be
:xogenously fixed at some level. We now have more complicated
orms for *S* and *I*, but to make them comparable in format to the
:arlier analysis, we will assume linearity:

$$S(r,Q) = \bar{s} + sQ + s'r$$
$$I(r,Q) = \bar{v} + vQ + v'r$$

For market-clearing (using ^ to denote the more general Keyne-
.ian solution):

$$\bar{s} + s\hat{Q} + s'\hat{r} = \bar{v} + v\hat{Q} + v'\hat{r}$$
$$\hat{Q} = (\bar{v} + v'\hat{r} - \bar{s} - s'\hat{r})/(s - v)$$

This is the *IS* curve, written in the multiplier format. The simple
nultiplier equation $\hat{Q} = (\bar{c} + \bar{I})/(1 - c)$ is generalised in two
ways, by the addition of the interest-rate dependency terms in v'
ind s', and by the divisor $(s - v)$ rather than $(1 - c)$. Observing
hat *s* is the marginal propensity to save out of additional income,
t is clear that $s = 1 - c$, so the difference in the divisor is the
ippearance of *v*, deriving from the dependence of *I* upon *Q*.

The multiplier formula is commonly used to show how output
:hanges when consumption or investment demand changes exoge-
ously; in the current model, we would associate that with shifts in
he *I* or *S* curves—for given *r* and *Q*, what is the impact of a shift in

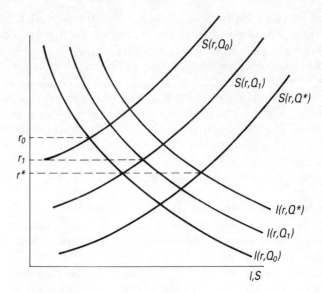

Figure 3.4a: *The general loanable funds market*

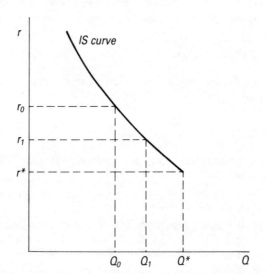

Figure 3.4b: *The IS curve*

Figure 3.4: *Derivation of the IS curve*

I or *S*. These shifts, in the linear form above, are encompassed in changes in $\bar{v}$ and $\bar{s}$, the 'exogenous' components of *I* and *S*. If $\bar{v}$ rises by one unit, or $\bar{s}$ falls by one unit, the change in equilibrium output is $[1/(s - v)]$ units, and in effect we have a generalised multiplier approach. These exogenous changes can be represented in the *IS* framework as shifting the entire *IS* curve to the right by the $[1/(s - v)]$ units; the multiplier then represents the change in output to a shift in *I* or *S* when *r* is fixed at some level.

This use of the multiplier, as representing the magnitude of shifts in the *IS* curve in response to a shift in *I* or *S*, is clarified when we apply this to the model with government fiscal policy. Consider a government, as before, that expends *G* (in real terms) and raises taxes in the amount *T*. This can be viewed as affecting the *I* and *S* curves in the following way: the government deficit *G* − *T* must be financed by borrowing, thus we have a new loanable funds demand curve $I(r,Q) + G - T$; the taxes as well affect household income, leaving a supply of loanable funds $S(r, Q - T)$. The market-clearing condition is that $I(r,Q) + G - T = S(r,Q - T)$. In the linear formulation, we can now solve for market-clearing as above:

$$\hat{Q} = (\bar{v} + G - T + v'\hat{r} - \bar{s} + sT - s'\hat{r})/(s - v)$$

and the effect of the fiscal policy, for a given interest rate, is to increase the associated market-clearing output by $(G - cT)/(s - v)$, recalling that $c = 1 - s$. This is exactly the same as the result in Chapter 2, but now the effect is to shift the entire *IS* curve rather than determine a particular output equilibrium.

3.5   THE MODELS TO THIS POINT

Most of the variables of interest in the neoclassical model were determined in the labour market: employment, output, and the division of the national income between wages and profits. The loanable funds market, through its equilibrium, then solves for the 'natural rate' of interest and the level of investment. This level of investment then operates to determine the growth of the economy; when investment exceeds that necessary to replace depreciation in the current capital stock, the expansion in the capital stock over time leads to increased productivity of labour and, in the labour market, to an equilibrium characterised by a higher real wage, employment, and output. The equilibrium in the loanable funds market can be affected by government actions, even if current national output remains at Q^*. As noted in the previous section, a government fiscal policy (now with $Q = Q^*$) changes the market-clearing condition to $I(r,Q^*) + G - T = S(r,Q^* - T)$; if the government runs a deficit, this should increase the demand for loanable funds and the equilibrium rate of interest, decreasing the equilibrium amount of private sector investment. The government might also follow 'incentive based' fiscal policies. An example is an investment tax credit designed to induce increased investment. This would increase I, for a given r, and lead to an equilibrium with a higher interest rate, but higher investment and presumably growth in the economy. Thus even in a neoclassical model there might be a role for government policy.

The Keynesian model generalises the notion of market-clearing in the loanable funds (and goods) markets. The market can be cleared by adjustments in r or in Q, and the IS curve shows all the combinations of r and Q (including r^*,Q^*) that are market-clearing. Looking at the loanable funds market in isolation, there is no particular reason to expect r rather than Q to adjust, and in that sense the Keynesian generalisation seems useful. If there is a reason to eliminate the points on the IS curve, other than r^*,Q^*, as equilibria, it must be found in the other markets. One suggestion is to view the IS curve from the goods-market perspective and to argue that if there is insufficient demand for goods at the production level Q^*, the price of goods should fall. But note that there is no immediate reason why this should restore demand. The insufficient demand arises either because investment is too low or consumption demand is too low. But in the model of investment, a fall in the price of machines and in the price of output goods essentially leaves desired real investment unchanged. In the model of saving, a fall in the price of goods today and that tomorrow leaves real saving unchanged. The price that is relevant in raising aggregate demand is the real interest rate, not the price of goods.

The Keynesian model to this point, if there is a price-adjustment problem, has the difficulty located in the labour market. If there are sales-rations deriving from insufficient aggregate demand, and these lead to a low-employment outcome in the labour market, why doesn't the real wage fall so that the fall in employment comes about from potential workers leaving the labour force rather than through involuntary lay-offs? This is a reasonable argument, but it still doesn't address the heart of the Keynesian problem—the low output and employment level in the economy.

Of course, our Keynesian model is still very incomplete. We have a locus, the *IS* curve, showing all the possible r and Q combinations that clear the loanable funds and goods markets. As yet we have no mechanism for determining which of those points is actually attained in the economy. The next step in completing the model is to introduce the money market, and here the price level of goods does play a potential role in aggregate demand.

As a final point in concluding our discussion on the loanable funds market, we note the very different role that investment has in a sales-rationed Keynesian equilibrium model, over the longer-term. In the neoclassical model where the economy is at full-employment each period, an increasing capital stock raises employment and output, along with the real wage. In a sales-rationed world, an increasing capital stock may merely substitute for employment, having a very different implication for the desirability of growth. This same differential impact, incidentally, arises in the case of technological progress, irrespective of investment. Technological progress in the neoclassical model leads to an increase in the productivity of labour and from that to a labour-market equilibrium with a higher real wage, employment, and output. But in a Keynesian sales-ration environment, the technological progress merely means that fewer workers are needed to produce the rationed output level; as with investment, technology substitutes for labour. Depending upon one's view of the economic environment, growth and technology can either be desirable or are to be feared.

4 The Money Market

In the development of the neoclassical model to this point, all of the real variables of interest have been determined. It remains to examine the nominal values, the price level and the rate of inflation. In the Keynesian model, in contrast, we have an *IS* curve but no basis for determining which point on that locus is attained, and therefore what r, Q and N define the outcome in the economy. Further determination of both models is provided by considering the asset markets in the economy—the markets for money and bonds.

The neoclassical model was traditionally closed by a simple model of the money market—the quantity theory of money. In keeping with this simplicity, we first develop the full neoclassical model with the quantity theory, and then consider how a generalisation of the theory of money might affect the analysis. This generalisation was provided by Hicks (1935) and Keynes (1936) and we will call it the Hicks–Keynes theory of money. The idea is that money is an asset, and holdings depend upon the opportunity cost—the return on alternative assets. This money-market model can be integrated into the neoclassical model or combined with the *IS* curve to further the description of the Keynesian model; like the dependence of investment upon output, the Hicks–Keynes theory of money is a generalisation of the traditional approach and is neither necessary nor sufficient for Keynesian results.

4.1 THE QUANTITY THEORY OF MONEY AND THE NEOCLASSICAL MODEL

That the neoclassical model has been solved for the real variables without the introduction of money is an important property of that model referred to as 'dichotomy': the 'real' and 'monetary' features of the model are separated and, in Marshall's terms, 'money is a veil' over the functioning of the real economy. An implication of this is denoted 'neutrality': the money market cannot have any effects on the (already solved) real variables, so a monetary policy is neutral with respect to those variables. The money market is of interest, however, since it will allow us to solve for the nominal variables, the price level and the rate of inflation.

In formulating the money market, money is to be viewed as a commodity just as labour, output, and loanable funds are commodities, and money similarly has supply and demand curves that can be solved for an equilibrium. The commodity of money is composed of a number of different goods, although the particular goods entering into an appropriate definition of 'money' is a matter of some contention. The basic definition is M_1, with the goods to be called money being actual currency (pound notes or dollar bills) and the amounts on deposit in current (chequing) accounts. A broader definition, M_2, includes as well the amounts held in deposit accounts, and there are other numerically denoted definitions. (There are some subtleties in the definitions that are beyond the interest of this book.) For our purposes it will be easiest to associate the term money with M_1, which can alternatively be described as those monetary assets that do not generally pay interest, or as those assets that can readily be used for transactions.

In the following subsections we briefly consider, respectively, the supply of money, the demand for money, the market equilibrium, and the roles for fiscal and monetary policy in the neoclassical model.

The Supply of Money

We will consider only briefly the factors underlying the supply of money. In this the Central Bank of the economy (the Bank of England or, in the US, the Federal Reserve Bank) is paramount since it controls the supply of currency and issues regulations controlling the behaviour of private banks. Insofar as the supply of money is associated only with currency, the Central Bank has complete control in determining how many pound notes or dollar bills to print and distribute to the economy, generally through open-market operations (where the Bank buys government securities with the money), although some monetarists refer, for heuristic reasons, to the 'money rain' (where the Bank hires helicopters to drop pound notes on the countryside). The difficulty in controlling the money supply has more to do with the other components included in definitions of money, and that is the issue we want to consider in the current subsection.

While currency supplies are fairly directly controllable by the Bank, the amount on deposit in chequing accounts (the other component of M_1) depends upon private decisions by individuals and banks, and the regulations that govern these accounts. One important regulation is that private banks must maintain a certain proportion of their outstanding chequing account balances in required reserves composed of particular, acceptable assets ('high-powered money'); denote this reserve ratio by R. Then, if chequing account balances are D, the bank must hold RD in required reserves. We will assume for simplicity that these are the only reserves held (i.e. banks do not hold excess reserves) and that they must be held in the form of currency (in practice, other assets are allowed). Then banks have a demand for currency: $C_B = RD$.

Households have some demand for M_1 composed of a demand for currency and a demand for chequing account balances. We will suppose that the division of the demand into these separate components follows the rule that households maintain a certain proportion c of their total holdings in the form of currency: $C_H = c(C_H + D)$, or $D = [(1 - c)/c] C_H$. Recalling that banks hold RD in the form of currency, we can write:

$$C = C_H + C_B = C_H + R\left[(1 - c)/c\right] C_H$$
$$C_H = \{c/[c + R(1 - c)]\} C$$

Define M_1 as $C_H + D$, the total household holdings of monetary assets, and observe:

$$M_1 = \{1 + [(1 - c)/c]\}C_H = \{1/[c + R(1 - c)]\} C$$

Holdings of M_1 are then the 'money multiplier' $\{1/[c + R(1 - c)]\}$ times C.

Implicit within this last formula are all the mysteries of 'money creation', the somewhat misleading term for the fact that a given amount of currency in the economy sustains a larger amount of M_1. It will be important for the later discussion, particularly with respect to real-balance effects and the 'inflation tax', to note that

demand deposits, the so-called 'created money', behave differently than currency held by the private sector as a whole (including
that held by banks). What happens with respect to demand
deposits is that banks have liabilities (equal to the outstanding
balances) and corresponding assets: the currency held in reserve,
loans outstanding, and bonds. Consider what happens with respect
to real private sector wealth when the price level in the economy
rises. The currency held by the private sector is worth less than
before in real terms, the real value of the demand deposits
declines, but so does that of the outstanding loans and bonds.
Insofar as the loans and bonds are private sector debts, the rise in
the price level harms the depositors at the bank but benefits the
debtors, leaving a zero net effect on the private sector except for
the decline in value of actual currency (or possibly government
bonds, depending upon whether one accepts the earlier Ricardian
equivalence proposition). The currency is a debt from the government to the private sector and the rise in the price level, by
lowering the real value of this debt, leaves the private sector worse
off; for this reason, the currency is referred to as outside money.
Inside money, on the other hand, has an offsetting liability within
the private sector, and a change in its value has no aggregate effect
on the private sector.

The model presented here for money supply is rather mechanis-
tic, and for that reason should not be taken to be a good
description of actual behaviour. Households must decide how
much money to hold in the form of currency and how much in
demand deposits (chequing accounts); we should not arbitrarily
assign a ratio c. More importantly, the behaviour of banks should
be examined from the viewpoint of optimisation. Banks have to
decide about holding excess, unrequired reserves. They have to
decide about their strategy in giving loans and in setting up
chequing accounts; the bank sets a return on a chequing account,
comprised largely of in-kind services such as free chequing, based
upon the return the bank can gain in loaning out the funds
involved. The money-creation process is properly viewed as a
market where the agents make decisions and supply and demand
operates.

That detail is unnecessary for our analysis, however. We merely
want to suggest that the Central Bank, through its control of the
monetary base (in our example, currency) and requirements

imposed upon private banks, can largely control the money supply when that is construed to include chequing accounts (and, for M_2, time deposits) as well as actual currency in circulation. In fact, we will in the discussion assume that the Bank simply determines the money supply; the reader will lose little in understanding most of the following if he associates money with currency outstanding and ignores the subtleties of the definitions of money.

The Quantity Theory of Demand for Money

The basis for the definition of M_1 is that currency and demand deposits can readily be used to complete transactions (the purchase of goods); further, individuals must generally hold purchasing power in these forms, in a non-barter economy, to engage in transactions. Early monetary economists therefore found it reasonable to suppose that households would hold money in proportion to their intended expenditures to facilitate the necessary transactions. In particular, if an individual intends to spend PT over a period, where T is the number of transactions and P the average amount spent per transaction, it seems reasonable to suppose that he will hold money as some proportion of this. If transactions in turn are some multiple of production, and we sum over individuals in the economy, we get a demand for money:

$$M_d = kPQ$$

in the economy. This is the 'cash balance' form of the quantity equation for the demand for money; an alternative form is written:

$$M_d V = PQ$$

where $V = 1/k$ is the velocity of money. In this form, money holdings multiplied by their velocity (or how fast they turn over) sustain purchases in the given amount.

Monetary Equilibrium in the Neoclassical Model

If the money supply is determined by the Bank at some level M_s, and the demand for money follows the quantity equation, setting supply equal to demand results in the equilibrium:

$$M_s = kP^*Q^*$$

where we set Q to Q^* since we are operating in the neoclassical context. The value of k is usually taken to be determined by various institutional factors (e.g. how many middlemen process a particular good, requiring money for the intermediate transactions, until it is finally consumed), and therefore is not a variable but a constant. Then the quantity theory of money has direct causality between the money supply and the price level. This is shown in Figure 4.1a where an increase in the money supply raises P. Indeed, a proportionality holds in that, for example, a 10 per cent increase in the money supply causes P to rise by exactly 10 per cent.

The proportionality suggests how to determine the inflation rate in the economy. The money supply, at a given time, determines P^* as M_s/kQ^*; its growth rate, if k and Q^* are unchanging over time, determines the rate of inflation π. More generally, by taking the log-derivatives of the supply–demand equality:

$$\pi = \dot{M}_s - \dot{Q}^*$$

the rate of output price-inflation equals the growth in the money supply less the rate of growth of output.

With these observations we can of course translate all the real values of variables, solved for in the labour and loanable funds markets, into nominal values by multiplying by the price level, or in the case of the interest rate, by adding the above rate of inflation to the real interest rate. The quantity theory completes the neoclassical model, in this way.

Besides the description of equilibrium in the money market given above, dynamic stories are often told about the transitional path to a new equilibrium when, for example, the money supply increases. Consider the case of a 'money rain': households collect the money from their back gardens, find themselves holding more money than they desire and rush out to buy goods with the excess. This drives up the price level since 'too much money chases too few goods'. This story is called the cash-balance mechanism, with the increased money supply causing households to buy additional goods. An alternative story, emphasised in the Hicks–Keynes approach to money, is that households try to buy other financial assets with the money, driving down the interest rate and through this interest-rate mechanism causing a decrease in saving (rise in consumption) and increase in investment, again leading to an excess demand for goods, raising their price. These stories are independent of the definition of equilibrium but may suggest what definition is appropriate, just as our discussion of *ex ante* and *ex post* clearing of the loanable funds market suggested that the Keynesian *IS* locus of equilibria might be appropriate. We will consider this later, after developing the Hicks–Keynes theory of money.

The Role of Fiscal and Monetary Policy

Since we have effectively completed the development of the neoclassical model, with some reservations about using the simple quantity theory to be expressed later, it might be useful at this point to consider the impacts of government policy in the model. The basic point is that if the government spends G in real terms, this will have to come out of the total full-employment output of the economy, requiring that consumption or investment falls. Further, the expenditure has to be financed in some way: by taxation, by borrowing, or by 'printing money'. We begin by examining the implications of these alternative ways of financing the expenditure, and then note that the necessary financing might have incentive effects changing output.

We consider the effects of taxation and borrowing in the context of the loanable funds market. If taxation does not have microeconomic incentive effects (e.g. a tax on labour might induce workers to decrease labour supply), it still has an effect on lowering disposable income and thereby saving by the function $S(r,Q - T)$. Borrowing raises the demand for loanable funds to $I(r,Q) + G - T$. If we consider the two extremes, we have as our loanable funds equilibrium:

(i) $T = G$: $S(r,Q^* - T) = I(r,Q^*)$
(ii) $T = O$: $S(r,Q^*) = I(r,Q^*) + G$

These need not (in the absence of the Ricardian equivalence proposition, which claims that in case [ii] the S curve shifts as well as households anticipate future taxes to repay the debt) entail the same equilibrium r (case [i] will generally show a lower equilibrium r), but both display an r higher than the equilibrium which would occur in the absence of government expenditure, and from that a lower level of investment—the government 'crowds out' private investment as shown in Figure 4.1b for case (ii). This may lead to a lower growth in the economy, reflected in lower real wages, employment, and output in the future (relative to the case

$G = 0$). Incidentally, a policy that has gained some vogue in the UK in recent years, financing the deficit with sales of state-owned enterprises, is largely identical to financing with borrowing. These sales tap the loanable funds market in the same way as borrowing.

Suppose instead that the government finances its expenditures by printing money, which it then uses to buy goods. If the government takes G out of an unchanged production of Q^*, the private sector allocation of goods for consumption and investment must have fallen by G—there must be either an implicit tax or implicit borrowing that has allowed this transfer of resources. What has happened is this: the increase in the money supply causes, through the quantity equation, prices to rise. In a neoclassical equilibrium (ignoring any incentive effects introduced by the government policy), there is no change in the real wage, but both the price level and the nominal wage have increased. Households are still worse off, because any nominally denominated assets have lowered in real value. For most such assets, this is merely a transfer from the lender to the debtor (if individual X has lent $10 to individual Y, the real value of this loan falls, making X worse off and Y better off), but there is one asset where there is no offsetting debtor in the private sector: currency. All the currency held by individuals in the economy is now worth less than it was before, because of the rise in the price level. The government has financed its expenditures by an implicit 'inflation tax' on money holdings. This tax then operates precisely as the general tax we considered above, entering into the savings function, lowering savings, and leading to an equilibrium with a higher r and lower investment.

The result, in the neoclassical model, that government expenditure (even if it doesn't change Q^*) raises interest rates and thereby lowers investment, explains the antipathy many monetarists have towards government spending. However, they see another serious problem arising from 'distortionary' effects of the financing used. Consider first a tax on wage-income used to raise the necessary revenues. This changes the incentive to work and is generally taken to decrease the labour supply—although, from the nature of household decision problems, such a tax may instead actually increase labour supply. In either outcome, the economy is no longer producing the efficient level of output Q^*. Recall our earlier discussion in Chapter 2 on the desirability of Q^*; if the income tax raises or lowers labour supply, and raises or lowers Q^*

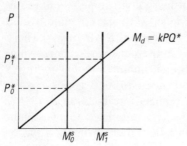

Figure 4.1a: *Effect of increasing money supply in the quantity theory model*

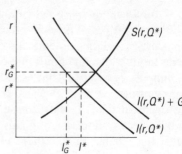

Figure 4.1b: *Effect of government borrowing G on the loanable funds market (raising r to r_G^* and lowering private investment to I_g^*)*

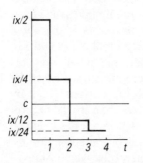

Figure 4.1c: *Marginal benefits and costs (c) of trips to the bank with optimal choice at $t^* = 2$*

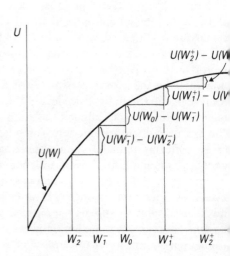

Figure 4.1d: *Case where it just pays to buy first bond $[U(W_1^+) - U(W_0) = U(W_0) -$ but not to buy second bond since $U(W_2^+) - U(W_1^+) < U(W_1^-) - U(W_2^-)$.*

Figure 4.1: *The quantity theory of money, the effect of borrowing on the loanable funds market, and the general demand for money formulation*

s a result, this is an inefficient outcome. The implicit inflation-tax
on money holdings, if an increase in the money supply is used to
finance government expenditures, has a related, although somewhat subtle, distortionary effect. The inflation-tax becomes a tax
on holding money, and as a result individuals will change their
behaviour, holding less money. This leads to inefficiencies in
transactions that become clear in a hyper-inflation period. Individuals, directly upon being paid, rush to the shops to unload the
depreciating currency.

The distortions caused by taxation are a 'deadweight loss' in that
the transfer of income from individuals to the government generally entails a certain loss along the way through the incentive effects.
Government expenditures can, of course, still be justified through
the traditional arguments in microeconomics, primarily the notion
of public goods (e.g. defence) which are not efficiently provided by
a competitive market.

In the discussion on the inflation-tax and on incentive effects we
avoided discussing government borrowing through bonds or other
nominally denominated instruments. The reason is that the analysis of this depends upon whether one accepts the Ricardian
equivalence proposition: do government bonds outstanding represent, to current households in the economy, a future tax-obligation
or repayment? If they do, they may have distortionary impacts
(individuals might anticipate, for example, that the bonds will be
repaid with a wage-income tax next year, so individuals might
increase their labour supply this year and take a long vacation next
year), but will not have a net inflation-tax impact on the economy.
If they do not, they are less likely to have incentive distortionary
effects, but will have a net inflation-tax impact. To see this latter
point, recall that inflation lowers the real value of a debt. The
holders of government bonds therefore find that their bonds are
worth less, in real terms, when inflation occurs. If, however, the
Ricardian equivalence proposition holds, individuals in the economy realise that future real taxes, to repay the bonds, will not
have to be as great, and the net effect on the private sector washes
out. Note that the inflation-tax on money holds in any case, since
no one expects the currency to ever be redeemed.

Given this discussion of the effects of the various policies, if one
accepts the need for government expenditure of a certain level,
how should that be financed? In the full-employment, neoclassical

world, government expenditure must entail a decrease in private expenditure (in the absence of incentive effects as discussed above); but it remains important whether that comes from consumption spending or investment, if we are concerned about the growth of the economy and the implications of that for real wages employment, and output. It is not contradictory that Keynesians in a time of full employment, favour taxation rather than borrowing (or its near-equivalent, the selling-off of national investments) Taxation operates through affecting disposable income of households, causing them to lower both consumption and saving. Borrowing operates directly on the loanable funds market, and in general leads to a greater relative impact on investment. Indeed, this dislike of full-employment deficits, financed through borrowing, is fairly general within macroeconomics; the dissenters largely lie in the 'supply-siders' who feel the disincentive effects of taxation are extreme to the point of actually lowering revenues when tax rates are increased, or those who accept the Ricardian equivalence proposition.

While Keynesians generally oppose full-employment deficits, this does not entail opposition to government borrowing during recessions. All of the above analysis was conducted under the assumption of full employment; in a Keynesian low-output environment, government expenditures need not come at the cost of private sector expenditures, and the analysis must therefore be different. Similarly, while almost all economists would oppose inflationary growth in the money supply during a period of full employment, using the inflation tax to finance expenditures, Keynesians would accept money-supply growth in a low-output situation when the growth would not necessarily be inflationary. even though it continues to raise revenues for the government.

4.2   THE HICKS–KEYNES THEORY OF MONEY

It will be recalled that after considering the simple multiplier theory, we noted a valid objection to the initial specification of savings as dependent only upon income, and investment as exogenous. These are variables deriving from agents' optimisation problems and should take account of the opportunity costs involved. Precisely the same objection can be raised with respect to the simple quantity theory of money. The demand for money should be derived as an optimising decision incorporating the opportunity cost of holding money. Hicks (1935) argued that holding wealth in the form of money is at the cost of depositing the sum in an interest-bearing account, and therefore the amount of money held should be inversely related to the interest rate.

There are two basic approaches to this dependence that really consider different asset choices: first, M_1 (currency and demand deposits) *versus* time deposits and, second, M_2 (currency, demand deposits, and time deposits) *versus* bonds. The models examining these choices are the transactions demand for money model, extending the quantity theory approach, and the asset demand for money model (i.e. the portfolio-allocation approach). We will develop these models and then show how the combination of these factors leads to the *LM* curve.

The Transactions Demand for Money

In the discussion of the quantity theory we supposed that individuals hold a proportion of the value of transactions in the form of money to facilitate those transactions; the proportion was taken to be given by institutional features of the economy. The analyses in Baumol (1952) and Tobin (1956) reformulate this as an optimisation problem facing the individual.

Consider an individual with a sum $x in his deposit account drawing interest and, for the moment, no holdings in the non-interest-bearing currency or chequing account. He intends to spend the $x evenly (the same amount each day) over the forthcoming period. One way of doing this is to transfer the $x to his chequing account at the beginning of the period, making a single trip to the bank. An alternative is to transfer only $½x at the beginning of the period, and then to make another trip to the bank halfway through the period, transferring the remaining $½x. The advantage of this alternative is that funds remain on deposit, drawing interest, for the first half of the period; the disadvantage is the cost of the second trip to the bank. The second alternative, further, entails a lower average money holding over the period since instead of running down the initial money holdings of $x over the period (giving an average money holding of $½x), he runs down $½x over each half of the period (giving an average money holding of $¼x).

The alternative possibilities, of course, include making three trips to the bank, then four, and so on. The effects of the alternatives are shown in Table 4.1. Note that the average holdings of assets by the individual, through the period, sums to $\frac{1}{2}x$ in each case, since he is spending the x evenly throughout the period; the different cases, however, divide this average holding between money and deposits in different proportions. As a result, there is a different amount of interest drawn in each case, and the column 'marginal interest' shows the increase in interest with each additional trip to the bank. This is diminishing, as seen from the chart.

Now suppose that each trip to the bank is equally costly at some amount c. There will come a point at which the marginal interest gain to another trip is less than c, and therefore the individual will not make that additional trip. For given i, x, c we can use the chart to calculate the optimal number of trips to the bank. This is shown in Figure 4.1c. The immediate implication, however, is that an increase in i (for given x,c) raises the marginal interest gains, and therefore leads to an increased number of trips to the bank. But this entails, from the average money holdings column, that the individual is, on average, holding less money for his given value of transactions. This is the basis for supposing that the transactions demand for money depends upon the interest rate.

The reader will note that this optimisation problem, in contrast to all the earlier problems, is solved in nominal, not real, terms. We can transform it to a certain extent into real terms. In evaluating the desirability of each additional trip, the individual compares $i(x/z)$ to c, where z is the denominator, specific to each additional trip, shown in the last column of the table above. Write x, the individual's total expenditures, as PQ, where P is the price level for goods and Q the real quantity of goods purchased. Now suppose that P doubles due to a general inflation, and the individual's real expenditures remain the same, but x doubles with the change in P. Since c is the cost of a trip to the bank, composed of the cost of transport and the value of the individual's time, it seems reasonable to suppose that c will double as well in the general inflation. But then the comparative values of $i(x/z)$ to c are unchanged, both doubling in absolute value, and the desirability of the additional trip is unchanged. The rise in P should then have no effect on the number of trips. But, returning to the table, the average money held (for a given number of trips), is proportional

Table 4.1: *Calculations for the transactions demand for money model*

Trips	Average money held	Average deposits	Interest	Marginal interest
1	$x/2$	0	0	—
2	$x/4$	$x/4$	$i\,(x/4)$	$i\,(x/4)$
3	$x/6$	$x/3$	$i\,(x/3)$	$i\,(x/12)$
4	$x/8$	$3x/8$	$i\,(3x/8)$	$i\,(x/24)$

to x, and the doubling in x doubles the amount of money held. The conclusion of all this is that a rise in the price level has no effect on the number of trips, but then the money holdings (and the average deposits) rise proportionately with P. An alternative way of stating this is that the real money holdings (dividing by P) are unchanged with the price level.

Of course, if x rises due to a change in the individual's quantity of purchases, Q, rather than P, there is no reason in the above calculation for c to rise, and therefore one is comparing, for each additional trip to the bank, a higher $i(x/z)$ to the given c—more trips are likely. But what happens to money holdings? Suppose that Q doubled, and as a response the individual went from 3 to 4 trips to the bank: his average money holdings would go from $x/6$ to $2x/8$, or $x/4$, so money holdings would actually rise. This example in fact reflects the general case; trips to the bank rise but not by enough to keep average money holdings from rising. This is easiest to see by using the calculus, as is done at the end of this subsection.

The analysis to this point suggests that we should write the real demand for money as:

$$(M/P)_d = L(i,Q)$$

where we introduce the notation L for the 'liquidity preference' function determining the real demand for money. This incorporates our observations that the demand for money holdings falls with the interest rate (as, for given expenditures, individuals make more trips to the bank, conserving on money holdings to gain the higher interest paid on deposits), the demand for nominal holding keeps proportionate to changes in the price level, so real holdings depend only upon the quantity of goods purchased, and do so in a positive relationship. The problem has been transformed into real terms with one very important exception: it is the nominal, not the real, interest rate that determines the real money demand. The reason for this is straightforward: the difference in return between an asset paying the interest rate i and a non-interest-bearing asset is i, whatever the inflation rate. If there is inflation, the interest-paying asset returns, in real terms, r, but the monetary asset returns $-\pi$, maintaining the differential of i.

Solving the Money-Holding Choice Problem with Calculus:
To use the calculus, we must transform the problem to eliminate the restriction that the number of trips takes on an integer value. We allow t, representing the number of trips, to take on any positive value. (This is not absurd, since the length of the period chosen in the text was arbitrary and, if we have for example ½ trip in a week, this is the equivalent of 2 trips in a month.) The following formulas hold:

    average money holdings $\frac{1}{2}x/t$
    average deposits $\frac{1}{2}x(1 - 1/t)$

(observe by inspection that the figures in the earlier chart meet these formulas). The individual maximises:

$$\tfrac{1}{2}x (1 - 1/t) i - ct$$

by choosing t. The first-order condition is found by taking the derivative with respect to t, and setting to 0:

$$\tfrac{1}{2}x(1/t^2) = c$$

Solve for t:

$$t = (xi/2c)^{1/2}$$

Average money holdings are then found by substitution in the earlier formula:

$$\tfrac{1}{2}x/(xi/2c)^{1/2} = (xc/2i)^{1/2}$$

It is seen that money holdings rise with the square root of x and fall with the square root of i; this 'square root law' is common to inventory problems. For a given c, then, a rise in x causes a (less than proportionate) rise in money holdings; this is the case we have associated with a real rise in expenditures. If c and x rise together, the case of a rise in the price level P, average money holdings rise in proportion, real holdings being unchanged.

The Asset Demand for Money

The model we have just considered followed the quantity theory of money in emphasising the transactions motive for holding money; it is really just a generalisation of the quantity theory to account for the opportunity cost of holding money—the nominal interest rate. Another use of money is as a store of value, an asset to be held as an alternative to such assets as bonds, equities (shares in firms), or physical assets. This 'precautionary' and 'speculative' demand for money (using the terminology in the *General Theory*) was formalised by Tobin (1958) in the portfolio-balance approach to asset holding.

Consider for simplicity an economy with just two assets available as stores of value (i.e. methods for individuals to hold their wealth, transferring their accumulated savings into the future): non-interest-bearing money and long-term bonds. Bonds are characterised by their maturity date, when the principal is repaid, and their coupon c_b (the sum paid as interest to the current holder, each period during the life of the bond). Bonds are traded in markets, and each bond has a market price P_b; from this one can calculate the current return as c_b/P_b. There is also the return to maturity, taking account not only of the current return but also the capital gains (losses) that arise if the current market price is below (above) the redemption value at maturity. We will also consider, for simplicity, a type of long-term bond known as the consol, which is distinguished by having no redemption date.

We consider the problem facing a household with an initial wealth W_0 to be allocated across the two assets; in contrast to the previous section, the household is not intending to expend any of this over the current period. Given that bonds pay interest and money does not, it would seem at first sight that the household should put all of its wealth into bonds. The reason it does not is that bonds are risky.

By the riskiness of bonds, we do not mean that there is some possibility of default. There are clearly bonds available (e.g. US Treasury bonds) that have no risk of default. Yet even these are risky in the following sense: the household could buy a bond today at the market price and, going to sell the bond in the next period, receive a much lower price. To see how this operates, consider a newly issued (at time 0) long-term bond. If the bond has a principal value of $100, and the current market interest rate is i_0, the coupon on the bond will be set at $c_{b_0} = i_0 \$100$. Now suppose that next year market interest rates have risen to i_1, and therefore newly issued bonds with a face value of $100 have a coupon of $c_{b_1} = i_1 \$100$. What happens to the price of the old (issued at time 0) bonds? They have a lower coupon, so clearly they are not worth as much as the newly issued bonds; the market price must fall to leave purchasers indifferent between the old bonds, with the lower coupon, and the new bonds.

The formula for the new market price of the old bonds is quite simple in the case of consols. For the consol with a coupon of c_{b_0} to be saleable at time 1, the market price must be such that the coupon gives a return equal to the market interest rate: $c_{b_0}/P_{b_1} = i_1$. An example might be helpful. Suppose that at time 0 the interest rate was 5 per cent, and therefore the $100 consol was issued with a coupon of $5, but at time 1 the interest rate has risen to 10 per cent, and new consols are issued at $100, with a coupon of $10. The old bond, with half the coupon of the new bonds, is then worth half as much, or $50. This shows how risky bonds can be. Generally, the percentage change in the price of the consol is the negative of the percentage change in the interest rate—if interest rates rise, for example, from 10 to 11 per cent, so that the percentage rise is 10 per cent, the bond falls in price by 10 per cent, giving a capital loss that offsets the interest for the year.

The extreme leverage of consols is mitigated in fixed-term bonds since the initial value of the principal is eventually repaid. Rather than equality of new and old bonds in the current return, as with consols, there must be equality in return-to-maturity. If the price of the old bond falls below its face value, there is an eventual capital gain upon redemption, and this is included in the return. If the maturity date is far in the future, the impact of changing market interest rates approaches that of consols; but as the maturity date becomes closer, the impact diminishes.

In any case, the return on a long-term bond (one that does not mature in the current period) in a given period can be written in percentage terms as $R = i + CG$, where i is the interest payment and CG the capital gain (or loss) on the bond. The household allocating its wealth across the two assets of money and bonds can observe the interest rate on bonds, but not the CG, which depends upon next period's interest rate. Suppose that the household expects the CG on average, over a number of years, to be 0, but that, in any particular year, it might take on the value x or the value $-x$, with equal probability. Further, x is a large number, so that $i - x$ is actually negative. Then, if the household puts its wealth into bonds, it gains (over holding money) on average, but in a particular year might end up with less.

Whether the household wants to take the risk associated with bonds depends essentially upon whether it is risk-averse with respect to the state of its wealth in a given year. With the initial wealth of W_0, depending upon how much the household has put into bonds and the particular outcome (whether x or $-x$ has resulted as the capital gain), the household ends the period with some wealth W_1. We will assume that the household makes its decisions on the basis of a utility function defined over W_1 with the curvature as shown in Figure 4.1d. This concave utility function displays risk-aversion, a gain of a certain amount adding less to utility than a loss of equivalent magnitude subtracts from utility, due to the diminishing marginal utility of wealth. While this entails that the household will not adopt a risky choice with an expected, or average, return of 0, we note that the expected return on bonds is $i > 0$, so the household may still allocate some or all of its wealth to bonds.

To determine the household's optimal allocation of wealth across the assets, we proceed in the usual way—starting from a 0 holding of bonds, will they buy the first bond, and then will they buy the second, and so on? Suppose that each bond costs \$100. For each bond, there is a 50 per cent chance that the household will gain the interest on the bond and a capital gain of x, increasing the initial \$100 to $(1 + i + x)$ \$100, and a 50 per cent chance that the household ends up with $(1 + i - x)$ \$100, which is less than \$100 by assumption. (Note the importance of the assumption that $i - x < 0$; otherwise, the bond is always profitable relative to holding money.) Now consider the purchase of the first bond. With 0 bonds, $W_1 = W_0$ since money bears no interest. With the first bond, there is an equal chance of ending up with an additional $(i + x)$ \$100 or losing the lesser sum $(i - x)$ \$100, leaving the household with the wealth values marked on Figure 4.1d as W_1^+ and W_1^-. But the household looks at the utility gains from this,

$U(W_1^+) - U(W_0)$ and $U(W_0) - U(W_1^-)$; if the former is greater, it pays to take the risk on the bond. In Figure 4.1d these are exactly equal, and the household is indifferent to purchase of the first bond. For the second bond that might be purchased, the dollar amount of the gain and loss remain the same, but the curvature of the utility function biases the household against the purchase as is seen from comparing $U(W_2^+) - U(W_1^+)$ and $U(W_1^-) - U(W_2^-)$ in the figure. The problem is that a second bond entails, in the event of capital losses, losses on top of the losses from the first bond, and therefore losses starting from a lower level of wealth, which (by the curvature of the utility function) entail a greater utility cost.

Now that we have the rule for optimal allocation of the wealth between money and bonds, we can examine how the household's allocation changes with respect to the interest rate on bonds. If i is higher, but the potential capital gains and losses x remain the same in value, it is intuitive that this makes it more favourable to hold bonds. Consider the first bond purchase shown in Figure 4.1d, where the potential utility gain and loss was equal, so that the household was indifferent to purchase. If i increases, then both W_1^+ and W_1^- rise, raising the potential utility gain and lowering the potential utility loss—it clearly becomes desirable to purchase the bond. From this, out of the given wealth, as i rises the allocation to bonds rises and the allocation to money falls. Once again we have an inverse demand for money with respect to the nominal interest rate. Further, it is the nominal interest rate that is relevant, since the real return to money is $-\pi$ and the real return to bonds (on average) $i - \pi = r$, but the difference in return is i.

The allocation towards money obviously also depends upon the size of the portfolio (the initial wealth of the household); heuristically, as the size of the portfolio rises (for a given i), we would expect the household to hold both more money and more bonds. Further, this choice should probably be independent of the price level in that if the real wealth of the household is unchanged, it should hold the same amount in real money and real bonds. We will write:

$$(M/P)_d = L(i, W/P)$$

The *LM* Curve

Our analysis in Sections 2 and 3 leaves us with two versions of the real money demand curve, both showing a dependence upon the nominal interest rate, but one incorporating the transactions demand based upon real income, and the other an asset demand based upon the allocation of real wealth. In the portfolio-balance model there was a demand for non-interest-bearing money as a store-of-value, independent of its role as a medium-of-exchange, since the only other asset, bonds, was risky. In a world with numerous assets—deposit accounts, short-term bonds(bills), equities, consumer durables (including housing), gold—some of which are essentially risk-free but bear interest, it is unclear why individuals would hold more non-interest-bearing money than was used for transactions purposes. A combination of the models into a 'general equilibrium over asset markets', as argued by Tobin (1969), might be appropriate. The individual must choose how much of his wealth to allocate to the different assets, taking account of their returns and risk. Much of the return to currency and chequing deposits derives from its use for transactions, just as much of the return from owning a house derives from living in it rather than from the capital appreciation. There is a further reason for solving the problem as a general equilibrium problem, with interrelated supplies and demands for all the various assets. We set up the supply of money supposing that a given amount of high-powered money sustained a certain amount of chequing account deposits. In fact, this is more complicated, since the available reserves can be used to sustain deposit accounts instead, and the supply side of money really depends upon the whole strategy of banks and other financial institutions.

Having said all that, however, we will adopt a demand function for money, for our analysis at this point, taking the form derived earlier (see p. 95):

$$(M/P)_d = L(i,Q)$$

with the demand for money in real terms depending positively upon national output and negatively upon the nominal interest rate. Macroeconomics is pursued by simplifying the structure of the aggregate model, primarily by ignoring interactions that are likely to be of small empirical importance. We will return to the general equilibrium approach later in this chapter.

To find an equilibrium in the money market, we combine our demand curve for real money with the assumption that the Central Bank chooses a real supply of money, and look for points where the market clears. In Figure 4.2a we have drawn a set of money

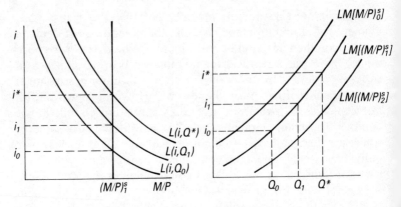

Figure 4.2a: *Combinations of i, Q that clear the money market for given $(M/P)_s$ and $(M/P)_d = L(i, Q)$*

Figure 4.2b: *The LM curve where $LM[(M/P)^s_i]$ corresponds to the case in Figure a*

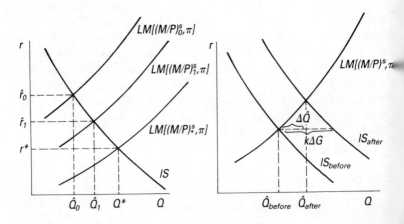

Figure 4.2c: *IS–LM equilibria for different real money supplies at common inflation rate*

Figure 4.2d: *'Crowding out' effect on Q increase with fiscal expansion but given real money supply, inflation*

Figure 4.2: *Derivation and application of IS–LM apparatus*

demand curves (each for a particular output level) with respect to the nominal rate of interest. For a given real money supply there are numerous combinations of i and Q that clear the money market, three of which are shown in the diagram for the real money supply $(M/P)_1^s$. The curve $LM[(M/P)_1^s]$, in Figure 4.2b, graphs the combinations. A change in the real money supply, from the Central Bank, shifts the entire LM curve, a rise causing the curve to shift to the right, as can be seen by working through the effects in Figure 4.2a. The LM curve will be combined with the IS curve of Chapter 3 in solving for equilibrium points.

4.3 THE *IS–LM* FRAMEWORK

The *IS–LM* apparatus was introduced by Hicks (1937) as a means of examining the Keynesian model and trying to contrast its structure with the neoclassical model. The approach solves for the equilibrium in the money and loanable funds markets simultaneously, determining the interest rate and output. This contrasts with the sequential solution method in the *General Theory* (the money market determines r, the loanable funds market determines Q from r, and the labour market determines employment) but represents a valid generalisation. In the following subsections we first construct the *IS–LM* apparatus, then show how the apparatus can be used to analyse fiscal and monetary policy, in the Keynesian environment, and, finally, examine the relation to neoclassical equilibrium.

The *IS–LM* Apparatus

We want to put the *IS* curve from Chapter 2 (see Figure 3.4b) on the same diagram as the *LM* curves from this chapter (Figure 4.2b), recalling that each *LM* curve relates to a particular real money supply from the Central Bank. There is one difficulty in doing this: the *IS* curve relates r and Q and the *LM*, i and Q, where i and r are related by $i = r + \pi$. We must therefore specify the rate of inflation or some mechanism for determining the rate of inflation. For the time being, it is simplest to suppose that the rate of inflation is exogenous, perhaps 0; in Chapter 5, we will address the issue again.

The *LM* curve, for a particular real money supply, graphed with i and Q on the axes can be redrawn with r and Q by shifting the *LM* curve down by the rate of inflation. Three examples of *LM* curves, for the same inflation rate but different real money supplies, are shown in Figure 4.2c.

To find the equilibrium in the loanable funds and money markets, for given real money supply and inflation, we look at the intersection of the *IS* and the appropriate *LM* curve. Because of the formulation, these represent potential Keynesian equilibria since r need not equal r^*, and Q need not equal Q^*. Addition of the money market to the Keynesian model allows us in this sense to solve for r and Q (recall that the loanable funds or goods market equilibrium condition, in isolation, left us with the whole locus of possible equilibria represented by the *IS* curve).

Fiscal and Monetary Policy in the *IS–LM* Framework

Suppose that the real money supply and inflation are such that the *IS–LM* intersection occurs at some low output $\hat{Q} < Q^*$, and the associated $\hat{r} > r^*$. In effect, the low real money supply leads to a high real interest rate and from that to a low-output equilibrium in the loanable funds (goods) market. It is immediate from the construction that an increase in the real money supply moves us to an *LM* curve further to the right, with an equilibrium displaying a lower r and higher Q. This shows the importance of monetary policy—the increase in real money operates through the 'interest-rate mechanism', lowering interest rates and by that increasing investment and consumption demand for goods.

Fiscal policy can be examined by reference to our discussion at the end of Chapter 3. An expansionary fiscal policy, one with a higher government expenditure or lower taxes, shifts the entire *IS* curve to the right by, for each unit increase in G, $1/(s - v)$, and for each unit fall in T, $c/(s - v)$, where c is the marginal propensity to consume out of income, s the marginal propensity to save ($s = 1 - c$), and v the marginal propensity to invest as national output rises. The effect, for an increase in G of magnitude ΔG, using the notation $k = 1/(s - v)$, is shown in Figure 4.2d. Both equilibrium r and Q rise. The resulting rise in Q, ΔQ, is less than the shift in the *IS* curve due to the interest rate rise—this is referred to as 'crowding out'. Demand for goods rises due to the increase in government demand, but the resulting interest rate rise lowers private investment, having a mitigating effect.

From the discussion, both expansionary fiscal and monetary policies raise equilibrium output. There are cases, however, where one or the other policy might be ineffective in this. If the *LM* curve was vertical, an expansionary fiscal policy shifting the *IS* curve to the right would not affect equilibrium output. If the *LM* curve was horizontal, an expansionary monetary policy (shifting the *LM* curve to the right is not meaningful) would have no effect. Hicks associated the vertical *LM* curve with monetarism and the horizontal with the Keynesian approach, thus, on the one hand, associating the two theories with claims about the slope of the *LM* curve and, on the other, identifying the theories with the ineffectiveness of monetary or fiscal policy. In fact, this was a highly misleading argument—we have already seen that the monetarist-neoclassical approach determines output at Q^* in the labour market, and neither monetary nor fiscal policy can affect that output, except perhaps through microeconomic incentive effects (if the government levies a tax on wage-income, workers might supply a different amount of labour). Monetary policy affects the price level, and fiscal policy affects the interest rate and from that the level of private investment and growth in the economy. Most Keynesians, in contrast, believe that both monetary and fiscal policy affect real output. We will consider further the relation of the *IS–LM* model to the neoclassical approach in the following subsection.

Returning to the general case where both monetary and fiscal policy affect the Keynesian equilibrium, is there any basis to prefer one over the other in practice? At first sight the expansionary monetary policy seems preferable in that it operates by increasing investment, while fiscal policy lowers investment. For a given current output, the monetary policy would seem to entail more growth in the future. The problem with this simple conclusion, however, is that the fall in interest rates benefits all interest-sensitive calculations such as housing and durable consumption goods. It might well be better to tailor a fiscal policy that directs the expansion specifically into capital-goods investment by such means as investment tax credits.

There is one final point to raise on policy issues. It might appear from the construction that a low-output equilibrium only occurs if the Central Bank lowers the real money supply; that is, the Central Bank could keep the economy at full employment simply by maintaining the money supply at the level $(M/P)^s_*$. The problem with this is that the *IS* curve will tend to shift around over time as factors change investment or consumption demand. The Central Bank, to retain full employment output Q^*, must stabilise the economy by constantly adjusting the real money supply so that the *LM* curve intersects the shifting *IS* curve at Q^* (the shift in the *IS* curve will change the r^* associated with full-employment output); the Central Bank must follow an activist policy.

The *IS–LM* Diagram and Neoclassical Equilibrium

The *IS* and *LM* curves can be viewed as generalisations of the simple multiplier model for the goods market and the simple quantity theory of money, in both cases introducing the role of the interest rate. The generalisation of the quantity theory to include the role of interest rates is generally acceptable to monetarists (see, for example, Friedman, 1958).

The *IS–LM* formulation is consistent with the Keynesian model, when the real money supply is too low, and is also consistent with the neoclassical model. For the given rate of inflation, there is a real money supply $[(M/P)^s_*]$ that sustains r^*, Q^*. The important issue is whether the generalisations contained in the *IS–LM* approach make the Keynesian low-output equilibria plausible.

The low-output equilibria arise when the Central Bank establishes too small a real money supply, driving up interest rates. The problem with this, raised by the monetarists, is that the Central Bank does not issue real money but nominal money, heuristically the number of pound notes in circulation. Suppose that the initial price level in the economy is P_0 and the Central Bank has issued an amount of money M_0. We are then at the *IS–LM* equilibrium in Figure 4.2c with output level $\hat{Q}_0$. The neoclassicals would argue that this low output level causes prices to start falling as firms compete for market shares (wages will fall as well due to the excess supply of labour), a process that increases the supply of real money for the given nominal supply M_0. This continues until the real money supply is restored to $(M/P)^s_*$, and the *IS–LM* equilibrium becomes r^*, Q^*. This is summarised as: the Central Bank determines the nominal money supply, but the market determines the real money supply.

The argument is a story of adjustment, with any low-output Keynesian equilibrium being transitional in nature. The only problem arises, as noted by Friedman as a possible explanation for the Great Depression, if the Central Bank follows a policy of responding to the falling price level by decreasing the nominal money supply still further. The best thing the Central Bank can do, it is claimed, is to follow a known rule for the growth of money to allow the market to adjust to shifts in the *IS* curve without having to deal with uncertainties about monetary policy.

The *IS–LM* formulation then poses the question about the legitimacy of low-output Keynesian equilibria as follows: does the price level adjust sufficiently rapidly (if at all) to restore full-employment output without serious transitional costs to the economy, or should the government attempt to stabilise against macroeconomic shocks reflected in shifts of the *IS* curve?

Stocks and Flows

We earlier stated that we would return to the general equilibrium approach to asset-holdings discussed in a previous section (see p. 101). We now want to do that in the context of trying to gain a fuller understanding of the *IS-LM* framework. In particular, we want to examine the *IS–LM* apparatus from a 'stocks' *versus* 'flows' perspective. The underlying problem is that we have defined a loanable funds market and a money market, but it is unclear what relationship the loanable funds market might have to the bonds market.

The *IS* curve is usually taken to concern 'flow' variables of saving and investment, which occur at some rate over time, and the *LM* curve 'stock' variables of money and bond holdings, summations of past flows. A household saves over time, increasing its wealth, which is then allocated across the various assets. Stocks and flows often create confusion, and are most easily understood by taking a particular period in time and examining what happens.

We consider an economy with only two assets for households to hold: money and long-term bonds (which are taken to be equivalent whether issued by the government or by firms). Money is denominated in pounds while bonds have a price P_b and a coupon payment c_b. Consider a particular household starting the period with asset holdings M_0 and B_0, earning wages over the period of Y_w, and, if it happens to hold shares in firms, receiving dividends from the firms in the amount d. (Note that we allow households to hold shares in firms, but not to trade them. This is done for simplicity.) This household will have to choose its consumption C (in real terms—PC in nominal) and end-of-period asset holdings M_1 and B_1, subject to its budget constraint. This can be written, in the absence of any taxes, as:

$$PC + P_b(B_1 - B_0) + (M_1 - M_0) = Y_w + c_b B_0 + d$$

The household has wage, interest, and dividend income which it expends on consumption and acquiring assets (saving). Depending upon the various prices in the economy, including the interest rate reflected in c_b/P_b, the household chooses some point along its budget line.

If we sum over all the households in the economy, total income will equal production Q. Now viewing the left-hand-side variables as aggregate, we write:

$$PC + P_b(B_1 - B_0) + (M_1 - M_0) = Q$$

and again the left-hand side is consumption plus saving. One thing we can do with this is to set the resulting amount of saving equal to the demand for loanable funds—since we are assuming no taxation, that is equal to firms' investment plus the government deficit or $I + G$. The loanable funds market is based upon getting this equality. That is not sufficient to clear both the bonds and money markets, however, since that requires that household acquire bonds in the amount of issue and money in the amount of issue. The LM curve is then about the division of the savings between the two assets; it is referred to as a stocks problem since, even if there is no saving, individuals may still want to change the proportions in which they hold their current stock of assets.

The IS–LM framework then takes the problem of clearing both the bonds and money markets, and puts this in the format of (i) having saving equal the total new issues of assets and then (ii) having saving divided between the two assets in the proportion in which they are issued. This clarifies the relationship between the IS–LM and the two underlying markets—the market for bonds and for money. To some extent the IS–LM approach creates artificial markets to aid the analysis, rather than strictly setting out supply and demand curves in the bond and money markets.

4.4 CONCLUSIONS

At this point we have constructed the basic neoclassical and Keynesian models. In the neoclassical case, we solved in the labour market for the real wage, employment, and output; one can then use the *IS–LM* summarisation of the loanable funds and money markets to determine the price level that sustains Q^*, and the associated interest rate. This can then be taken back to the explicit loanable funds market of Chapter 3 to determine the level of investment, which is interesting in its implications for the future growth of the economy. The Keynesian model works in a different way. Here the monetary authority sets the real money supply which, through the *IS–LM* framework, solves for equilibrium output and the real interest rate. The output level is then sustained in the labour market, with employment adjusting to that level necessary to produce the output. In terms of equilibrium conditions, the neoclassical model imposes full employment as a condition (with respect to the *IS–LM* framework), removing any efficacy of monetary policy in affecting output; the Keynesians allow the full locus of *IS* curves to be potential equilibria.

Beyond the imposition of equilibrium conditions, however, there are stories about the adjustment processes in the economy that attempt to legitimise one or the other of the models. The neoclassical story is that the Central Bank issues a nominal rather than real money supply; if, at the current price level this leads to a low-output equilibrium, that would cause firms and workers to lower their price and wage demands, thus increasing the real money supply and restoring the aggregate demand and output in the economy. Keynesian economics basically does not accept this story, or views the transitional period as being sufficiently long that any ultimate neoclassical equilibrium is not of particular interest. In particular, if the economy constantly suffers macroeconomic shocks of one sort or another (reflected in the *IS* curve), no neoclassical equilibrium would ever be reached; the economy would always be on some transitional path.

A somewhat stronger Keynesian position would actually view a low-output *IS–LM* equilibrium not as a transitional point but as an outcome that is self-sustaining over a reasonably extended period of time. This runs into a legitimate neoclassical counter-argument.

If firms cannot sell their output, why don't they lower the price? If workers cannot sell their labour, why don't they lower their wage? There seems to be a strong case that some adjustment should occur.

From this it would seem that the neoclassical *versus* Keynesian debate is really about adjustment processes—about whether quantities or prices adjust to a change in macroeconomic conditions (perhaps a fall in the money supply) and with what speeds. These are the issues that we want to consider in the following chapter. In many ways, however, that discussion will not be satisfactory to answer the issues but will merely rephrase them. The problem is that the adjustment process ultimately comes down to individual behaviour, requiring the same careful microeconomic foundations analysis that characterises the derivations of the labour-market supply and demand curves, and the *IS* and *LM* constructions.

APPENDIX TO CHAPTER 4: REAL-BALANCE EFFECTS

The reader may have noted that the effects of price level change in the *IS–LM* apparatus, as described in this chapter, do not correspond entirely to the real-balance effects discussed in section 1.2 (see pp. 6–20). There we argued that a recession might be self-correcting since firms would respond to the excess supply of goods, and workers would respond to the excess supply of labour by lowering nominal prices and wages. This would increase real wealth in the following sense: money holdings by individuals in the private sector are a net wealth. Unlike government bond holdings, if one accepts the Ricardian equivalence principle, the fact that the government need never tax in future to redeem currency issue implies that money holdings represent a net wealth to the economy. The real value of this net wealth depends upon the real stock of money holdings in the economy; as these rise, the wealth in the private sector rises. One might think, and Patinkin (1965) has argued, that this rise in real wealth with a falling price level in a recession will lead to increased consumption demand for goods. The real-balance effect, then, might be to increase consumption expenditure from a given income, shifting the *IS* curve to the right and thereby leading to a restoration of the neoclassical equilibrium in the *IS–LM* diagram.

This contrasts with the current argument that the main restorative feature, with a falling price level, lies with the shifting of the *LM* curve. The argument is that the given nominal money becomes more effective for transactions purposes, and individuals will only hold the increased real money if the interest rate falls, leading to a movement along the *IS* curve, with increased investment and consumption spending. Both effects of course might be present, and they really represent complementary phenomena.

5 Price and Quantity Adjustment

At the end of the previous chapter we suggested that the difference between the Keynesian and neoclassical approaches might be in their view of the adjustment processes in the economy. A way of clarifying the distinction between the two is to take a particular example—the response of the economy to a fall in the nominal money supply. If the price level adjusts immediately, there will be no recession, as the *LM* curve (dependent upon the real money supply) remains in its original position. If the price level adjusts slowly, there will be a recession, but unless if some other dynamics of the system deepen the recession faster than price adjustment ends it, there is a self-correcting mechanism in the economy. For a true, persistent Keynesian equilibrium, there must be some reason why prices do not adjust at all, or the adjustment is insufficient to restore the neoclassical equilibrium.

If one wants to formulate a Keynesian approach, in this context, one has to deal with the issue of price adjustment. One way of doing this is the fixed-price approach, where it is simply assumed that nominal prices are given, and the resulting outcome is examined; since prices do not adjust in response (for example) to a monetary shock, quantities must. We have already utilised this approach in our analysis, but it will be helpful to restate it in a relatively complete version. The useful feature of the fixed-price approach is that it clarifies an important issue: the distinct features of mis-set real wages and nominal prices. Following the logic of the real-balance effect, the 'wrong' nominal price level leads to an inadequate aggregate demand reflected in 'sales-rations' at the firm level. This then determines whether the economy is underproducing relative to neoclassical equilibrium. A separate yet related

112

issue is in whether this underproduction is reflected in actual unemployment of labour, or whether the real wage is sufficiently low such that the labour supply has fallen to the (reduced) labour demand. The issues are related in a way that is clarified by reconsidering the labour-market formulation in the *General Theory* as discussed in Chapter 2. The real wage has implications for the firm's desired production level. If the real wage is sufficiently high, then the firm optimally cuts its production (on marginal-productivity/real-wage comparison grounds) to just the level of aggregate demand, and the sales-ration is not an independent force; the real wage then in effect determines whether the firm is 'happy' with its sales-ration or whether it will attempt, perhaps by lowering its output goods price, to raise sales. The level of the real wage may then induce nominal price adjustment that restores aggregate demand. Clarifying these relationships is one of the purposes of this chapter, since it is important for our later analysis.

The simple fixed-price approach has, however, two problems. To provide an adequate theory, the basis of price determination must be explored. In addition, it is impossible to understand what nominal price rigidity means in a period of inflation when prices are clearly changing, and the model needs further extension in this direction. A way of extending the approach is to follow an argument raised by Tobin (Sept./Oct. 1972) that the Phillips curve defines the price-adjustment path; it is the 'missing equation' that determines how price and quantities adjust over time with respect to a monetary (or other type of) shock. This makes explicit the notion of slow price adjustment over time and, further, the model is applicable to an inflationary period. The difficulty is to provide a theoretical backing for the Phillips curve; this can be done to some extent with *UV*-curve analysis examining the dynamics of the labour market, and the application of standard Walrasian excess-demand price-adjustment assumptions to wage-setting.

The problem, as viewed by the neoclassicals, is that in general this labour market is not in equilibrium. The original form of the Phillips curve postulated that nominal wage-inflation would increase as unemployment fell, but this sort of adjustment might not lead to a restoration of Walrasian equilibrium if nominal prices were adjusting as well, leaving the real wage mis-set, and further, the fall in nominal prices might just equal the rate of fall of the nominal money supply, leaving aggregate demand unchanged. The neoclassicals argued that this failure of adjustment arises since the process is improperly specified—it is more properly formulated as one of relative or real wage adjustment in response to dis-equilibrium unemployment. As long as unemployment differs from the 'natural' or equilibrium rate, there is an incentive for firms to change their wage offers relative to the price level. This can be frustrated only if an accelerating inflation or deflation leaves a gap between target real wages and actual real wages.

For there to be a continuing disequilibrium, there must be some process that is preventing adjustment. To the neoclassicals this can only be a temporary confusion brought about by, for example, unexpectedly high inflation. The Keynesian notion is that some other factor might be preventing the adjustment. One of the conclusions of this book will be that contracting can serve as that factor.

5.1   THE FIXED-PRICE APPROACH

The fixed-price approach takes the nominal price level P and the nominal wage W to be given and, at least for the relevant time span, unchanging. The approach was suggested by the arguments in Clower (1965) and Leijonhufvud (1968) that prices are slow to adjust in comparison with quantities. The model was further developed by Barro and Grossman (1971) to consider the resulting 'quantity constrained' equilibria. It should be noted that we implicitly used this sort of model in our 'sales-rationed' labour market in Chapter 2, and the discussion here will be very similar to that, differing in that the IS–LM approach is now incorporated.

The basic structure of the model is perhaps best understood in a three-quadrant diagram (Figure 5.1a), where we begin with the IS–LM analysis and use the resulting equilibrium output to determine sales-rations operating on the labour market. Assume that the growth rate of the money supply and the rate of inflation are zero, and that there is a given nominal money supply. We then draw the set of LM curves (in the i,Q quadrant) corresponding to different real money supplies as the nominal price level P changes. Given an IS curve, we can then find (for each P) the IS–LM equilibrium output level Q which represents a potential output sales-ration pertinent to the labour market, carried into that market in our diagram by means of the production function in the lower right-hand quadrant.

If P is such that the $IS-LM$ equilibrium output level $\hat{Q}$ is less than the neoclassical equilibrium Q^* (i.e. $P > P^*$), there is an associated $\hat{N}$ representing the maximum number of workers whose output can be sold. With the sales-ration, actual employment still depends upon the real wage in the labour market. Employment may be limited by the sales-ration, by the real-wage-determined labour demand (the MPL curve), or by labour supply. For each sales-ration there are associated values of the real wage, w_0 and w_1, such that for real wage rates between w_0 and w_1, employment is determined by the sales-ration at $\hat{N}$; for real wage rates above w_1, the MPL condition limits employment below $\hat{N}$; and for wages below w_0, labour supply limits employment below $\hat{N}$. Note that when the $IS-LM$ equilibrium dictates the neoclassical output level Q^*, w_0 and w_1 become equal, at w^*—any wage other than the neoclassical equilibrium w^* entails a fall in employment. Should the $IS-LM$ equilibrium be at a $Q > Q^*$, N^* remains the maximal employment level sustainable in the labour market, at a wage of w^*. (In fact, this case becomes somewhat more complicated since there will be underproduction of goods relative to demand, and the resulting rationing may cause workers to supply less labour at a given wage since they are unable to spend their current income, thus compounding the problem.)

The three-quadrant diagram allows us to associate with each P, and its $IS-LM$ equilibrium, the appropriate values of w_0 and w_1. These values are graphed in Figure 5.1b. We have labelled three regions in the diagram: 'classical unemployment' occurs when the real wage is above the relevant w_1 values, so that the real wage limits employment (below N^*) along the MPL curve; 'Keynesian unemployment' occurs when the sales-ration determines output levels; and when the real wage is below w_0, so that labour supply limits employment, we have 'repressed inflation'. Of these 'regimes', the classical unemployment case is one we discussed in Chapter 2, where high real wage rates 'price workers out of jobs'; the only new feature is that the concept is here extended to cases where aggregate demand (from the $IS-LM$ equilibrium) is insufficient to sustain full employment anyway. The Keynesian regime follows our earlier sales-ration approach to the labour market. The

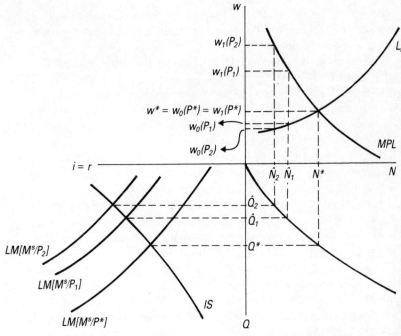

Figure 5.1a: *The three-quadrant diagram for determining* w_0, w_1 *values corresponding to price levels*

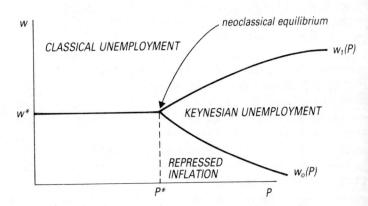

Figure 5.1b: *The three regimes*

Figure 5.1: *Fixed price analysis*

low-wage, labour-supply limiting case, is new to our discussion; this is denoted as repressed inflation since there is excess demand in both the goods and labour markets.

Beyond this exercise of labelling regimes, the framework can be applied to monetary and fiscal policy shifts. As is intuitive, these policies are effective only in the Keynesian regime, where the sales-ration (determined by the *IS–LM* equilibrium) is pertinent. If unemployment is caused by insufficient aggregate demand, an expansionary monetary or fiscal policy can decrease it; if it is caused by an excessive real wage, it is the real wage itself that must be lowered; and if it is caused by an insufficient real wage, again it is the real wage that must be changed.

The sales-rations approach to the Keynesian labour market is a natural one in showing how aggregate demand leads to unemployment, and it was for this reason that we adopted it in Chapter 2. While the model is inadequate in not providing any basis for the price rigidities, we can use it to consider how the economy might adjust from a Keynesian unemployment position. There are two features of this relative to a Walrasian, neoclassical equilibrium: P is too high, so that there is inadequate demand and sales-rations, and w is too high, so the inadequate demand becomes reflected in Keynesian involuntary unemployment. Neoclassical economists would expect that because of the excess supply of labour, w will start to fall, and continue to fall (for given aggregate demand) to the appropriate (for the given P) w_0. However, as w falls, firms recognise the large divergence between the *MPL* and the low real wage, and will seek to expand their sales by lowering their output price; this then leads to a restoration of aggregate demand, for the given nominal money supply. To gain Keynesian results there has to be some failure in these adjustment processes. This could just be a failure of firms to lower their prices faster than the money supply is falling, so that the sales-rations remain binding. Alternatively, one could be in the position of the original *General Theory* labour market as discussed in Chapter 2—the real wage could fail to adjust, so that firms had little incentive, on a marginal-productivity/real-wage comparison, to try and gain further sales. The rest of this chapter will examine adjustment processes. The difficulty, however, is that very little formal microeconomic modelling is involved, and one is really choosing between behavioural equations on an *ad hoc* basis. To go beyond this, one has to give firms price-setting and wage-setting powers, and to examine their optimal behaviour.

5.2   THE PHILLIPS CURVE AS THE MISSING EQUATION

The neoclassical objection to a Keynesian *IS–LM* equilibrium was that, for a given nominal money supply determined by the Central Bank, the nominal price level in the economy would adjust, increasing the real money supply to the point where the *IS–LM* equilibrium occurs at Q^*. The adjustment process, and the speed of the process, is left largely undefined. A way of specifying this, suggested largely by Tobin, is to integrate the Phillips curve into the model. In fact, we will be able to define Keynesian equilibria, allowing for price adjustment by the Phillips curve, corresponding to different nominal monetary policies, where we define the policy as an initial nominal money supply and a constant rate of growth of the money supply into the future. Equilibrium will be reached when the nominal price level is growing at the same rate as the nominal money supply (so that the real money supply is unchanging), but this equality will occur at differing output levels, depending upon the growth rate of money.

The Phillips curve derives from Phillips (1958), and was further developed in Lipsey (1960). It is an observed empirical relationship between nominal wage-inflation and the unemployment rate, with wage-inflation increasing as unemployment falls. For our purposes in this section it will be easier to work with a simpler relationship where the rate of increase of nominal wages, wage-inflation, represented by ω, is an increasing function of output: $\omega(Q)$. The heuristic reasoning is that a higher output will be associated, in a Keynesian framework, with lower unemployment and this will lead to an upward pressure on nominal wages. We will return to the basis for the Phillips curve later in this chapter. For now, we add another assumption—that firms mark up prices as wages rise so that $\pi(Q) = \omega(Q)$, where π is the earlier-defined rate of price-inflation.

We begin with a technical point about the *IS–LM* analysis. Recall that the position of the *LM* curve in the r,Q quadrant depends upon both the real money supply and the rate of inflation (since the pertinent interest rate for money-holding decisions is i, the nominal interest rate, differing from the real interest rate r by π). Since we will want explicitly to incorporate inflation into our analysis, it will no longer be appropriate to assume that the inflation rate is fixed or zero as a means of drawing a single LM curve pertinent to each real money supply. Rather, for each real money supply there are numerous LM curves, each conditional upon a different π; several of these are drawn, for a fixed real money supply, in Figure 5.2a. But the Phillips curve, drawn (upside-down) as $\pi(Q)$ tells us which LM curve is pertinent at each output level. Combining the appropriate points from the various LM curves gives us a new locus, the LM^* curve for that real money supply, incorporating the differing rates of inflation as Q varies. For each real money supply, there is a different LM^* curve, and (as with the LM curves) a higher real money supply shifts the LM^* to the right; two of these are drawn in Figure 5.2b. These LM^* curves can be used in the same way as our earlier LM curves in solving for an $IS–LM^*$ equilibrium.

We will want to use this Phillips-curve-augmented Keynesian model in two ways: first to show the adjustment process in the economy to a one-time change in the nominal money supply, and then to examine how the growth rate in money might sustain differing real output equilibria. Technically, these issues are referred to as the 'neutrality' of money and the 'superneutrality'. The model will show non-neutrality of money in the short run (a one-time change in the nominal money supply causes short-run real effects), long-run neutrality (after the adjustment is complete, the real effects disappear) but not superneutrality (a higher growth rate in the nominal money supply over time sustains a higher real output level).

First consider what happens when the growth rate of the money supply is normally zero, and we begin from a long-run equilibrium with zero-inflation marked as Q_{ni} with the associated $(M/P)_{ni}$ in Figure 5.2b (the subscript ni signifies the non-inflationary output equilibrium). There is a one-time jump in the nominal money supply, but no continued growth from that point. If P could immediately jump, it could restore $(M/P)_{ni}$ and the equilibrium output Q_{ni}. However, the Phillips curve will instead dictate a slow adjustment of prices. Writing the original money supply as M_0 and price level as P_0, the increase in M to M_1 will cause the LM^* curve

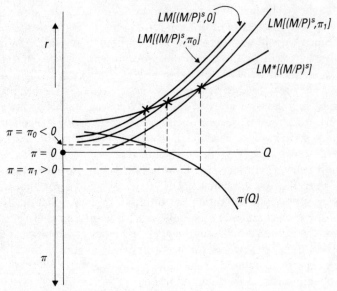

Figure 5.2a: *Derivation of the LM* curve for a particular real money supply (note that distance between the LM curves equals the rate of inflation)*

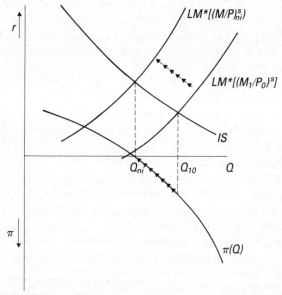

Figure 5.2b: *Phillips-curve adjustment to a nominal money supply increase*

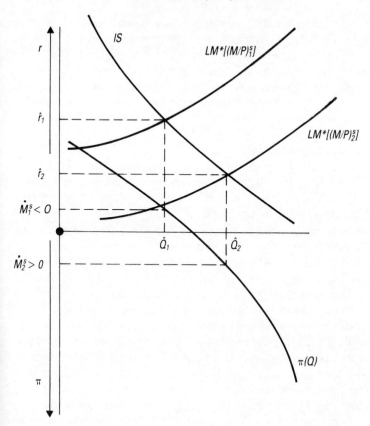

Figure 5.2c: *Long-run Keynesian equilibria with different rates of monetary growth*

Figure 5.2: *The Phillips-curve-augmented Keynesian model*

to shift outwards to the position appropriate to the real money supply M_1/P_0, an equilibrium with the higher output level Q_{10}. But, by the Phillips curve, this higher output causes nominal wages (and, by the mark-up condition, prices) to start rising, shifting the LM^* curve back to the left; the adjustment process continues until P has adjusted to some P_1 where $M_1/P_1 = M_0/P_0 = (M/P)_{ni}$. Alternatively, reversing the signs, a one-time fall in the nominal money supply causes a short-run recession until the fall in output leads to falling prices that restore the real money supply to the Q_{ni} level. Money is non-neutral in the short-run, but the output effects set in motion adjustment in nominal prices that restore the *ni* equilibrium. Note that we have been careful to refer to Q_{ni} rather than Q^*, the neoclassical equilibrium; they will be the same only if the Phillips curve dictates that Q^* is the non-inflationary level of output, and without exploring the underlying basis for the Phillips curve, we have no way of judging this.

Alternatively, we can use the LM^* curves and the Phillips curve to solve for the Keynesian equilibrium appropriate to a given initial nominal money supply and specified rate of growth (not necessarily zero) in the nominal money supply. In a persistent Keynesian equilibrium, the values of $\hat{r}$ and $\hat{Q}$ will be maintained over time, requiring that the point of intersection of the IS and LM^* curves be unchanging over time. Since the LM^* curve is conditional upon the real money supply, this stationarity occurs if M/P is unchanging, requiring in turn that the rate of inflation must equal the growth rate in the nominal money supply. But then for a persistent equilibrium each monetary policy, with its associated nominal growth rate, mandates a particular point on the Phillips curve—the one associated with that rate of inflation—just as the zero rate of growth mandates the non-inflationary output level. The appropriate level of output is then sustained in the IS–LM^* apparatus by the real money supply M/P that causes the LM^* curve to intersect the IS curve at that level of output. This is shown in Figure 5.2c for two possible nominal money supply growth rates, $\dot{M}_1^s < \dot{M}_2^s$. A higher growth rate in the nominal money supply leads to a higher long-run Keynesian equilibrium output level, a lower real interest rate, and a higher real money supply figure; money is not superneutral since the higher growth rate has real effects. This is of course an 'equilibrium' result, and one can discuss the transitional paths from one long-run equilibrium to another—a natural extension of our analysis for the zero-growth case. In particular, if the nominal money supply starts to grow more rapidly, the immediate effect is to cause the real money supply to start growing, shifting the economy to an LM^* curve to the right of the original, leading to an IS–LM^* point with higher output and thus by the Phillips curve, higher inflation (but still possibly less than the rate of growth of the money supply). This process continues until the new long-run equilibrium is eventually reached.

The combination of the *IS–LM* apparatus with the Phillips curve to provide a complete model of Keynesian equilibria, incorporating inflation, seems on the surface to meet the neoclassical objection to our earlier Keynesian equilibrium. As output falls short of Q^*, there is a deflationary tendency with wages and prices falling; the problem arises that when this fall corresponds to the rate of fall in the money supply, there is no adjustment of real variables. The weakness of this argument is that we have not provided a theoretical basis for the Phillips curve but merely assumed its form and existence, and the associated price-dynamics. For example, our mark-up assumption doesn't allow real wages to change at all, and we are restricted to examining changes in nominal prices and wages. We will therefore turn to the issue of providing labour-market foundations for the Phillips curve.

5.3   THE *UV* CURVE AS A BASIS FOR THE PHILLIPS CURVE

Economic theory in general has not devoted much attention to the issue of price-setting by individual agents in the economy. Rather, there has been a reliance upon definitions of equilibrium, with prices taken to adjust (by the 'invisible hand') to sustain the equilibrium. The dynamics felt to underlie the price-setting, and achieving the equilibrium, is known as Walrasian price-adjustment: the price of a good rises (falls) as a function of the excess demand (supply) for that good. By the standard definition of equilibrium, there is no excess demand or supply at that point, and therefore the price tends to remain there. In contrast, a position of excess demand (supply) leads to a rising (falling) price, which may tend to restore the equilibrium position.

If we apply this Walrasian price-adjustment principle to the labour market, we could take the nominal wage to rise over time as a function of the excess demand for labour, which can be measured as the number of vacancies (V) less the number of unemployed (U) seeking those vacancies, at the current wage rate. (It might seem more natural to define the excess demand for labour as total labour demand less total supply, but if we subtract actual employment from total labour demand we get the number of vacancies, and if we subtract it from supply, we get the number of unemployed, so both measures are the same.) Walrasian price-adjustment principles then suggest that nominal wage changes should depend upon the excess demand, $V - U$, and we adopt the wage-adjustment equation: $\omega = f(V - U)$, with the rate of wage-inflation ω depending positively on the excess demand for labour, $V - U$.

The purpose of this section is to show that, starting from this Walrasian price-adjustment formulation, we can derive a traditional Phillips curve with ω depending upon unemployment rates, and further can derive an $\omega(Q)$ 'Phillips curve' as used in the previous section. For the traditional Phillips curve, we must relate $V - U$ and the unemployment rate in the economy, to be denoted by u. A literature has developed suggesting that this be done by means of the UV curve. The UV curve arises from the notion that when vacancies are scattered throughout the economy, and the unemployed are searching for those vacancies, successful matchings generate new hires, H; while it is unlikely that all the vacancies will be located by unemployed workers, it seems reasonable that an increase in U will increase the likelihood of each vacancy being found, and thus increase the number of new hires. Similarly, an increase in V should increase H, so we write: $H(V,U)$, with H depending positively upon both V and U. On the other hand, it is likely that other workers will be losing their jobs through redundancies, quits, or retirements. Subtracting this number (a slightly better model, with similar results, would make this some fraction of current employment N), we can write the net change in employment as $\Delta N = g(V,U)$, and graph this as a set of curves in Figure 5.3, each curve showing all the combinations of V and U that achieve a particular change in employment over the economy. Insofar as we are interested in persistent equilibria, we can focus upon the curve that is associated with $\Delta N = 0$, and we will call this the UV curve, the combinations that maintain the level of employment in the economy.

In Figure 5.3 we have superimposed the wage-adjustment equation $\omega = f(V - U)$ as a set of lines each showing the U, V combinations that entail a particular rate of wage-inflation. (For each ω, $V - U$ must be a constant, giving the linear form.) From this, each point on the UV curve is associated with a particular rate

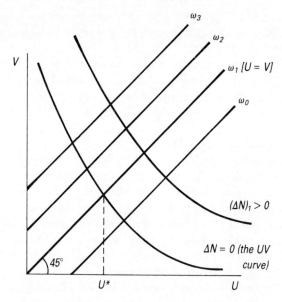

Figure 5.3: *The UV curve and wage-inflation lines*

of wage-inflation, and these combinations could be graphed as a form of Phillips curve relating ω to U, the unemployment level; examination of the figure shows that a lower U is associated with a high rate of wage-inflation, so the resulting Phillips curve is downward-sloping. To turn this into a traditional Phillips curve— with ω depending upon u, the unemployment rate—we will need to know total labour supply in order to calculate the $u = U/L_s$ corresponding to each ω. For our purposes now it will be easiest to assume a vertical labour supply curve at some amount L; a higher U then entails a higher unemployment rate u as well, and thus a higher u as associated with a lower ω. A further translation is to observe that employment $N = L - U$, and therefore a higher U is associated with a lower N, but from the production function $Q(N)$, it is also associated with a lower Q—a lower Q results in a lower ω, as we initially supposed in section 5.2. The UV curve, and the Walrasian price-adjustment assumption, can then be used to justify the Phillips curve and its applications in the previous section. A given unemployment rate, maintained over time (i.e.

on the *UV* curve) leads to a certain rate of inflation since the excess demand for labour depends upon the particular combination of *U* and *V* on the *UV* curve.

The role of employment and unemployment stationarity in the analysis may not be entirely clear. To understand it better, suppose that in fact employment in the economy is growing (and therefore unemployment is falling); we are not then on the *UV* curve, where employment is unchanging, but at some point above it, with higher vacancies. The implication of this is that, for a given current unemployment rate, if employment is increasing, there is a greater excess demand for labour and therefore a greater rate of nominal wage increase. This is the phenomenon of 'Phillips loops' where, during a recovery, the Phillips curve should lie above that in a decline. In fact, precisely the opposite has been observed: as a recovery slows, the Phillips curve seems to shift outwards, a higher inflation rate being associated with a given rate of unemployment. It was this 'instability' of Phillips curves over the late 1960s and early 1970s that led to the neoclassical resurgence in macroeconomic theory as discussed in the following section.

5.4   THE EXPECTATIONS-AUGMENTED PHILLIPS CURVE

The basis for the Phillips curve developed in section 5.3 depends upon the Walrasian form for the wage-adjustment equation; in particular, nominal wages were taken to rise in response to an excess demand for labour measured by $V - U$. Neoclassical economists have responded that the form adopted is inappropriate; that a firm changes its nominal wages in order to change its relative wage and thereby recruit more or less labour. Therefore, depending upon what it expects other firms to do, it will set a higher or lower change in its wage offers. This turns out to be a powerful change in assumptions and leads to the notion of a 'natural rate' of unemployment. In this section we will examine this argument, and then consider in section 5.5 whether the sectoral model presented by Tobin (Mar. 1972) successfully counters these arguments.

The neoclassical form of the Phillips curve arises from the argument that if firms have an excess demand for labour, they will not just bid up nominal wages at some given rate but will also be trying to raise their relative wage. To do this, if the firm expects other firms to be raising wages at the rate ω^e, they will use this as the benchmark for setting their own wage rates—higher if they want to increase recruitment, lower if they are willing to lose workers to other firms. Averaging over firms, we have a nominal wage-adjustment equation: $\omega = f(V - U) + \omega^e$. It is immediate that if expectations are accurate, this can only be met when actual wage increases equal the expected, requiring that $f(V - U) = 0$. The neoclassicals then view this as the only possible equilibrium and argue further that this balance, with firms not seeking to change their relative wages, can only occur at $L_d = L_s$, requiring from $V = L_d - N$ and $U = L_s - N$ that $V = U$. In Figure 5.3, we are on the 45-degree line through the origin ($U - V$), and to be on the UV curve as well, U must equal the marked U^*; for a fixed labour supply L, we have a *natural rate of unemployment* $u^* = U^*/L$. At this natural rate there is no pressure for real wages to change, and because we are on the UV curve, no pressure for employment to change. We have indicated the natural rate with the * notation reserved for neoclassical equilibria; it is certainly the case that labour supply and demand are equal as in a neoclassical equilibrium. It is less clear perhaps how this corresponds to our earlier $N^* = L_d(w^*) = L_s(w^*)$. An obvious change is that there are 'transitional' vacancies and unemployment due to the imperfectness of the matching process discussed in section 5.3. A less obvious problem is that there are very many ways in the labour market that u^* might be sustained. It might happen, if aggregate demand allows, at the w^* such that labour demand, when marginal product determines labour demand, equals labour supply; alternatively, it might happen at a sales-rationed Q and N, but one where w has fallen to the point where, because of workers leaving the workforce, u is still at the low level u^*. A separate argument is necessary as to why, if aggregate demand is low, the low real wage leads firms to lower nominal prices as well. This argument could be made on the basis that, with a low real wage, firms have great incentive to lower their relative output price to gain sales, and this lowers nominal prices until aggregate demand is restored.

For further discussion it will be helpful to replace $f(V - U)$ with the associated function $F(u)$, showing the pressure on wages with respect to the unemployment rate—$F(u)$ can be derived from $f(V - U)$ using the translation of the previous section. Further, if one accepts the neoclassical argument, $F(u^*) = 0$. While the neoclassicals see u^* as the only sustainable rate of unemployment over time (since with their wage-adjustment equation it is the only equilibrium), they have suggested that there might be divergences in the short run due to expectational errors. We can write the 'expectations-augmented Phillips curves' as $\omega = F(u) + \omega^e$, and graph a number of these in Figure 5.4a, where each curve's position depends upon the level of expectations ω^e. This leads to the argument about accelerating inflation if the government attempts to maintain some unemployment rate $u_0 < u^*$. If initial inflationary expectations are at zero, so that the relevant Phillips curve is the one $F(u)$, the unemployment rate u_0 is associated with a wage-inflation in excess of expected wage-inflation. Either expectations are validated, which requires that unemployment return to u^*, or actual wage-inflation exceeds the expectations. If the latter, inflation-expectations for the following period will presumably increase, moving the economy onto a higher Phillips curve. The low unemployment rate can only be sustained if inflation keeps accelerating so that expectations lag behind the actual outcome. The only unemployment rate where this is not occurring is u^*, and the long-run Phillips curve, where $\omega^e = \omega$, is vertical at u^*. Government attempts to lower unemployment lead to a higher ultimate inflation level, when u^* is finally restored. This need not mean, however, that the government should avoid attempting to lower the unemployment rate temporarily. It is still left with a short-term trade-off between unemployment and inflation—it can lower unemployment temporarily at the cost of a permanently higher rate of inflation (which in turn can only be lowered by a temporary recession raising u above u^*). This may be a desirable strategy if u^* is not the 'efficient' unemployment rate as defined in Part II of this book. Alternatively, and less desirably, the government may attempt to use the short-term trade-off for immediate political benefit, in a 'political business cycle'.

The accelerationist story does, however, depend upon the expected inflation term entering the wage-adjustment equation with a coefficient of unity. If we define a general wage-adjustment equation with a 'feedback coefficient' of λ, so that $\omega = F(u) + \lambda\omega^e$, provided that $\lambda < 1$, we can still solve for a long-run Phillips curve where $\omega = \omega^e$ and u need not equal u^*. The long-run Phillips curve can be written: $\omega = F(u)/(1 - \lambda)$. While this is steeper than the short-run curves in Figure 5.4a, it remains a downward-sloping trade-off.

It is important to note that both the wage-adjustment equation in the previous section, with $\lambda = 0$, and the expectations-augmented equation in this section, with $\lambda = 1$, are arbitrary, neither being based upon a model where agents choose prices in a well-formulated optimisation problem. The search story in Part II is intended to provide a better microeconomic foundation for the neoclassical natural rate and expectational-error accelerationist story. Contracting will similarly provide a basis for a Keynesian wage-adjustment story, with the staggered-contracts approach providing in effect a $\lambda < 1$, and our equilibrium-recession story an argument about why the zero wage-adjustment position may not occur at u^*. In the following section we will consider two early arguments as to why the neoclassical approach may be limited in impact.

5.5 SECTORAL PHILLIPS CURVE MODELS

While the wage-adjustment equations discussed to this point are arbitrary, they have another feature: they are aggregative over the entire labour market. We will now consider a pair of approaches that, while largely accepting that wage adjustments should be in relative terms with respect to excess demand, still go beyond the simple natural rate result by introducing the notion of sectoral Phillips curves, where each sector adjusts wages depending upon the excess demand in that sector. We begin with a 'dispersion of unemployment' argument in Lipsey (1960) and then turn to the 'nominal wage floors' approach in Tobin (Mar. 1972).

Consider an economy with two equally large sectors, a and b, so that average wage-inflation can be written: $\omega = (\omega_a + \omega_b)/2$. Suppose also that each sector raises wages, relative to the expected rate of wage-inflation ω^e, according to a Phillips curve $\omega_i = F(u_i) + \omega^e$ where i equals either a or b. This is of course the 'neoclassical' adjustment equation with a feedback coefficient on ω^e of unity. Further suppose that the function $F(u_i)$ takes on the form in Figure 5.4b, and in particular has the curvature shown (this curvature is typically found in empirical analysis). We have drawn the Phillips curve for the case where ω^e is initially zero, and want to ask what unemployment rates are consistent with maintaining this. One answer is $u_a = u_b = u^*$, so that $F(u_a) = F(u_b) = 0$ and $\omega_a = \omega_b = 0$. This clearly meets the non-accelerationist definition of a natural rate of unemployment, with the average rate of unemployment in the economy being $(u_a + u_b)/2 = u^*$. But now suppose that unemployment in sector a falls to $\bar{u}_a$ and that in b rises to $\bar{u}_b$, where these (as seen in Fig. 5.4b) lead to wage-inflation rates in each sector of $\omega_a = c$ and $\omega_b = -c$. Average wage inflation is again zero, but because of the curvature of the sectoral Phillips curves, this is associated with an average unemployment rate in excess of u^*. A greater dispersion of unemployment rates across the economy means that the natural rate of unemployment, from the accelerationist point of view, is higher. While this suggests that a government policy of diminishing sectoral disparities might be desirable, it of course does not really address the issue of a long-run trade-off between inflation and unemployment.

That issue is addressed in the argument by Tobin, which follows a suggestion in the *General Theory* that workers are generally willing to accept real wage decreases arising from a rising price level, but resist a nominal wage fall. Keynes' claim is that workers are concerned about their relative wage. If prices rise, leading to a real wage fall, workers in a given sector expect other groups of workers to suffer the same change; on the other hand, if they agree to a nominal wage fall, they might expect that they will be losing their relative position. We will model this by making an assumption of nominal wage floors, that nominal wages are strictly rigid downwards, a stronger assumption than adopted by Tobin, who sees the floors as temporary in nature within a given sector.

To understand the model, it will be useful to write the divergence of actual wage-inflation from expected as $\rho = \omega - \omega^e$; this must be zero in an equilibrium. Or in terms of averages over our two sectors, $(\rho_a + \rho_b)/2 = 0$. The importance of the nominal wage floors is that, depending upon the rate of inflation in the economy (at an equilibrium so that $\omega = \omega^e$), the floors are more or less binding in relative terms. The maximum rate at which relative wages can fall in a sector is the aggregate rate of increase ω, with nominal wages unchanging and inflation lowering their relative value.

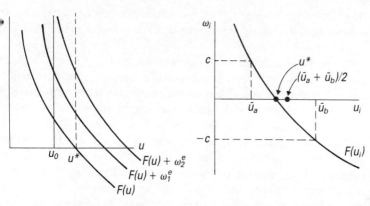

Figure 5.4a: *Expectations-augmented short-run Phillips curves and vertical long-run Phillips curve*

Figure 5.4b: *Role of dispersion of sectoral unemployment rates*

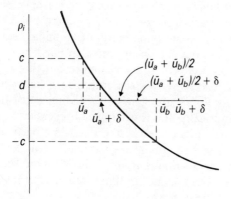

Figure 5.4c: *The Tobin wage-floors sectoral model*

Figure 5.4: *The long-run Phillips curve under alternative wage-adjustment formulations*

Now consider the earlier sectoral unemployment rate $\bar{u}_a$ and $\bar{u}_b$, as shown in Figure 5.4c, with the Phillips curve drawn showing the relative wage changes that would occur in the absence of nominal wage floors. The average relative wage change calculated would be zero, so $(\bar{u}_a + \bar{u}_b)/2$ would be an equilibrium average unemployment rate. However, the existence of nominal wage floors means that the relative wage fall of $-c$, for sector b, can occur only if $\omega \geq c$. Thus $(\bar{u}_a + \bar{u}_b)/2$ is an equilibrium only for wage-inflation in excess of c.

But suppose ω happens to equal some smaller amount d. Then $\rho_a = c$, but $\rho_b = -d$, giving a positive average rate of relative wage increase. If the dispersion of unemployment remains the same in the economy, an equilibrium can be found by increasing both sectoral unemployment rates by some amount δ, to $\bar{u}_a + \delta$ and $\bar{u}_b + \delta$, as shown (Fig. 5.4c). Since $\bar{u}_b + \delta > \bar{u}_b$, the nominal wage floor remains binding and ρ_b remains at $-d$; but $\bar{u}_a + \delta$ now entails $\rho_a = d$, and the average rate of relative-wage inflation is zero. Thus the lower rate of inflation ω is associated with a higher equilibrium average rate of unemployment. This implies that the government can lower unemployment from $(\bar{u}_a + \bar{u}_b)/2 + \delta$ to $(\bar{u}_a + \bar{u}_b)/2$, by increasing the rate of nominal money growth (and thus sustained inflation in both wages and prices) from d to c. In other words, there is a long-run Phillips curve trade-off.

As noted, our assumption here of nominal wage floors is stronger than the one Tobin presents. In particular, he suggests that these floors are temporary in nature but that the stochastic nature of the economy keeps putting new sectors into excess supply so that floors are generally binding somewhere in the economy. Empirically, this is what one observes in the economy—only after a sustained period of recession in a particular industry do workers agree to nominal wage cuts. The difficulty remains, however, that the assumptions are arbitrary in the sense that they are not derived from agents' optimal, rather than perhaps empirically observed, behaviour.

5.6 CONCLUSIONS

For an economy to remain in a recession, with involuntary unemployment, two things must happen: real wages must not fall to transform the involuntary unemployment into voluntary withdrawals from the workforce, and nominal prices must not fall to restore the real money supply and aggregate demand. These are related issues since the level of the real wage will affect firms' desire to increase production and sales, which they presumably try to effect by lowering their nominal price. The neoclassical argument is that if there is involuntary unemployment, there is a tendency for real wages to fall and eliminate this; if there are binding sales-rations, firms have an incentive to try to lower their output price, which in turn raises the real money supply and increases aggregate demand. The Keynesian model depends upon some failure of these adjustment processes.

The Phillips curve, in its original form, could be used to construct the following sort of argument about a balanced deflation in a recession. Nominal wages would be falling in response to the excess supply of labour, but nominal prices would similarly be falling as firms seek to increase their market share by lowering their output price—if both of these are changing at the same rate, real wages are stationary and the involuntary nature of unemployment remains. Further, if the nominal money supply is decreasing at this rate, the real money supply is unchanging, and aggregate demand remains at its depressed level. Although agents are trying to change their relative prices, they fail to do so as other agents are doing the same. The accelerationist argument is that this balanced deflation cannot occur, since agents will take account of the expected behaviour of other agents and adjust their rate of price and wage change to include this; the deflation would be accelerating and would then surpass in magnitude the nominal money supply changes and restore aggregate demand and output.

The neoclassical argument against 'money illusion' is a strong one and not easily dismissed; it is reasonable that agents, in their price-setting, should take account of their expectations of other agents' behaviour. From this, one is led to something of a dismissal of the Phillips curve as a basis for Keynesian theory. The limitations on adjustment underlying Keynesian phenomena must be of a different, 'real' nature. We will eventually argue in this book that contracting begins to provide such a model—one that follows Keynesian theory in basing economic fluctuations upon aggregate demand but without the money illusion component of the Phillips curve model.

That the monetarists have provided an effective rebuttal to the prevailing post-war Keynesian model (the aggregate-demand/Phillips-curve synthesis) does not of course mean that their analysis is the appropriate alternative. The neoclassical approach is lacking in an explanation for the observed, sustained divergences in unemployment from the natural rate. Search theory and the new classical school have further developed the idea of the 'expectational errors' Phillips curve to address this issue, and we will examine the adequacy of that approach in the following chapter.

Part II
Search and Contracting
Models of Unemployment

Introduction

The primary weaknesses of the neoclassical and Keynesian models should now be clear. The neoclassical model with its equilibrium 'full employment' or natural rate of unemployment bears little relationship to empirical observation. The model, if it is intended to be applicable to a real economy, must be extended to explain why observed unemployment rates vary widely over time and why restrictive monetary policies lead to recessions. The Keynesian model, on the other hand, needs a theoretical foundation for its assertions about the failure of price and wage-adjustment to restore a neoclassical equilibrium. It is not enough to assume price or wage rigidities, but these must be shown as the result of optimising decisions on the part of individual agents in the economy.

The search and contracting models arose as detailed studies of the labour market designed to serve precisely these ends. Search models attempt to explore in a fundamental way the labour-market processes leading to a natural, frictional rate of unemployment, and (with rational expectations) the information problems that might lead to short-run observed Phillips curves. The contracting models, in contrast, were developed to show how firms and workers would contract to maintain a fixed wage, irrespective of demand conditions. Workers are taken to be risk-averse, and firms insure them against variations in their wage rate. There was great initial excitement that this was the beginning of an explanation for the wage rigidity that, in turn, would provide a foundation for Keynesian economics.

The purpose of this part of the book is to clarify how these two sorts of models operate, how they relate to each other, and the implications for macroeconomic analysis. Both models can be based upon a conception of the labour market that we have seen, in rudimentary form, in the previous chapter—the economy is composed of numerous sectors facing stochastic shocks that shift job opportunities between the sectors. Due to information restrictions or mobility limitations, unemployment arises as workers move slowly across the sectors. Where the models differ is in their view of how firms and workers come together in the labour market.

The search model is based upon the neoclassical idea of price-rationing. If a particular firm wishes to expand its workforce, it raises the wage rate it pays, and if it wishes to decrease its workforce, it lowers its wage rate; workers then respond to relative wages in moving between sectors of the economy, being temporarily but voluntarily unemployed as they search for a new and better-paying job. The contracting model views separations as enforced, involuntary redundancies—the wage remains fixed, as part of the optimal strategy of the firm, and the firm then decreases its workforce by lay-offs. In the sense of showing how involuntary redundancies—job-rationing—arises in the economy as optimal behaviour on the part of agents, contracting models have been relatively successful.

Surprisingly, however, both approaches can lead to exactly the same outcome in terms of unemployment, and in fact achieve the 'efficient' rate of unemployment, differing only in the particular mechanism by which it is sustained. Demonstrating wage rigidity and involuntary unemployment is not the same thing as constructing a Keynesian model. The reason for this is that the price system, in a competitive economy, is just one way of sustaining the neoclassical equilibrium real outcome. An effective command economy could, by regulation, achieve exactly the same outcome by ordering agents to produce and consume in the appropriate amounts. The optimal contracts signed between workers and firms, in the original contracting models, include agreements that the firm ignore the wage and marginal productivity comparison (of the neoclassical labour market) in deciding how many workers to retain, but follow the previously agreed levels of employment. Wage and employment decisions are separated.

In fact, there are good theoretical reasons for disbelieving both the 'efficient' search and contracting models. A more adequate search model takes account of the fact that, in general, an unemployed worker has very little bargaining power with a firm where he is seeking a job. The simple search model generates unemployment as workers voluntarily quit their current jobs, when the wage is lowered, to accept unemployment to search for a new job. Workers in the real economy, however, recognise that they have far better bargaining power with potential new employers by searching on-the-job, without voluntarily relinquishing their current job; the notion of voluntary search unemployment collapses. The only way to sustain a functioning labour market is for firms to enter into explicit or implicit (the firm develops a reputation for how it treats its workers) contractual arrangements; it is in the firms's interest to enter into such contracts. The problem is that fully optimal, efficient, contracts are extremely complicated in their employment and lay-off compensation commitments; for this reason actual contracts are likely to be simpler and less efficient in nature. A literature has recently developed considering limited contracts, under the rubric of 'asymmetric information' contracting. The interesting feature of these contracts is that they display inefficiently high unemployment.

The microeconomic analysis has a number of major conclusions. The first is that wage rigidity and involuntary unemployment arises naturally in the labour market due to imperfections that would exist in a search economy. The analysis also suggests that the role of unemployment benefits and trade unions has been overemphasised in terms of effects upon the equilibrium rate of unemployment. On the macroeconomic side, we argue that the neoclassical approach to expectational errors in creating a short-run Phillips curve is not particularly plausible. Interestingly, in the staggered contracts approach, the same effects can be shown in a more convincing framework. More importantly, contracts can be used, in the model of equilibrium recessions, as the basis for a more Keynesian model of the macroeconomy.

6 Search Equilibrium: the New Classical View

Search theory arose as a formalisation of the idea of frictional or transitional unemployment. It allows for a concrete analysis of equilibrium unemployment rates, and an examination of whether unemployment is subject to monetary policy. There are two important issues in determining whether a monetary (or fiscal) policy to lower unemployment is desirable. The policy must be effective in actually lowering unemployment, but, further, it must be shown that otherwise the unemployment rate would be too high. This requires developing some notion of 'efficient' unemployment as a benchmark. We begin this chapter with a discussion of the underlying stochastic economic environment that leads to transitional unemployment, and construct the benchmark 'efficient' criterion.

The efficient, or desirable, unemployment arises as workers shift sectors (being temporarily unemployed in the process) in response to shifting job opportunities, moving from declining to expanding industries. The driving force behind unemployment, in this view, is real sectoral shocks. (We will later introduce other bases for unemployment.) Here we follow the arguments in Lucas and Prescott (1974) that labour markets, through competitive wage-setting, will provide workers with the incentives to move voluntarily in the efficient numbers. The resulting equilibrium, or natural, rate of unemployment is more or less constant over time, the only difference in a particular period being which sectors are expanding and which declining. A different sort of unemployment arises, following Lucas (1975), if there is monetary policy uncertainty as well. An uncertain monetary policy may lead to uncertainty about inflation and relative wages; for example, a fall in

140

inflation may lead workers in a high-productivity and high-wage sector to think that their relative wage has fallen when it has not, and that they should move to another sector. Similarly, a high inflation may fool them into thinking that their relative wage is high, and that they should remain where they are even though in fact wages elsewhere are higher. This sort of unemployment differs in amount each period (depending upon the inflation rate), and leads to the appearance of a Phillips curve. However, workers cannot be fooled systematically—if inflation remains high, they come to expect this and unemployment returns to the natural rate. This is of course just the expectational-errors story of the previous chapter, with divergences in unemployment arising due to expectational errors that cannot persist indefinitely. Here, however, it arises in a carefully constructed model, and its basis is clearer. The implications for monetary policy are twofold: there is policy ineffectiveness (since workers cannot be fooled systematically, the apparent Phillips curve is not a real policy trade-off), and since it was supposed that the equilibrium in the absence of the monetary policy confusion was efficient, such a policy would be undesirable anyway, the only desirable policy being one that removes the monetary uncertainty.

The approach presented in this chapter is labelled the 'new classical' school. There are a number of substantive features of this model: labour markets generally achieve efficient unemployment, except for monetary policy uncertainty; the model makes some concession to observation in that it provides a basis for divergences from the natural rate of unemployment; and there is no role for a systematic monetary policy. These are the properly controversial facets of the approach. Two other features, however, are not objectionable, although one (rational expectations) has been the centre of much controversy. The basic stochastic sectoral model of the labour market is a legitimate one, although we ultimately argue that it must be extended to incorporate aggregate demand uncertainty as well. Rational expectations is something we have already adopted implicitly, and will continue to assume, as we discuss later in this chapter.

6.1   A STOCHASTIC SECTORAL MODEL OF THE ECONOMY

The essentials of a model of transitional unemployment are that there are distinct sectoral labour markets (possibly disaggregated to the level of individual firms) and that there is some element that causes job opportunities to shift between the sectors. We will take the simplest case of two sectors, and we will further suppose that each sector is composed of one firm (although the firm will behave competitively and not use any monopoly or monopsony power). The two firms are identical in terms of their production function, which takes on the simple form used in Chapter 2: $Q(N)$, $Q'(N) > 0$, $Q''(N) < 0$ (i.e. the production function is concave). The shifting of job opportunities is represented by the idea that the output of each sector sells at a random price depending, presumably, on shifts in the relative demand for the two goods. We will assume that there are only two possible prices for each good, $p^+ > p^-$, that each price is equally likely to obtain in a sector, but that each sector ends up with a different price. That is, if we take a particular sector, it *ex ante* faces a random price for its output, but *ex post* it will have one of the price levels and the other sector the other. It will be convenient to refer to the sector that draws the high price as the + sector, with price p^+, and the sector with the low price as the − sector, with price p^-. We will consider a period of analysis of length one, starting from time 0 and going to time 1. The price facing a sector remains the same over this period.

The next set of specifications concerns the behaviour of labour in the economy. There will be a total of L identical workers, each with a zero disutility of work, so that the labour supply curve in the aggregate is vertical at L. The workers are initially evenly allocated between the two sectors with $L/2$ in each. The basis for this assumption is that we are taking the intitial allocation to occur before the sectoral output prices are learned, and therefore at a point in time when both sectors are identically placed. A worker initially allocated to one sector can move to the other sector (if he learns, for example, that employment opportunities are better there), but this takes time. In particular, the time it takes to move between the sectors will be θ, expressed as a fraction of the total period (of length one) lost in moving. This time will be considered as spent in unemployment.

We now want to consider the optimal ('efficient') amount of unemployment in this economy. Since there is no disutility of work, we can measure the total social welfare by the value of production: $p^+Q(N^+) + p^-Q(N^-)$. This is the total surplus produced in this economy which can be divided among the participants. For economic efficiency, where we are not concerned with the distribution of the product across agents, this figure should be maximised. Since $p^+ > p^-$, it adds to the value of production if N^+ is high relative to N^-, but our cost of mobility means that shifting workers into the high-price sector entails a loss of total labour services available to the economy (by the amount of unemployment). These factors must be balanced in determining the optimal allocations.

It should be obvious that if any labour shifting is desirable, it should be from the − sector to the + sector (and further, the workers should move as soon as possible, at time 0, arriving in the other sector at time θ). If we denote the number of workers moving to the + sector as S, we can write the total labour services used in each sector over the period as:

$$N^- = L/2 - S$$
$$N^+ = L/2 + (1 - \theta)S$$

Note that when a worker moves between the sectors, the − sector loses his services over the entire period, but the + sector gains his services for only the proportion of the period remaining, $(1 - \theta)$. This is the sense in which the shift is costly.

Substituting these equations into the value of production formula, we have $p^+Q[L/2 + (1 - \theta)S] + p^-Q(L/2 - S)$ as the objective function to be maximised with respect to the value of S. The rule for optimally shifting workers is immediate: a worker should move from the − sector to the + sector if his marginal value product in the latter, after adjusting for the moving (unemployment) time, exceeds what it would be in the former. Consider whether, starting from the equal initial allocation $N^+ = N^- = L/2$, any workers should move. At this point, the last worker in the − sector produces the marginal value product $p^-MPL(L/2)$, where the $MPL(N)$ schedule is derived from the production function $Q(N)$, and is downward-sloping as in Chapter 2. If the worker moved to the + sector, he would produce $(1 - \theta)p^+MPL(L/2)$, ignoring the fact that his marginal product is actually slightly lower than this at $MPL[(L/2 + (1 - \theta)]$. For the first worker to optimally move, it must be the case that $(1 - \theta)p^+MPL(L/2) > p^-MPL(L/2)$, or the ratio p^+/p^- must exceed $1/(1 - \theta)$, which of course exceeds one. Efficient unemployment then arises whenever the sectoral prices are sufficiently different to compensate for the moving time.

For efficiency, workers should continue to move until there is equality between the relevant marginal value products.

$$(1 - \theta)p^+MPL(N^+) = p^-MPL(N^-)$$

or

$$(1 - \theta)p^+MPL[L/2 + (1 - \theta)S] = p^-MPL(L/2 - S)$$

which can then be solved for the efficient unemployment level S. This is shown diagrammatically in Figure 6.1. From the initial allocation of $L/2$ workers in each sector, the case in Figure 6.1 shows that some movement is optimal since $(1 - \theta)p^+MPL(L/2) > p^-MPL(L/2)$. A positive S lowers N^- by that amount and raises N^+ by $(1 - \theta)S$; the optimal S is shown where the resulting N^- and N^+ values meet the (adjusted for moving time) marginal value product equality condition.

The point of the discussion is that in general there is an optimal shifting of labour, at the cost of some unemployment, due to shifting opportunities (reflected in output prices) across the sectors in the economy. The optimal unemployment level, when there is no disutility of work, is defined as the level where the value product (i.e. the GNP) of the economy is maximised. A higher amount of unemployment lowers GNP; perhaps surprisingly, a lower amount also lowers GNP. This is an important point—too low a rate of unemployment is just as bad as too high a rate!

6.2   AN EFFICIENT MARKET EQUILIBRIUM

The analysis in the previous section examined the efficient level of unemployment in the economy, where efficiency is defined by the usual economic criterion of maximising net social benefit. The efficient level, to be denoted S^*, depends only upon the underlying economic environment. It may or may not be sustained by the market system (or any other particular economic system). This is

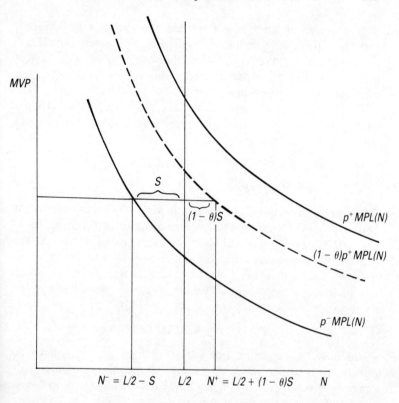

Figure 6.1: *Efficient allocation of labour in the sectoral model*

the issue we now want to pursue—is S^* attained as a market equilibrium?

The equilibrium attained in an economy depends upon the market structure. For example, a monopolistic equilibrium is usually inefficient, but a competitive market system (under certain assumptions) achieves efficiency. Following Lucas and Prescott (1974), we will show that a competitive market system can be designed to attained S^*. In Chapter 8 we will consider why this formulation of a search market is perhaps not very convincing.

In the structure of the problem in section 6.1 there are two times when a worker might take on employment in a sector and two sectors. This suggests a market structure with four competitive markets, one for each sector at each time. In fact, the market in the − sector at time θ will be inactive and can be ignored. Introduce three wage rates corresponding to the active markets: w_0^-, w_0^+, w_θ^+. We argue that the competitive wage rates, achieving supply and demand equality in each market, sustain the employment allocation of section 6.1.

The demand for labour in each market is given by the marginal value product curve as drawn in Figure 6.1. Being on the demand curve for labour then entails that:

$$w_0^- = p^- MPL(N^-) \; w_0^+ = p^+ MPL(N^+)$$
$$w_\theta^+ = (1 - \theta)p^+ MPL(N^+)$$

The supply curves are slightly less immediate. The important point is that a worker, initially allocated to a sector, will remain there unless if he can gain a higher wage by moving to a different market (at time θ). If workers shift from the − market at time 0 to the + market at time θ, it must be the case that $w_\theta^+ \geqslant w_0^-$; if some remain in the − sector, equality must hold. But then a competitive solution is:

$$w_0^- = p^- MPL(N^-) = (1 - \theta)p^+ MPL(N^+) = w_\theta^+$$

—precisely the condition that earlier defined S^* when that was positive. It is straightforward to show that the market solution will similarly give $S^* = 0$ when no amount of shifting could bring equality between the two marginal value products. The competitive solution achieves efficiency because the worker receives, in his wage, the marginal value product (as adjusted for the time remaining to work) and therefore has the appropriate incentives to move when this would be higher elsewhere; all unemployment is voluntary.

Our interim conclusion is that competitive labour markets sustain the efficient level of unemployment, and there is therefore no need for government intervention if we accept that these markets are functioning properly. We will of course return to this issue in the sequel. For now we observe that this efficient, market level of unemployment should be understood as an equilibrium level and as such can be treated as other equilibria in economics are treated. In particular, this 'natural rate' changes with the underlying economic environment. It is straightforward to observe that an increase in price dispersion (a rise in p^+ relative to p^-)

increases S^*. A fall in θ, representing perhaps increased efficiency in labour market processes, may also raise S^*.

This last result suggests that it might be helpful to move from S^*, the efficient level of unemployment, to a new variable s^*, the rate of unemployment. Since the S^* workers moving between sectors are unemployed for the duration of their move, θ, we define s^* as $\theta S^*/L$, the ratio of time spent in unemployment to total available labour time. (This transformation holds as well for any arbitrary S into s.) Using this new definition, we observe that the fall in θ, while raising S^*, may in fact lower s^*. When the cost of moving falls, the efficient number of movers rises, but the actual total time spent in moving may decrease.

The 'comparative statics' effects discussed are important to a neoclassical model. Since observed unemployment changes dramatically in the economy, if one wants to adopt a 'natural rate' model, that model must include some explanation for such changes. There have been claims that the rise in unemployment rates over the 1970s can be ascribed to an increased price dispersion due, for example, to oil price shocks and to demographic changes that have led to greater inflows into the labour market (a greater number of new workers have to be allocated over the firms in the economy).

6.3 PRICE DISPERSION, THE SHORT-RUN PHILLIPS CURVE AND THE EQUILIBRIUM BUSINESS CYCLE

The reader may have noted that in our analysis in the previous two sections we have written the p and w variables in lower case, our earlier notation for real, rather than nominal, values. The reason is that the important factor in determining the efficient unemployment level and rate is the relative value productivity of workers in the two sectors—a worker should move only if his productivity in the other sector, adjusted for the period of unemployment, is higher than if he remains in his current sector. This depends, in the example of the previous sections (an alternative interpretation is that the physical productivity in each sector is subject to a random element), upon the price of the good in the + sector relative to that in the − sector, p^+/p^-. Multiplying both p's, and (in section 6.2) all the w's, by a common factor leaves the solution unchanged. In that sense, the model depends only upon real or relative prices, and shows the usual neoclassical neutrality with respect to a monetary inflation that raises all prices (including wage rates) in proportion. The prices and wages discussed in effect are the nominal price for each good, and the wage in each sector at each time, divided by the general price level P.

In this section we explore by an example the problem raised by Friedman (1968) and Lucas (1973), that agents may not be able to distinguish between relative price changes, the pertinent feature of the allocation in the previous sections, and general inflation, which does not affect the efficient (and should not affect the market) allocation. To examine this, we will switch to nominal output prices in each sector and suppose that there are three possible output prices in each sector: $P_3 > P_2 > P_1$. Further we will suppose that these are related as $P_3 = aP_2 = a^2P_1$, where $a > 1$. The possible outcomes are further restricted in supposing that there are only two contingencies: (A) one sector faces P_3 and the other P_2, or (B) one sector faces P_2 and the other P_1. We will suppose that each case (A and B) is equally likely, and that within the case each sector is equally likely to have the higher price. An important feature of the example as constructed is that case A represents a general inflation with respect to B, all prices having risen by a, but with sectoral relative prices $P_3/P_2 = a$ or $P_2/P_1 = a$ being the same in either case. The problem is otherwise unchanged from section 6.1.

If the output price levels in both markets are observable as in section 6.1, both cases A and B lead to the same efficient and market outcomes, the ones following the analysis in sections 6.1 and 6.2. The new assumption is that workers initially in a particular sector can only observe the nominal price in that sector and not the general rate of inflation (equivalent, in our simple example, to observing the nominal price in the other sector as well). A worker in a sector might observe any of the prices P_3, P_2 or P_1 as the output price pertinent to his sector. If he observes P_3, he can infer, from the two possible cases, that the other sector must be facing P_2, and therefore that he is the high price sector; if he observes P_1, he is in the low-price sector. But suppose that he observes P_2—either a general inflation has occurred and he is in the low-price sector, or no inflation has occurred and he is in the high-price sector. He has no way of knowing, and if he decides to move to the other sector, it is just as likely that he is moving in the wrong direction as in the right one.

It might seem from the last observation that a worker observing P_2 as the output price in his sector should never move. Surprisingly, perhaps, that is not the desirable strategy. We will analyse this problem by considering efficient rules for workers to follow, where efficiency is defined by the criteria in section 6.1. As in section 6.2, there are wage rates that will sustain these efficient outcomes, and we will in this section suppose that the efficient solution is in fact attained as an equilibrium. The efficient rules take the following form: a certain number of the workers in a sector observing a particular output price should move to the other sector. It is obvious that a worker observing P_3, since he is necessarily in the high-price sector, should not move. We therefore denote by S_2 the number of workers observing P_2 that should move, and by S_1 the number observing P_1 that should move.

The criterion for efficiency will need to be more explicitly stated since we will have to trade-off 'efficiency' in the two outcomes— cases A and B—and will therefore need to balance the effects of an employment rule over the two cases. Consider a particular employment rule, in case B, that leads to employment of N^+ in the high-price sector (the one with output price P_2) and N^- in the other (with P_1). If the same employment levels were maintained into case A, nominal national income would rise by the factor a since the high-price sector now faces $P_3 = aP_2$ and the low-price $P_2 = aP_1$. To make the national income figures comparable, we must deflate the latter by the general rise in prices, the factor a. We can then write 'real' national income in each case as: $p^+Q(N^+) + p^-Q(N^-)$, where $p^+ = P_2$ and $p^- = P_1$, and N^+ and N^- will be subscripted to denote whether it is the employment outcome in case A or B; these will in general differ for a given moving rule reflected in the values of S_2 and S_1. Since each case, A and B, is taken to be equally likely, we write our expected, or average, welfare as:

$$1/2[p^+Q(N_A{}^+) + p^-Q(N_A{}^-)] + 1/2[p^+Q(N_B{}^+) + p^-Q(N_B{}^-)]$$

We will then choose moving rules, S_2 and S_1, to maximise this expression.

Given these rules, in case A, some workers will observe P_2 (none will observe P_1) and the resulting shifting of labour leads to:

$$N_A^+ = L/2 + (1 - \theta)S_2 \text{ and } N_A^- = L/2 - S_2$$

In case B, some workers will observe P_2 and others will observe P_1, leading to:

$$N_B^+ = L/2 + (1 - \theta)S_1 - S_2$$

$$\text{and } N_B^- = L/2 + (1 - \theta)S_2 - S_1$$

The group S_2, in this case, are moving in the wrong direction. The problem is that the rules for workers shifting can only be based upon their observed output price, and not upon additional information about whether a general inflation (case A) has occurred, since that information is assumed to be unavailable.

The gains from increasing S_1 and S_2 can be written:

$$S_1: \frac{1}{2} \{(1 - \theta)p^+MPL[L/2 + (1 - \theta)S_1 - S_2]$$
$$- p^-MPL[L/2 + (1 - \theta)S_2 - S_1]\}$$

$$S_2: \frac{1}{2} \{(1 - \theta)p^+MPL[L/2 + (1 - \theta)S_2]$$
$$- p^-MPL[L/2 - S_2] - p^+MPL[L/2 + (1 - \theta)S_1 - S_2] +$$
$$(1 - \theta)p^-MPL[L/2 + (1 - \theta)S_2 - S_1]\}$$

and, provided these expressions are positive when the relevant S is zero, the levels of the Ss are set to bring them (the marginal gains) into equality with zero, as with the choice of the single S value in section 6.1. While these formulae are somewhat complicated, the two major conclusions of interest are relatively straightforward.

The first conclusion of importance is that unemployment is lower (or the same if $S_1 = 0$) in case A, the case of the general inflation, than in case B. To see this, observe that the unemployment in case A comes exclusively from the workers observing P_2 and then moving, S_2. In case B we continue to have S_2 but in addition have S_1 unemployed who observe P_1, so the total must be higher. Examination of the expressions for gains from moving in fact shows that S_1 can equal zero only if S_2 equals zero as well. This is intuitive, since S_2 is the rule that contains 'waste' in the sense that workers will occasionally be moving in the wrong direction, while S_1 only occurs in case B and is definitely in the correct direction. Thus, if unemployment is ever relevant, it is lower in case A.

The second conclusion is that this new environment definitely lowers welfare in comparison to that in section 6.1, and further lowers it (or just maintains it) in each outcome. In each case (A or B), national income is maximised by the S^* calculated by the rule in section 6.1, where all the unemployed are moving from the low-price to the high-price sector. In case B, therefore, where some unemployed are moving in the wrong direction, welfare must be lower, and in case A, only if $S_2 = S^*$ is national income maximised. This welfare loss is unavoidable, and is due to the additional restriction on information imposed in this section.

To examine the implications of the two conclusions, it is helpful to consider what might underlie the economic environment in this section. One approach is to introduce the simple quantity theory of money and suppose that the Central Bank determines the nominal money supply. By the quantity theory, nominal national income and the money supply are related by a constant factor for money-holding, k; in our two cases, we have:

$$M_A^s = k[P_3Q(N_A{}^+) + P_2Q(N_A{}^-)]$$
$$M_B^s = k[P_2Q(N_B{}^+) + P_1Q(N_B{}^-)]$$

as the nominal money supplies that sustain the given employment and output levels. Now suppose that the Central Bank adopts the following policy rule: set the money supply randomly, with equal probability, at either M_A^s or M_B^s. If workers can only observe the output price in their own sector, and cannot observe the nominal money supply, this leads to the environment discussed in this section. From our second conclusion above, however, this is a bad policy in that a lowering of the randomness of the policy would increase welfare.

But suppose instead that the Central Bank observes, following our analysis, that the high 'inflation' case A is associated with a lower unemployment rate than case B. It might then use this Phillips curve to adopt a monetary policy which maintains M_A^s over time. Here we run into a problem known as the 'Lucas policy critique'. If the high money supply is maintained over time, the uncertainty about which case is pertinent (A or B) will disappear from the economy since it is always in case A, and therefore unemployment will attain the section 6.1 equilibrium S^*. As long as the Central Bank follows the random monetary policy, it observes that low unemployment is associated with high prices and the high money supply M_A^s. If it concludes on that basis that there is a viable trade-off between high prices and unemployment, and adopts a policy of maintaining M_A^s, the policy does not have the intended effect since the observed behaviour of the economy was conditional upon the prior random policy.

How adequate is this model as an explanation for observed macroeconomic phenomena? The major shortcoming has to do with the information structure assumed, the inability of agents to distinguish between relative price effects affecting their sector and a general price inflation. They must not be able to observe the general price level (in our simple example, the price in the other sector) or the nominal money supply which, by the quantity theory, allows them to deduce the general price level. It is reasonable to ask how long these sorts of expectational errors can persist. To answer this question, Lucas (1975) has suggested that the expectational errors, even if they do not persist for very long, can set in motion real actions that have persistent effects over time. As an example, firms observing that their price has gone up might misperceive this to be a rise in their relative, or real, price, in place of an actual general inflation. On this basis they might invest in new capital equipment, raising productivity of labour and thus leading to higher employment in the future. This is the model of the 'equilibrium business cycle'. This still requires an initial, substantial miscalculation about general inflation that is not entirely plausible. We will examine in Chapter 9 an interesting variant of this Lucas information problem, where agents in the economy must attempt to distinguish between real and monetary aggregate shocks to the economy, and are limited in their responses by previous contractual agreements. That model, the 'staggered contracts' approach, replicates the Lucas results in a somewhat more plausible framework.

There is a further limitation on the Lucas results that should be discussed. We have assumed in this section that aggregate price uncertainty depends only upon the money supply in a quantity theory formulation. This can be extended by returning to the *IS–LM* apparatus. In that approach, an increase in the money supply requires a rise in P for the economy to remain at the Q^* level of output. But a rightwards shift in the IS curve, due perhaps to an increased propensity to invest or consume or to a more expansionary fiscal policy, also requires (for a given nominal money supply) a rise in P for the $IS–LM$ intersection to remain at Q^*, since the rise in P shifts the LM curve to the left. Thus the unexpected inflation driving the Lucas problem and leading to inefficient levels of unemployment can arise either through an uncertain monetary policy or through unpredictable shifts in the IS curve. This is interesting since it provides, even in the 'policy neutrality' framework of the Lucas approach, a justification for an activist monetary policy. If the government 'has an information advantage' in that it observes any shifts in the IS curve while private agents do not, it can neutralise these by an activist monetary policy—if the IS curve shifts to the left, for example, a rise in the money supply allows Q^* to be maintained without any fall in P that would otherwise lead to excessively high unemployment as workers, misperceiving this to be a fall in their sectoral position, quit jobs inefficiently. This idea of an activist 'stabilisation policy' is one of the major conclusions of the staggered contracts model, and it is interesting to note that it holds in the original Lucas framework as well.

6.4 RATIONAL EXPECTATIONS AND POLICY INEFFECTIVENESS

The model presented in section 6.3 presents a more adequate basis for the 'expectational errors' approach that we associated with the monetarists in Chapter 5. In section 6.3, the errors are unavoidable in that the information about whether the economy is facing case A or B (a general inflation or not) is simply not available, and agents must do their best subject to the non-availability of that information. The result, if we assume as we have done that the efficient outcome (subject to the availability of information and hence called the 'second best' efficient outcome) is attained as an equilibrium, is that welfare is lower than under the greater information availability of sections 6.1 and 6.2; further, the model displays an apparent Phillips curve, but does not allow a monetary policy trade-off along the Phillips curve. This last result is the 'policy ineffectiveness' implication usually associated with the new classical school. Much of the literature, however, uses a different (more heuristic) form of the approach to make similar points, and emphasises the notion of 'rational expectations'. We will follow the analysis in Sargent and Wallace (1975) as representative of this school.

We begin with the adoption of the 'Lucas supply function':

$$y_t = a_0 + a_1(m_t - m_t^e) + a_2 y_{t-1} + u_t$$

where y represents the deviation of real output from the 'equilibrium' level, m is the growth rate of money and m^e the expected growth rate, and u is an error term (uncorrelated over time) drawn from a distribution with a mean of zero. The equation is presented in the standard form of an econometric result where a_0, a_1, a_2 are taken to be estimated coefficients. The role of u is to represent any randomness in the system. The basic argument underlying the equation is that unexpected growth in the money supply leads to unanticipated inflation, which, through the sort of expectational-errors mechanism of the previous section, leads to a temporary decrease in unemployment and increase in real output. If the money-supply growth is predicted, however, these effects do not occur (in the terms of the previous section, agents know that case A has occurred). The increase in output may cause a compensatory decrease in the following period ($a_2 < 0$) or may lead to some follow-on business cycle effects ($a_2 > 0$). These follow-on effects are clarified by noting that the stipulated 'Lucas supply function' differs from our model of the previous section. There any divergence of unemployment from the natural rate led to a decrease in the GNP measure; here the phenomenon is due to 'intertemporal substitution effects'. Agents are confused not about sectoral price and wage relativities but about wages in this period relative to those next period. Thus, in a period of unanticipated inflation workers may think that their real wage has risen, so they supply more labour, intending to cut their labour supply next period when they anticipate that the wage will return to the normal level. The unanticipated inflation then causes an increase in output this period but a follow-on negative effect next period.

The Central Bank is assumed to follow some rule for monetary policy:

$$m_t = g_0 + g_1 y_{t-1} + v_t$$

where the money supply grows at the rate g_0 except insofar as the Bank adopts some sort of attempted stabilisation policy. If y_{t-1} was low, the Bank might want to expand the money supply more rapidly ($g_1 < 0$), thinking that this might induce higher output this period. The v term represents a randomness arising, perhaps, from incomplete control over the money supply and, like u, is taken to have a zero mean and to be uncorrelated over time. The coefficients g_0 and g_1 are policy choices by the Bank.

The basis of the rational-expectations approach is that private agents use any available information in forming expectations. Consider an agent trying to predict the money supply growth so that he can in turn predict inflation and choose his actions accordingly. If the Central Bank is following the stipulated rule, an agent observing past money supply and income values should be able to deduce g_0 and g_1. He will then predict that money supply will grow in the current period t by:

$$m_t^e = g_0 + g_1 y_{t-1}$$

If all agents are rational in their predictions, we can substitute this value for expected monetary growth, and the formula for actual monetary growth, into the Lucas supply function:

$$y_t = a_0 + a_2 y_{t-1} + u_t + a_1 v_t$$

The monetary policy parameters g_0 and g_1 simply drop out—it makes no difference whatever values the Bank chooses. This is the policy-ineffectiveness result of the rational-expectations literature. Private agents compensate for any predictable policy actions by the Central Bank and in that way negate them. Of course, the argument only applies to predictable (from past actions) policy measures. A new policy, a sudden change in g_0 and g_1, will have short-term effects until the new values are learned by the private sector, as argued by Taylor (1975).

Rational expectations has become something of a controversial concept in macroeconomic theory, yet the basic principle should not be that contentious. It is a simple extension of basic economic methodology to suppose that maximising agents choose their information-acquisition and expectations-formation actions just as rationally as they choose their other actions. The difficulty has largely resided in the models used to present the rational-expectations approach. They tend to assume a free availability of information, or in any case not to make very clear the underlying structure of the economy that limits information. In this sense the model in section 6.3 is strongly preferable to that in the current section. Further, as is obvious, the implications of rational expectations depend upon the particular model in which it is embedded. In the new classical models, rational expectations lead to the policy-ineffectiveness result, but there is no reason to think that it must do so in other models where the impact of the policy does not depend exclusively on expectational errors. The reader will note that we have in fact adopted rational expectations (in the sense of not relying upon expectational errors) implicitly throughout the book, and we will continue to do so. A proper Keynesian model should not depend upon expectational errors (except in the sense that the information is really not available) any more than it should depend upon an irrational wage or price rigidity.

6.5   CONCLUSIONS

This chapter has introduced the notion of an efficient unemployment rate as workers move between sectors in response to shifting job opportunities. The unemployment arises since information is not immediately available and the initial allocation of workers does not reflect the output prices eventually learned for each sector. The efficient (subject to information availability) unemployment rate s^* can be sustained by competitive sectoral labour markets. While we have labelled this as a search equilibrium, it is really a story of segmented labour markets, the 'island' story in Phelps (1970). We will consider the more common, 'dynamic monopsony', search models in Chapter 8 and find that they do not support the notion that the labour market will be efficient; indeed, they suggest a serious market failure that naturally leads to contracting in the economy.

The basic information problem underlying efficient unemployment can be compounded, as in section 6.3, by introducing inflation uncertainty in addition to relative price uncertainty. Workers are uncertain as to whether an observed price or wage change in their current sector represents a relative change or is merely due to a change in general inflation. As we have seen, this leads to an apparent Phillips curve, with the general inflation associated with the relatively low unemployment rate, but there is nonetheless no policy trade-off for the monetary authorities. Rather, the only desirable policy action is to minimise the uncertainty of inflation since the additional uncertainty leads to lower welfare than in the model of section 6.1 and 6.2; this can be done, in a quantity theory framework, by improving control of the money supply (eliminating money supply uncertainty) or, interestingly, in an *IS–LM* framework, by using an activist stabilisation policy of using the money supply to offset shifts in the *IS* curve.

While this Lucasian model is certainly not Keynesian, it is interesting in that it extends the neoclassical approach a bit closer towards empirical reality, and also suggests a very important information problem that is pertinent to macroeconomic understanding. The model does allow for a Phillips curve of a sort, and therefore is consistent with differing observed unemployment rates over time. The problem is that the information difficulties in the model are not particularly plausible; in a sense, rather than agents having too much information (as is the common objection to rational-expectations models), they seem to have too little. If agents can observe either the actual inflation rate, or the rate of growth of the money supply, the short-run Phillips curve disappears and the economy returns to s^*. To be more specific, the difficulty is that workers observe the price in their own sector (after the inflation has or has not occurred), but not the price in the other sector. But since the inflation has already occurred, they should be able to observe other prices without much effort, or to observe the contemporaneous money supply figures. We will return to the issue of the macroeconomic validity of the approach, and the improvements provided by introducing contracting, in Chapter 9.

The other implausibility of the model is that it supposes that all unemployment is due to workers voluntarily leaving their jobs to search and move to a job with higher wages. This is clearly not in accord with actual practices in the labour market, where workers face involuntary redundancies and difficulties in locating vacancies. This difficulty can be overcome by introducing an efficient contracting model as discussed in Chapter 7, that otherwise behaves exactly the same as the current search model.

7 The Contracting Model

An important feature of the search analysis in the previous chapter is that workers move voluntarily in response to higher anticipated wages and that there are competitive markets where supply and demand for labour equate. There is no involuntary unemployment. A worker is temporarily unemployed, in transition, as he moves into a sector where he anticipates a higher wage due to his higher productivity in that sector. This contrasts with the *UV*-curve models presented in Chapter 5, where workers are indeed engaged in search, but they are searching not for a higher wage but for a job vacancy. It might seem that one way of constructing labour markets resulting in *UV*-curve, and Keynesian, behaviour is to adopt an assumption of wage rigidity. If real wages do not adjust to restore a competitive equilibrium in labour markets, jobs are likely to be rationed—there will be involuntary unemployment and job-seekers will be concerned with locating vacancies and less concerned about the wage rate on offer. The problem, however, is that this rigidity seems on the face of it to violate the rationality assumption that we impose on economic agents—if there is an excess supply of labour, why doesn't the wage fall?

For this reason it was felt to be rather exciting when Azariadis (1975) and Baily (1974) noted that wage rigidities might be explained as rational behaviour of firms operating under 'implicit contracts'. It was in the interest of firms, even without a union contract limiting their behaviour, to maintain their reputation in terms of employment practices, and that as a result they would have implicit agreements with workers to, for example, not lower wages if the demand for their product fell. The basic argument is that a worker joining a firm intends to remain over an extended period of time, and in deciding whether to accept a job considers not just the wage rate today but what wage rate he might expect to gain in future, and whether he runs a large risk of lay-off. A firm with a reputation of maintaining wage rates and employment even under adverse demand conditions can more easily recruit workers today—in effect, it pays a lower wage on average because it insures workers against fluctuations in their employment conditions in the future.

While the contracting literature does display rigid wage rates and resulting involuntary redundancies, this does not immediately mean that the model has Keynesian macroeconomic implications. Two features of the early models were particularly troubling in this respect. Real, rather than nominal, wages seemed to be rigid, so one might still expect the real-balance argument to operate as to why a neoclassical equilibrium should be restored over time; the contracting approach provides a direct theory of the involuntary nature of unemployment but not of the maintenance of low-output Keynesian equilibria. Secondly, employment under adverse demand conditions actually equals or exceeds that obtaining under what might be called a neoclassical or Walrasian equilibrium, the sort of efficient outcome discussed in Chapter 6. The second problem, the employment implications of contracting, has recently been dealt with in the 'asymmetric information' contracting literature as discussed in Chapter 9, and we will in Chapter 10 consider how this revised contracting model can lead to Keynesian implications.

The main purpose of this chapter is to show how the basic contracting model relates to the efficient search construction of the previous chapter. We present two contracting models, one without risk-aversion and one with. The former, although not common in the literature (it is discussed in Baily, 1977) is the more interesting for our purposes in clarifying the relationship between search and contracting; in particular, we show that the model gives precisely the same unemployment outcome as the efficient competitive labour markets of Chapter 6. It differs only in that the unemployment becomes involuntary rather than voluntary; that is, in mechanism rather than outcome. Further, since the contracting is based upon internalising what might otherwise be a monopsonistic market failure, as clarified in Chapter 8, contracting can be expected to arise naturally in the labour market. The risk-aversion model is in fact somewhat less interesting, and we include it mainly because it is the normal approach in the literature; we also consider, in section 7.5, how contracting might differ if done explicitly with trade unions rather than, as in the original contracting literature, on an individual basis with potential workers.

There is a final point that is important. Much criticism has appeared in the literature against both the search and contracting models on the grounds that they are partial equilibrium in nature—they consider the behaviour of one firm without considering the full market environment and the interrelationships across the firms in the economy. This can be important, as in the previous chapter, where we observed that the price uncertainty generating unemployment had to be a relative price uncertainty, with one sector being favoured over another; a general inflation would have entirely different effects—this was, however, only clear because we set up the model as an, albeit very much simplified, general equilibrium model. While it is appropriate, in solving for equilibrium, to first consider the behaviour of each agent in isolation, one cannot draw equilibrium conclusions from this until one aggregates the behaviour patterns of the different agents into an equilibrium. That is the approach that we will adopt throughout the book.

7.1   A BASIC CONTRACTING MODEL

We will begin by considering the behaviour of a single firm in the same stochastic output-price environment as in the previous chapter, and show its optimal contracting behaviour. Later in the chapter we will place the individual firms into the general equilibrium of Chapter 6 and examine how the results of that chapter are changed.

The firm has a production function $Q(N)$ as before and faces a random (real or relative, since we will not introduce the Lucasian inflation uncertainty) output price, either p^+ or p^- with equal probability 1/2. Unlike the model in Chapter 6, the firm will have a more active role in decision-making (rather than just comparing the marginal product to the wage in a competitive sectoral labour market). In particular, before it learns its output price, it will sign contracts with workers committing itself to how it will behave once it learns its output price (what wage it will pay and how many workers it will employ)—the firm is able to make 'contingent' commitments. The standard assumptions of the contracting model arise from the notion that there is imperfect mobility in the economy and that firms end up with attached workforces. Thus each firm at the beginning signs some number N_0 of workers to contracts; once it learns its output price, the firm will not be able to hire more than this number of workers and, further, any laid-off workers will be unable to obtain jobs elsewhere. We will follow these assumptions in this section, to replicate the standard contracting results, and then return to assumptions more in accord with the Chapter 6 model to show how contracting and search relate.

The firm thus chooses how many potential workers N_0 to sign to contracts, and the contract offer composed of the real wage in each outcome (again, without inflation uncertainty, this is equivalent to offering given nominal wages), w^+ and w^-, and employment in each outcome, N^+ and N^-, where we have not prejudged whether these employment targets are reached by wage adjustment (e.g. setting w^- so low that the requisite number of workers quit) or by involuntary lay-offs. The firm takes account of the fact that N_0 will limit the employment figures: $N_0 \geqslant N^+, N_0 \geqslant N^-$. An important feature of the problem is that the firm must offer its contracts before it knows whether it will actually face p^+ or p^-. This is a problem of choice under uncertainty (e.g. if the firm knew that it would face p^-, it would presumably choose a low N_0, but not knowing this must balance out its N_0 choice over the optima for the two price outcomes), and the firm can be taken to choose its contract offers to maximise expected (a synonym for average) real profits over the two eventualities:

$$[p^+Q(N^+) - w^+N^+ + p^-Q(N^-) - w^-N^-]/2$$

When the output price is learned, the firm then carries out the relevant part of the contract, the committed wage and employment levels contingent upon that output price. We will discuss later why the firm actually commits itself in this way.

For a contract to be feasible, the contingent wage and employment levels must be attractive to workers. We assume that potential workers (who are assumed to be identical) can gain a real value G if they go elsewhere in the economy. They compare this to the value of the preferred contract, which is fully described by w^+, w^-, N^+, N^-, N_0. Using these values, a worker can calculate the chance of unemployment (whether voluntary or involuntary) in each outcome as $u^i = (N_0 - N^i)/N_0$ for $i = +, -$. If unemployed at the firm, the worker (since he cannot obtain another job) will gain a leisure value of $d < G$. We will assume in this section that a potential worker is interested in his expected real income:

$$[(1 - u^+)w^+ + u^+d + (1 - u^-)w^- + u^-d]/2$$

where in each outcome he has the probability $1 - u^i$ of being employed and getting the relevant wage w^i and the probability of u^i of being unemployed and gaining only the leisure value d. Workers will accept the contract offer so long as the expected (or average) real income, including any leisure value gained during unemployment, exceeds the opportunity cost G.

This represents a completely specified maximisation problem for a firm. It wants to choose an optimal contract that maximises expected profits subject to two constraints: the contract values must leave a worker's expected real income in excess of G, and employment levels in each outcome cannot exceed N_0. The easiest way to approach this problem is to observe first the rigid wage result: whatever values of N_0, N^+, N^- are chosen by the firm, an optimal contract (as discussed below, there are other contracts that are just as good) displays total wage rigidity $w^+ = w^-$. To see this, observe that the firm's expected profits (once it has chosen its employment levels) can be written as the average revenues less the average wage bill over the two possible outcomes, $[w^+N^+ + w^-N^-]/2$. The average wage bill represents the cost of production, and we can view the firm's optimisation problem in two steps: cost-minimisation and, then, profit-maximisation. Cost-minimisation in this case (once N^+ and N^- are determined) involves the choice of wage rates w^+ and w^-—the firm chooses these to minimise its average wage bill, subject to having a feasible contract that potential workers will accept.

The 'cost of production', the expected wage bill $[w^+N^+ + w^-N^-]/2$ can be presented as a budget line in Figure 7.1a, and the firm would like a line close to the origin, representing the least cost of labour. The problem is that the feasibility constraint must be met. As noted, potential workers will accept the contract offer if the expected real income (including leisure value gained during ay-offs) $[(1 - u^+)w^+ + u^+d + (1 - u^-)w^- + u^-d]/2$ exceeds the value obtainable elsewhere in the economy, G. Multiplying through by N_0 and substituting for each u^i, the feasibility constraint becomes:

$$[w^+N^+ + w^-N^- + d(2N_0 - N^+ - N^-)]/2 \geq GN_0$$

This then determines the feasible combinations of w^+, w^- for given values of N_0, N^+, N^-, and is graphed in Figure 7.1a. Interestingly,

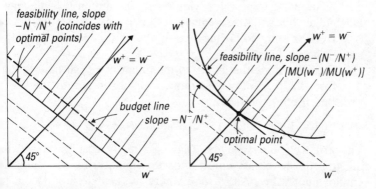

Figure 7.1a: *Optimal w^+, w^- combinations include the rigid wage solution under risk-neutrality*

Figure 7.1c: *Optimal w^+, w^- combination is the rigid wage solution with risk-averse workers*

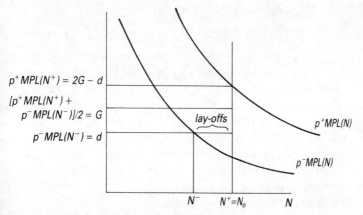

Figure 7.1b: *Efficient lay-offs in the contracting model*

Figure 7.1: *Contracting solutions*

the constraint (when met with equality) has exactly the same slope as the potential budget lines, and coincides with one budget line—the minimum feasible labour wage bill budget. The implication is that it does not matter how the wage bill is paid, with respect to the wage rate in each outcome—the firm can choose the point on the feasibility constraint where $w^+ = w^-$, having a rigid wage policy, and end up on the same budget line as with a varying wage rate. The rigid wage policy is a possible optimal contract, although there are other contracts with a varying wage (the other combinations of wage rates lying on the minimum feasible wage bill budget line) that are equally as good. (When we introduce risk-aversion in the following section, the rigid wage contract is the unique optimal contract.)

We can calculate the expected minimum wage bill paid by the firm from the feasibility constraint, and substitute into the firm's expected profit expression:

$$[p^+Q(N^+) + p^-Q(N^-) - 2GN_0 + 2dN_0 - dN^+ - dN^-]/2$$

The firm will maximise this (having already cost-minimised by meeting the feasibility constraint with equality) by choosing the employment values N_0, N^+, N^-, where the actual employment in an outcome cannot exceed the size of the attached workforce N_0. First suppose that N_0 is predetermined at some very large number and consider how the firm chooses the actual employment levels N^+ and N^-, calculating the gain to raising each as:

$$N^+: [p^+MPL(N^+) - d]/2 \qquad N^-: [p^-MPL(N^-) - d]/2$$

The firm would set each N^i so that these marginal gains become zero with the marginal value product equal to the leisure value d. If, however, N_0 is not so large, and is less than an N^i meeting the $MVP = d$ condition, the N_0 limit is binding and the firm would fully employ the available workforce. In other words, there is full employment (of the N_0 signed workers) in each outcome if the marginal value product would exceed the leisure value d; otherwise employment is reduced to the level such that the MVP equals d. The marginal value product curves are shown in Figure 7.1b and it is straightforward that $N^+ \geqslant N^-$.

Now consider the choice of N_0. Starting from zero, consider when it pays the firm to stop raising N_0. The marginal value product of the first worker is very large in both outcomes p^+ and

p^- and should exceed leisure value d—the first worker should be employed in either outcome and adds $[p^-MPL(N_0) + p^+MPL(N_0)]/2$ (the average marginal value product) to expected revenues and G to costs. As the firm continues to increase N_0, it will either hit a point where (raising $N_0 = N^+ = N^-$) the average marginal value product equals G, or the marginal value product in the bad outcome falls to d. If the former occurs first, the optimal contract is a full-employment one with $N_0 = N^+ = N^-$ such that $[p^-MPL(N_0) + p^+MPL(N_0)]/2 = G$. If the latter occurs first, the firm might still raise N_0, but now only in order to continue raising N^+ beyond N^-. From this point, an increase in $N_0 = N^+$ gains expected revenues of $p^+MPL(N^+)/2$ and raises expected wages by $G - d/2$, where the $d/2$ represents the leisure value gained by the new workers when unemployed in the p^- outcome. The firm will stop raising N_0 when:

$$N_0 = N^+: p^+MPL(N^+)/2 = G - d/2$$

$$N^-: p^-MPL(N^-)/2 = d/2$$

This solution is shown in Figure 7.1b and entails (adding the two equations), as before, that the average marginal value product equals G, the opportunity cost of a worker signing the contract, with lay-offs in the p^- outcome to the point where the marginal value product equals d, the opportunity cost of leisure.

When will the optimal contract actually entail unemployment? It must be the case that for the N such that $p^-MPL(N)/2 = d/2, p^+MPL(N)/2 > G - d/2$. With algebraic manipulation we have: $p^+/p^- > (2G - d)/d$, a condition that the two price possibilities be sufficiently far apart. (Recall that a similar condition held for the analysis in Chapter 6.) Thus, if p^+ is sufficiently greater than p^-, we end up with a contract with unemployment.

Summarising the results to this point, an optimal contract allows for a rigid wage that does not depend upon the output-price outcome; workers are signed to contracts until the average marginal product equals the opportunity cost to signing the contract, G; and unemployment occurs whenever the marginal value product falls below d. Since these contracting rules follow a comparison of marginal value products with the appropriate opportunity cost, they meet intuitive conditions of efficiency. We will return to this question later when we modify the model to be more directly comparable to that in Chapter 6. For now we consider in what sense the model explains involuntary lay-offs. We have separately shown that the contract allows for a rigid wage, and that there are cases where $N^- < N_0$, so that there is unemployment. But if the rigid wage exceeds the worker's alternative d, this unemployment must be through involuntary lay-offs. That the feasible rigid wage w must exceed d can be seen by rewriting the earlier equation:

$$[w^+N^+ + w^-N^- + d(2N_0 - N^+ - N^-)]/2 \geq GN_0$$

as:

$$(w - d)(N^+ + N^-)/2 \geq (G - d)N_0 > 0$$

The wage w exceeds G to compensate workers for the times when they will be unemployed and only gaining d. The implication is that workers will be 'unhappy' about being laid off and receiving d rather than the wage w, and the lay-offs must therefore be involuntary. Of course, this strategy of having a fixed wage and using involuntary lay-offs is just one possibility; the firm can alternatively (but without any gain from doing so) lower the wage in the bad outcome to d, so that workers are indifferent to lay-off, and raise the wage in the good outcome to compensate. The argument nonetheless makes involuntary lay-offs consistent with optimising behaviour, which was the objective.

In the discussion to this point we have assumed the existence of contracts rather than justifying them. The question is why firms must commit themselves in advance to wage and employment levels in the way that we have supposed. The answer to that is relatively simple in the current context, where we have assumed that a worker who starts out at this firm, if he is not employed at the firm, remains unemployed gaining a leisure value d. In the absence of commitments about wages and employment prospects no worker would 'attach' to a firm. In attaching to a firm, the worker loses his possibility of going elsewhere and, by our assumption, gaining G. Thus the firm would gain monopsony power and, in the absence of a binding commitment to wage rates, it could lower the wage for its attached workers to d, the minimum needed to get an attached worker to actually work in preference to leisure. But the potential worker would anticipate that and therefore would not attach to the firm. This possibility of using monopsony power is often referred to in the literature as *ex post* suboptimality, in that it pays the firm to renege on its contract. Usually it is assumed that some reputation mechanism prevents the firm from doing this; by reneging today, the firm gains a reputation for 'exploiting' workers and it becomes more difficult, and therefore more costly, to hire in the future. While we have considered the case here, where there is no later mobility, we will find in Chapter 8 that it is precisely a monopsony problem, in the search context, that leads firms to voluntarily offer contracts.

A final point relates to the terminology of 'implicit' contracts. Observation of the economy indicates that non-unionised employees rarely have explicit commitments from their employer about future wages and lay-off possibilities, and the current model is meant to be applicable to non-unionised as well as unionised firms (the actual role of unionisation being discussed in section 7.5). The argument is that the commitments may be 'implicit' and constitute norms by which a particular firm operates, preserving its reputation for good labour practices. But because of this notion of implicit contracting, one cannot immediately judge by simple observation whether these sorts of commitments actually occur in the economy.

7.2 THE ROLE OF RISK-AVERSION

The model in section 7.1 differs from the usual contracting models in the literature in that there is no mention of risk-aversion. The more standard models assume that firms are risk-neutral (they seek to maximise expected or average profits as in section 7.1) but workers are risk-averse (they seek to maximise expected utility rather than income). This leads to a risk-sharing basis for contracting that is often thought necessary to explain the existence of contracts in the economy; in contrast, we have already argued that there is a monopsony power argument for contracting, and we will strengthen this argument in Chapter 8. However, since the risk-sharing approach is the common one in the literature, we want to examine it. Introduction of risk-aversion will change our results in section 7.1 in two ways. In section 7.1 the firm could optimally set a contract with a rigid real wage, but could also choose from equally profitable (feasible) contracts with varying wages; with worker risk-aversion, the rigid wage contract is uniquely optimal.

In addition, the earlier approach led to employment levels that seemed intuitively efficient, with workers signed to contracts *ex ante* to the point where their expected marginal value product equalled their opportunity cost to signing the contract, G, and were then possibly laid off *ex post* if their marginal value product in the bad outcome p^- fell below their opportunity cost to actually working, the leisure value d; in contrast, the risk-aversion assumption will lead to suboptimally low unemployment in the bad outcome.

We introduce worker risk-aversion by assuming that they have a concave utility function over their real income in a period: $U(y)$, $U'(y) > 0$, $U''(y) < 0$; the utility function has the shape we have previously given the firm's production function, giving it the property of diminishing marginal utility of income. This corresponds to risk-aversion since a loss in income entails a higher utility loss than an equal gain in income would raise utility, so the individual will avoid risk. Given a number of possible outcomes, the individual will seek to maximise his expected utility rather than just his expected income. A potential worker will now decide to accept a contract if his expected utility from the contract exceeds $U(G)$, the utility of the alternative job. This means that the feasibility condition from section 7.1 must be rewritten:

$$[U(w^+)N^+ + U(w^-)N^- + U(d)(2N_0 - N^+ - N^-)]/2 \geqslant U(G)N_0$$

Since the firm's objective remains the same, it will continue to maximise expected profits subject to the (now rewritten) feasibility condition on wages and lay-offs. As in section 7.1, we begin by showing the rigid wage result and then consider the firm's optimal contract offer in terms of employment levels. For given contract values of N_0, N^+, N^-, the feasibility condition can be graphed as a relationship between w^+ and w^-, as in Figure 7.1c. In contrast to Figure 7.1a, this is no longer a straight line, due to the curvature of the utility function. The condition can be viewed as an indifference curve, and the slope at any point is the marginal rate of substitution calculated in the usual way. If w^+ were to rise by a unit, the worker's expected utility would rise by $N^+ MU(w^+)/2$, where MU is the marginal utility of another unit of income starting from w^+; if w^- rises by a unit, the utility gain is $N^- MU(w^-)/2$. To keep expected utility the same if w^+ rises by Δw^+ (so that utility would rise by $N^+ MU(w^+)\Delta w^+/2$), w^- must fall by some amount Δw^- (lowering utility by $N^- MU(w^-)\Delta w^-/2$), with the ratio being:

$$MRS(w^-, w^+) = (N^-/N^+)/[MU(w^+)/MU(w^-)]$$

with $MU(w^+)/MU(w^-)$ greater than one if $w^+ < w^-$ and less than one if $w^+ > w^-$ due to the diminishing marginal utility of income. The resulting feasibility condition as drawn in Figure 7.1c has the usual shape of an indifference curve. The firm, as in section 7.1, wants to minimise its total expected labour budget, for given employment values. The budget line from section 7.1 is given as: $[w^+ N^+ + w^- N^-]/2$, and therefore has the slope $-N^-/N^+$ as drawn in Figure 7.1c. The budget is minimised at a point of tangency where this slope equals that of the feasibility condition:

$$[MU(w^+)/MU(w^-)] = 1$$

Due to the concave utility function, marginal utilities of incomes can be equal only if the incomes are equal; thus the optimal contract must include wage rigidity with $w^+ = w^-$.

In the sense of assuring wage rigidity and from this the involuntary nature of any unemployment, the addition of worker risk-aversion seems to strengthen the contracting model. However, it has another implication that is not as desirable from a Keynesian viewpoint: the unemployment level in the bad outcome p^- is below the intuitively efficient outcome in section 7.1. To examine this, we will suppose that the N_0 and N^+ values have been optimally chosen, and note that the rule for lay-offs in section 7.1 was that lay-offs should occur in the p^- outcome as necessary to raise the marginal value product $p^- MPL(N^-)$ to d. We argue that, given the same values of N_0 and N^+, the rule now is to have a higher N^- and therefore fewer lay-offs (less unemployment).

Consider the marginal gain to increasing N^-. First we gain $p^- MPL(N^-)/2$ from increased production, including the factor of $/2$ which appears in expected profits to reflect the probability of the p^- outcome. But what happens to the wage bill? In section 7.1 it rose by $d/2$, the leisure value foregone by the new worker, since the expected wage bill could be written as $(G - d)N_0 + (N^+ + N^-)/2$. Now, however, the wage bill rises by some amount that maintains the feasibility condition:

$$[U(w^+)N^+ + U(w^-)N^- + U(d)(2N_0 - N^+ - N^-)]/2 = U(G)N_0$$

Recalling the rigid wage result, this condition can be rewritten:

$$[U(w) - U(d)](N^+ + N^-)/2 = [U(G) - U(d)]N_0$$

so the change in N^- must leave this unchanged, requiring that w falls by some amount to compensate for the rise in N^-. A unit rise in N^- would raise the left-hand side of this by $[U(w) - U(d)]/2$ and a rise in w would raise this by: $MU(w)(N^+ + N^-)/2$. We can write the change in w in response to a rise in N^- as: $-[U(w) - U(d)]/[MU(w)(N^+ + N^-)]$. The expected wage bill changes by this, multiplied by $(N^+ + N^-)/2$, plus the actual wage payment to the newly employed worker, $w/2$. We have:

$$\{-[U(w) - U(d)]/MU(w)+w\}/2$$

to compare to the gain in expected revenue $p^- MPL(N^-)/2$. If the expected wage bill change is less than d, we have the excessively high N^- result. That this is the case follows from the concave shape of the period utility function. Note that, if $[U(w) - U(d)]/MU(w)$ exceeds $w - d$, we have our result. But $U(w)$ exceeds $U(d)$ by some amount which represents the sum of the marginal utilities of each unit of income in excess of d, and this can be represented as the average marginal utilities of these units times the number of units, $w - d$. But since MU is declining with each additional unit of income, the average marginal utility must exceed $MU(w)$, and therefore the expression exceeds $w - d$ as required.

This result on excessively low unemployment, since N^- is high relative to the given N_0, is fairly intuitive. Workers do not like risk, and since the firm is risk-neutral, it can optimally provide insurance to workers, in effect collecting the premium for the insurance by a lower average wage over all outcomes. One form of insurance is to protect against a wage that varies with the output price facing the firm, the state of demand for the firm's product. But this still leaves employees with a lay-off risk, the risk that the will only gain leisure utility $U(d)$ rather than the utility from the fixed wage $U(w)$. It is optimal for the firm to provide some further insurance against this risk by raising N^- above the 'efficient' level. The result is however unfortunate for a model attempting to b Keynesian, and the literature quickly pointed out that in fact the firm could provide further insurance at a lower (in fact, zero) cost by means of lay-off compensation payments.

Suppose that in addition to specifying the wage and employment rules in the contract, the firm also commits itself to lay-off compensation payments c^+ and c^- for the two output prices. It is a simple extension of our earlier arguments that the way to minimise the expected wage bill, including the compensation payments, is to guarantee the worker a fixed total income (including his leisure gains) over all the outcomes by setting $w^+ = w^- = c^- + d = c^- + d = G$. In this case, raising N^- by one unit saves $d/2$ on the expected wages bill (paying $c^- = G - d$ to the worker rather than $w^- = G$) as in section 7.1, and we obtain the 'efficient' level of unemployment again. A further problem arises, however. The compensation payments leave workers indifferent to lay-offs, and lay-offs are therefore not involuntary in the earlier sense that the worker is worse off as a result.

Given that our discussion of the optimal solutions in sections 7.1 and 7.2 has been somewhat heuristic in nature, below we present a solution of the problems by calculus.

Solution of the Optimal Contract Problem with Calculus Methods

We will examine the contracting problems of sections 7.1 and 7.2 using Kuhn–Tucker formulations. We write the problem more generally to include numerous possible output prices, indexed by i, each price ($p_i > 0$) having an associated probability of occurrence $z_i > 0$. We also add the formal assumption that $Q'(N) \to \infty$ as $N \to 0$ to ensure that solutions contain strictly positive employment values. In the first instance, in each problem, we will merely look for a solution that meets the first-order conditions, and will then consider whether this is in fact the optimal contract at the end of this section (i.e., are the first-order conditions necessary and sufficient).

Section 7.1: The firm seeks to maximise expected profits:

$E_i[Q(N_i) - w_iN_i]$ which is notation for

$\Sigma_i z_i[p_i Q(N_i) - w_iN_i]$

This maximization is subject to the constraint that actual employment cannot exceed the number of attached workers N_0 and the feasibility constraint on potential workers being willing to sign the contract:

(i) $N_0 \geqslant N_i$ for each i

(ii) $E_i[w_i N_i + d(N_0 - N_i)] \geqslant G N_0$

There are also the non-negativity conditions $N_i \geqslant 0$, for each i. Multiply each constraint (i) by the appropriate z_i for convenience, and write the Lagrangian function L with multipliers λ_i (on each constraint (i) as multiplied by z_i) and μ (on (ii)):

$$L = E_i\{[p_i Q(N_i) - w_i N_i] + \lambda_i(N_0 - N_i) + \mu[w_i N_i + d(N_0 - N_i) - G N_0]\}$$

The firm's instruments are the N_i and w_i values and N_0, with first-order conditions:

(a) $\partial L/\partial N_i = 0$: $p_i Q'(N_i) - w_i - \lambda_i + \mu(w_i - d) \leqslant 0$ for each i
   [with equality if $N_i > 0$]
(b) $\partial L/\partial w_i = 0$: $[-1 + \mu]N_i = 0$ for each i
(c) $\partial L/\partial N_0 = 0$: $E_i[\lambda_i] + \mu(d - G) = 0$

Consider a possible solution with each $N_i > 0$. From (b), (a) can be written:

(a') $p_i Q'(N_i) = d + \lambda_i$

and from (a'), (b), and (ii):

(c') $E_i[\lambda_i] + d = E_i[p_i Q'(N_i)] = G$

Interpreting these, either N_i has a marginal value product of d or (if $p_i Q'(N_0) \geqslant d$) $N_i = N_0$; N_0 is chosen such that the average marginal value product equals G. The assumption $Q'(N) \to \infty$ as $N \to 0$ ensures that there are $N_i > 0$, $N_0 > 0$ meeting these first-order conditions.

Section 7.2, without layoff compensation payments: Under work risk-aversion the problem changes only in that constraint (ii) becomes:

(ii) $E_i[U(w_i)N_i + U(d)(N_0 - N_i)] \geqslant U(G)N_0$

The first-order conditions are:

(a) $p_i Q'(N_i) - w_i - \lambda_i + \mu[U(w_i) - U(d)] \leqslant 0$ for each i
   [with equality if $N_i > 0$]
(b) $[-1 + \mu U'(w_i)]N_i = 0$ for each i
(c) $E_i[\lambda_i] + \mu[U(d) - U(G)] = 0$

Again consider possible solutions with each $N_i > 0$ [the assumption on $Q(N)$ will ensure such a solution]. Then (b) requires that each w_i be the same value—the rigid wage result; write w for this wage. To see the overemployment result, suppose that there is an unemployment outcome $0 < N_i < N_0$; then, from (b) into (a):

$$p_iQ'(N_i) - w + [U(w) - U(d)]/U'(w) = 0$$
$$[p_iQ'(N_i) - d] + [U'(w)(w - d) + U(w) - U(d)]/U'(w) = 0$$

We must show that the second term is positive. But from (ii), $w > d$, and using the concavity of U: $U(w) - U(d) > U'(w)(w - d)$.

Section 7.2, with lay-off compensation payments: The introduction of compensation payments changes the firm's objective function to:

$$E_i[p_iQ(N_i) - w_iN_i - c_i(N_0 - N_i)]$$

and constraint (ii) to:

(ii) $E_i[U(w_i)N_i + U(c_i + d)(N_0 - N_i)] \geq U(G)N_0$

The first-order conditions become:

(a) $p_iQ'(N_i) - w_i + c_i - \lambda_i + \mu[U(w_i) - U(d)] \leq 0$ for each i
  [equality if $N_i > 0$]
(b) $[-1 + \mu U'(w_i)]N_i = 0$ for each i
(c) $E_i[\lambda_i] - E_i[c_i] + \mu[U(d) - U(G)] = 0$
(d) $\partial L/\partial c_i = 0: -(N_0 - N_i) + \mu U'(c_i + d)(N_0 - N_i) = 0$ for each i

Again we look for a solution with $N_i > 0$ each i. Conditions (b) and (d) are met with $w_i = c_i + d = G$. Substituting into (a) and (c) gives:

(a') $p_iQ'(N_i) = d + \lambda_i$
(c') $E_i[p_iQ'(N_i)] = G$

as in the section 7.1 case.

'Second-order' conditions: The problems all have quasi-concave objective functions and convex constraint sets, except for the following difficulty: at an $N_i = 0$, any wage w_i becomes feasible (since it does not matter to expected income), and similarly (in the last problem), at $N_i = N_0$, any c_i is feasible. This represents only a technical difficulty however since a convex set

can be constructed from contracts that are just as good—our first-order conditions described above do represent optimal contracts. The first problem, because of the non-strictly concave objective function and the linear constraint set, does not however describe a unique optimal contract in that many wage combinations are consistent with the (unique) employment conditions.

7.3   IS THE CONTRACTING MODEL KEYNESIAN?

To understand the contracting model, it is important to also understand exactly what lies behind the rigid wage result, and the very special sense in which the result holds. These are not the rigid wages assumed in the fixed-price model, and it would be a serious analytical error to say that contracting justifies the use of the fixed-price framework. The two basic differences are that contracting specifies fixed real not nominal wages, and further includes rules about employment levels that differ from the simple marginal-product/real-wage comparison rules of Chapter 2.

In this it is helpful to recall how we approached the problem. We supposed that the firm had first determined optimal employment levels, and then the firm determined how to achieve this at the least labour cost by varying w^+ and w^-. In section 7.1 this division did not matter in the least, so the firm might just as well set a rigid wage over outcomes, while in section 7.2, it was uniquely optimal to set a rigid wage due to worker risk-aversion. The point is that varying the wages over the two outcomes had no economic incentive justification. The firm's available labour supply was exactly the same, at N_0, irrespective of the wage set. Setting a higher wage to attract a larger workforce does not operate in the model since the firm does not face an upward-sloping labour supply curve. The only thing that matters, in achieving a given workforce size, is the average wage over outcomes, so that the N desired workers will accept the contract.

In the following section we shall show that in fact the risk-neutrality contracting model (henceforth the 'efficient contracting' model) gives precisely the same results as the 'efficient search' model of Chapter 6, when placed in the same environment. Where the models differ is that contracting leads to involuntary redundan cies in contrast to the voluntary quits of search. We shall see in Chapter 8 that our earlier search model, when reformulated in a more plausible manner, leads to a market failure that gives firms incentives to contract, and in Chapter 9 that there are limitations on contracting that arise in the actual economy that can potentially lead to Keynesian results as explored in Chapter 10.

The models we have considered to this point in this chapter have, however, not followed the economic environment of Chapter 6, but rather one more in keeping with the standard contracting literature. They have differed in a fundamental manner: in Chapter 6 unemployment arose efficiently as a mobility process, with workers separating from an unfortunate firm (with a low output-price) to move to another firm where their productivity and wages would be higher, passing through a state of unemployment in the interim; in this chapter the rationale for unemployment ever occurring is quite different—workers become unemployed when the value of their leisure exceeds their marginal value product at the firm. This is similar to the traditional neoclassical labour market of Chapter 2, where at equilibrium not all potential workers are actually employed since the real wage is such that labour supply at $L_s(w)$ includes those workers whose leisure value is less than w, and not those whose leisure value exceeds w. An increase in the marginal productivity schedule, $L_d(w)$, would lead to an equilibrium with higher employment as the new, higher equilibrium real wage induced further labour force participation. We make this point since there has been a tendency to confuse 'real productivity shocks', and their effect on employment, with Keynesian phenomena as we will discuss below. The labour-supply formulation we have assumed in sections 7.1 and 7.2 does differ from the Chapter 2 upward-sloping labour supply curve, since we are now assuming that all workers are identical having the same leisure value d. Suppose that there are a total of L potential workers in the economy. Then our aggregate labour supply curve is horizontal at d, and then vertical at L for all real wages above d—it is L-shaped.

The reason we introduce the aggregate labour supply curve is that we need to formulate a 'general equilibrium' contracting market for further interpretation of even this non-mobility contracting, where the equilibrium is in effect *ex ante*, an equilibrium occurring in the contract-offering market. Suppose that there are f

firms, identical *ex ante* (they need not end up with the same output price but run the same chances over output prices). There will then be a contracting labour market, where the firms make their contract offers to sign up their desired number of workers. We can now interpret the earlier value G of a worker's opportunity cost in signing a contract—it is the market price for labour in the sense of being the expected income (in section 7.1) or the expected utility (in section 7.2) that a firm's offer must meet in order to be competitive with other firms' offers. An equilibrium is reached at some G such that each firm makes an offer with a value to the worker of G, and makes the offer to some number N_0 of potential workers, such that summing up the N_0's over all the firms leads to a demand for 'signees' of the available workforce L (assuming of course that the equilibrium occurs at a $G > d$ and therefore with all the potential workers signing contracts with some firm).

The demand for workers is downward-sloping for the usual reasons. Recall that each firm offers a contract to the N_0 workers such that the average marginal value product (including any leisure gained in unemployment) equals G. Then, if the market G is lower, the firm attaches a higher N_0 to meet the average marginal value product equalling G condition. After the market for contracts clears, each firm has its number of attached workers and follows the lay-off rule in the optimal contract: in the absence of risk-aversion, it lays off its workers into unemployment to the point where the marginal value product equals leisure value d; if there is risk-aversion, it lays off somewhat fewer workers. Contracting models of the sort in sections 7.1 and 7.2 are then readily interpretable as general equilibrium models.

We are now in a position to clarify why the fixed wages in the contract are real rather than nominal, and how the p^+ and p^- outcomes can be interpreted (and, perhaps more importantly, what would be an improper interpretation). Suppose we follow the Chapter 6 interpretation, and view p^+ and p^- as real or relative prices, so that some sectors have high prices and others low (with, extending the Ch. 6 approach to f firms, $f/2$ firms facing each relative price). Firms will care about their real profits and workers their real income, in general, since workers directly and firms indirectly (through their disbursements to shareholders) care about the ultimate consumption good value of their income; any general nominal changes through inflation are irrelevant. The contracting result is then for real wage rigidity, with lay-offs when the real productivity of workers in a particular sector falls below their real leisure value. As in Chapter 6, each period the unemployment level will on average be the same, so the model does not address cyclical fluctuations. These might possibly be addressed, remaining within the real framework, by assuming that a firm faces a good or bad marginal value product curve not because of changes in relative prices (demand shifts in favour of a different sector) but because of changes in real physical productivity. All sectors might then together, in a given period, be unlucky and face the equivalent of a p^- price (the marginal value product of labour falls), so unemployment might be high in some periods and low in others. But in what sense is this idea of a general fall in real productivity, an 'aggregate productivity shock' rather than an 'aggregate demand shock', Keynesian? That it is not Keynesian does not mean, of course, that it has no explanatory power. It might be very pertinent in explaining the effects of the oil price shocks of the 1970s. A rise in the real price of imported oil might be viewed as an excise tax on each sector in the domestic economy, in effect lowering net real productivity in each. However, this is precisely what would happen in a simple neoclassical labour market of the form in Chapter 2—it is exactly equivalent to a downwards shift in the labour demand curve, leading to lower employment; contracting just explains why the fall is effected through involuntary lay-offs rather than falling real wages causing workers to voluntarily depart from the market. As in the following section, the efficient (with risk-neutral workers) contracting model differs from a neoclassical model only in the mechanism rather than the result. Interestingly, the risk-sharing contracting model of section 7.2 would result in less unemployment than the neoclassical model, as workers are partially insured against lay-offs.

We have discussed the idea of aggregate productivity shocks in some detail since much recent literature (e.g. the staggered-contracts approach in Ch. 9) seems to view them as the basis of a Keynesian approach. We now want to turn to another possible interpretation of the models above, meant to be Keynesian in nature, but again unsustainable as such. Why is it that the contracts cannot be nominal in nature, so that an inflation might result in the bulk of sectors drawing a nominal P^+ (switching to our earlier upper-case notation for nominal prices) and, with a fixed nominal wage W, then leading to higher employment, with lay-offs and high unemployment when a low nominal P^- is drawn by the bulk of sectors? In the absence of a Lucas information problem in distinguishing between real and nominal prices (which would in fact have precisely the same effects as in the previous chapter), we might view this possibility as one where all the sectors together draw a nominal price, either P^+ or P^-. But then the optimal contract, if firms and workers care only about their real incomes, is to set a full employment contract with a rigid wage at the marginal physical product of the N_0^{th} worker. The changes in nominal prices are simply irrelevant. It is only if workers or firms care about nominal incomes (rather than real) that a different result ensues, and there is no convincing reason as to why agents should in general care about nominal values.

There are two further possibilities that we will discuss later in the book. The staggered-contracts literature (Ch. 9) introduces a variant of the Lucas information problem, but one where agents are unable to distinguish between aggregate (rather than sectoral) real and monetary shocks. That information problem, combined with limitations on contracts (it would not suffice if efficient contracts were possible), can lead to partially indexed contracts where monetary policy is non-neutral. There again, however, there is nothing that appears to be an aggregate demand shock except for the sort of effect of a shifting of the *IS* curve on the price level as discussed in the Lucas model. The introduction of a proper aggregate demand mechanism is the primary aim of Chapter 10, where we suggest that all sectors can draw a low marginal value product of labour curve due to a fall in aggregate demand, in a monopolistically competitive world with imperfect contracting. To establish the imperfections in the labour market that justify the assumption of imperfect contracting used in both the staggered contracts model and in Chapter 10, we must first examine why the efficient search story of Chapter 6 is not plausible (Ch. 8), and why the efficient contracts of this chapter are generally not available as a substitute (Ch. 9).

In the following section we will place contracting fully into the mobility environment of Chapter 6. However, our detailed discussion of the non-mobility model, up to this point in the chapter, will be useful since later models will naturally tend to imply immobility. Indeed, for our macroeconomic models in Chapters 9 and 10 we will make an even stronger assumption, that leisure value is zero. This will put us firmly, in a sense, in a Keynesian world, since the absence of mobility will remove the search rationale for unemployment, and the zero leisure value will similarly eliminate the leisure-value marginal-value-product comparison for unemployment. In the contracting models of this chapter, a zero leisure value would lead to contracts with invariant full employment (assuming that the marginal value product of labour is always positive). It is only limitations on contracting that will then produce inefficient unemployment of workers with a positive marginal product but a zero leisure value—any unemployment will, in that sense, be Keynesian.

7.4 THE CONTRACTING MODEL WITH MOBILITY

To reinforce the point that contracting *per se* does not alter the employment outcomes of the earlier search model, we will now place the efficient contracting model of section 7.1 into the environment of Chapter 6; in particular, after time θ, workers can obtain a new job at another firm. Contracting then occurs at time 0, when neither firms nor workers know the output price pertinent to the particular firm; at time θ we will suppose that firms can again hire (knowing their output price) in some competitive market with a real wage w_θ. Of course, equilibrium in that market requires that the wage equal the marginal product at those firms that are hiring then, the firms that have the high output price p^+. If each of the f identical *ex ante* firms had signed N_0 workers to contracts and hire some number H_θ at time θ, they will in the p^+ outcome end up with a total workforce (adjusting for the unemployment time) of $N_0 + (1 - \theta)H_\theta$ and therefore $w_\theta = (1 - \theta)p^+ MPL[N_0 + (1 - \theta)H_\theta]$. Firms will of course take account of this opportunity for further hiring in their original contract offers. They will also take account of the change in laid-off workers' opportunity cost, which is no longer leisure value d but rather w_θ.

The mobility problem changes the firm's optimal initial contract offers in an obvious manner. From the N_0 attached workers, the firm will continue to follow the rule of laying off workers in the p^- outcome if their marginal value product would be less than their opportunity cost; now, instead of d, this is the wage they would get by moving and therefore lay-offs will occur to the point where $p^- MPL(N^-) = w_\theta$. Now consider the choice of N_0. In raising this the firm gains the average marginal value product over the outcomes, including the w_θ gained by laid-off workers, and where the marginal value product in the p^+ outcome now takes account of any later hirings; $p^+ MPL[N_0 + (1 - \theta)H_\theta]$. It chooses N_0 such that the average marginal value product equals G, which in equilibrium will be set such that the firm chooses to sign $N_0 = L/f$ workers to contracts (and firms in the aggregate then attach the entire workforce).

From the condition on later hirings and the rule on lay-offs, we have the two conditions:

$$w_\theta = (1 - \theta)p^+ MPL[N_0 + (1 - \theta)H_\theta]$$
$$w_\theta = p^- MPL(N^-) = p^- MPL(N_0 - H_\theta)$$

Setting these equal then gives precisely the condition on H_θ that we had on S^* in Chapter 6. The only difference here is that the firm can contract with its initial workforce N_0 to set a fixed wage and then use involuntary lay-offs in the p^- outcome to achieve the workforce N^-. The proper mobility between sectors occurs not because of workers responding to wage signals, but due to involuntary lay-offs.

7.5 TRADE UNIONS

The contracts we have discussed to this point are essentially commitments, implicit or explicit, made to individual workers. These workers forego their potential wage elsewhere in the economy, G, to receive a set of commitments that have equivalent value—they gain no additional surplus from the contract, the contract being designed to maximise the firm's profit subject to potential workers accepting the offer. We now want to consider how the outcome might differ if the contracting was with organised trade unions. This is important for two reasons: many neoclassical economists have blamed unions and associated high real wage rates for high unemployment; second, analysis of this case will clarify the separation of wage and employment commitments that is important for understanding the features of our earlier, individual bargaining contracts.

The fundamental difference between contracts negotiated by unions, and those with individual workers, is that unions can reasonably expect to gain a surplus for their members over the 'competitive alternative' G—unions should be able to gain monopoly rents for their members through their combined bargaining power. We will examine this maintaining the earlier structure as much as possible. We consider a union with M members, working for the same firm; the members are identical and risk-neutral expected-income maximisers. They could gain G elsewhere in the economy by leaving the union and the firm, but only gain leisure value d if laid-off. The basic points can be made in the absence of uncertainty, where the firm and the union know in advance the output price at the firm, p. Observe that under individual contracting this case would lead to full-employment at a wage G, with an N_0 such that $pMPL(N_0) = G$. Refer to the employment level meeting this condition as N^*—the union leads to underemployment if the resulting employment is less than N^*; it leads to actual unemployment if employment is less than the union membership M (which will be specified below).

Now consider a union with an arbitrarily fixed membership M which may exceed or fall short of N^*. The expected income, including leisure value, of each union member is:

$$(N/M)w + [(M - N)/M]d$$

where the member gains the negotiated wage w with a probability of being employed equal to total employment over membership size and gains leisure d with the given probability of unemployment. The union can be taken to maximise this expression or equivalently the total income of its members:

$$wN + (M - N)d$$

In the literature a typical approach is to adopt the simple monopoly union model where the union is taken to have total power to choose the real wage, with the firm then having total power to choose the employment level in response. The union maximises the expected real income of its members subject to a labour demand curve from the firm—this is the traditional monopoly problem and the optimal rule is to set the marginal revenue equal to marginal cost (in choosing the quantity, in this case of labour, to supply), with the wage set then being the point on the demand curve that leads to this quantity. Since the marginal cost of supplying labour is the leisure value foregone, we have the point marked as w_u and N_u in Figure 7.2a, provided of course that $M \geqslant N_u$. Monopoly power is effective in the case where w_u exceeds the competitive wage G and then N_u will be less than N^*, the underemployment result. If the membership size $M \leqslant N_u$, we have full employment of members (the union may be associated with underemployment but not actual unemployment); if $M > N_u$, we have actual unemployment of members and further this is inefficient (in terms of our discussion earlier in this chapter) since workers are being laid-off even though their marginal product exceeds their leisure value.

If this were the end of the story one could conclude that unions may create underemployment and unemployment. The problem is that both the firm and the union could agree to a contract that is better than the w_u,N_u outcome. This arises in the 'bilateral monopoly' model of union behaviour when we allow the parties to agree to both wage and employment commitments. Relative to the possible contract (w_u,N_u), the union would prefer any contract (w_c,N_c) meeting the condition:

$$w_c N_c \geqslant w_u N_u + d(N_c - N_u)$$

since each member's expected income, including leisure value, is higher. The firm would prefer any contract such that:

$$p[Q(N_c) - Q(N_u)] \geqslant w_c N_c - w_u N_u$$

Contracts meeting both conditions, and thus preferred by both parties to the monopoly union outcome, are shown in Figure 7.2b. Provided that $pMPL(M) \geqslant d$, the only contracts that are not dominated by some better contract are those with full employment. To see this, take any proposed outcome (w,N) with unemployment but $pMPL(N) > d$. Combining the conditions for a dominating contract, such a contract exists if:

$$p[Q(N_c) - Q(N)] \geqslant d(N_c - N)$$

Raising N_c from N meets this condition provided that $pMPL(N) > d$. Bilateral monopoly thus implies that there will be full employment of union members, provided that that meets the efficiency condition that the marginal product exceeds the leisure opportunity cost d.

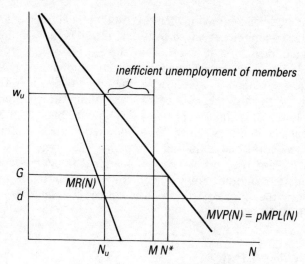

Figure 7.2a: *The monopoly union model and unemployment among union members*

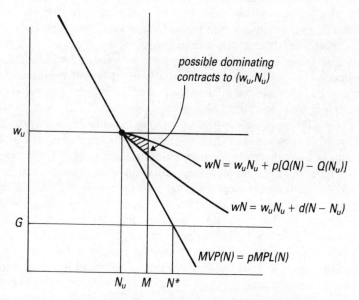

Figure 7.2b: *Bilateral monopoly solution range*

Figure 7.2: *Union wage and employment determination*

Our study of contracting then suggest that if employment as well as wage commitments can be made, there will be full employment of union members, in contrast to the simple monopoly union model. The only possible undesirable effect of unions is that M might be less than N^*. Otherwise, the effect of the union would simply be to raise the wage above G. without affecting employment levels. It is important to note just how the bilateral monopoly contract operates, since this follows our earlier individual contracts in the bad output-price outcome—the wage is fixed, but firms do not use this wage in a marginal-value product/wage equality to determine employment. Rather, following the optimal contract, they employ workers whose marginal value product is less than the wage.

7.6   CONCLUSIONS

The basic results in this chapter are that the efficient contracting model (either the risk-neutrality case in section 7.1 or the risk-aversion but compensation payment case in section 7.2) replicates competitive labour markets in employment outcomes but differs in its fixed wage and the involuntary lay-offs that achieve the efficient outcome. The case of risk-aversion without lay-off compensation payments, with its inefficiently low unemployment, will not be of much interest for our later analysis.

Thus this approach, which at first sight seemed very Keynesian, upon reflection seems less so. There are the two apparent problems in using this model to derive Keynesian results: the rigid wage is a real one, not a nominal one, and in any case there are separate employment commitments so that employment in the low output-price case exceeds that mandated by a marginal-product/real-wage comparison. That the rigid wage is real rather than nominal divorces the two earlier mentioned problems with a Keynesian equilibrium—if there is unemployment, why doesn't the real wage fall; if there is a Keynesian low-output equilibrium, why don't nominal prices and wages fall, raising real balances, shifting the *LM* curve to the right and restoring the neoclassical equilibrium. We are left with the second question and will seek to address it in Chapter 10 using the limited contracting model of Chapter 9. We now repeat the important point that showing a rationale for involuntary unemployment is not the same as showing Keynesian aggregate demand-based low-output equilibria.

The serious problem in establishing Keynesian equilibria will in fact be the employment rules dictated by the efficient contract. In Chapter 9 we will consider the major argument in the literature as to why the efficient contracts of this chapter might be implausible. This argument is based upon the enforceability problem of contracts. Once the firm has agreed to the optimal contract, which is *ex ante* in its interest in lowering the average labour cost it faces over both good and bad output-price outcomes, it still has an incentive to renege *ex post*. It has an incentive to lower the agreed fixed wage to the minimum amount necessary to get its attached workforce to actually remain—either the leisure value d or the wage obtainable elsewhere in the economy, net of mobility costs (in our formulation, the period of unemployment before the new job is begun). Even if it doesn't violate the real-wage agreement, however, it has an incentive to cut back employment in the bad outcome below the agreed level to the point where the marginal value product equals the wage. If the efficient contract is unenforceable (either through a reputation mechanism or legally), a second-best contract might be adopted. The asymmetric information contracting literature, discussed in Chapter 9, argues that the second-best contract might well contain excessive unemployment. Before turning to that argument, however, we want to strengthen the case for contracts as a natural phenomenon in labour markets even in the absence of trade unions. This can be done, as in the following chapter, by observing that monopsonistic market failure tends to arise in search markets and that firms optimally respond to this by offering commitments.

8 Search and Inefficiency

The search model presented in Chapter 6 may seem unusual to those conversant with the standard search literature introduced in Phelps *et al.* (1970). This is because there are two distinct search stories: the segmented markets (islands parable) story of Chapter 6, and the dynamic monopsony search to be considered in the present chapter, with Mortensen (1970) as an example. In Chapter 6 workers had to decide whether to move between segmented competitive labour markets which might be viewed as 'islands'—it takes time to move between the islands and this time can be viewed as unemployment. But on arrival on the new island, the worker simply enters the competitive labour market, obtaining a job at the competitive wage. A more plausible scenario, perhaps, is one where an unemployed worker searches by applying to different firms, each of which makes a job-offer with some associated wage; expanding firms might offer higher wages, and the searcher might do well to keep looking for such a firm, remaining unemployed in the meanwhile. Unemployment in this story is a productive activity in the sense of learning information about the wage offers throughout the economy.

In this chapter we present this form of search, beginning with (as we did in Ch. 7) a formulation meant to be representative of the standard literature (sect. 8.1), and then in section 8.2 placing the model into the environment of Chapter 6 to examine how the model fundamentally differs from the efficient search approach of that chapter. The major result is that search, when workers have to apply to individual firms and no longer can rely on a competitive sectoral market, leads to inefficiency. This inefficiency, which might be characterised as a monopsonistic exploitation, actuall leads to too low an unemployment rate—workers have little incentive to search for new jobs since they anticipate being 'exploited' in the new job and not receiving the full benefit of their search. Interestingly, as we discuss in section 8.3, contracting arises naturally in this environment as those firms wishing to recruit new workers can do so only by making commitments in advance of search. The points made in this chapter derive primarily from Diamond (1981; Apr. 1982) and Frank (1985).

8.1 A PARTIAL-EQUILIBRIUM SEARCH MODEL

The basis of the current model is that there are a large number of firms in the economy offering different wage rates; while potential workers know the distribution of wages in the economy, they do not know which particular firm pays which wages and can gain this information only by applying to the firm and learning its wage rate. For simplicity we assume that search can occur only by the unemployed. (It is necessary, for the model to generate unemployment, that the costs to search are less for the unemployed than for someone searching on-the-job, an assumption that has been objected to by Tobin [Mar. 1972]; otherwise, a searcher would accept the first job-offer and continue to search while employed.) All potential workers are identical and, upon application, receive a job-offer from the firm. This last assumption is not as restrictive as it might seem since the job-offer might be one with a very low or zero wage and therefore be equivalent to no job-offer at all.

Consider an unemployed person seeking a job. When he accepts a job he is taken to remain there until retirement, and therefore any wage-offer is a lifetime wage offer. To find a job, the searcher applies at numerous firms, one at a time, and either accepts or rejects the offer; each application takes a period of time θ. In keeping with the traditional search literature we will temporarily (for this section only) assume that the worker discounts the future at an interest rate r (per time period θ).

The searcher perceives that he might receive, upon application to a firm, any of a number of possible wage-offers: w_0, w_1, w_2, ..., w_k, where the increasing subscript denotes a higher offer. Further, he associates a probability a_i with each possible offer w_i. The searcher must choose whether to accept a given offer w_j or to reject the job and continue searching. We define w_r, the reservation wage, as the minimum wage-offer that he will accept. In an unchanging environment, the searcher's reservation wage is unchanging over time.

We can calculate w_r by considering what happens when the searcher starts his search with the rule that he will accept anything above w_r. Upon his first application, the probability that the searcher receives an acceptable offer can be written as the sum of the probabilities of all offers above w_r: $A_r = a_r + a_{r+1} + a_{r+2} + \ldots + a_k$. Then $(1 - A_r)$ is the probability of receiving an offer below w_r and therefore the probability that he declines the offer. The acceptable offers have an average value that can be written:

$$\bar{w}_r = (a_r w_r + a_{r+1} w_{r+1} + \ldots + a_k w_k)/(a_r + a_{r+1} + \ldots + a_k)$$

To actually solve for w_r, we introduce the notion of the 'return function'. Arbitrarily denote the expected gain to search from the beginning as some value V. The return function observes that V is composed of the return to a successful initial application and the return gained from further search if the initial application is unsuccessful, again V because of the unchanging environment (but since this occurs θ later, we must discount the latter term):

$$V = A_r \bar{w}_r + (1 - A_r)[V/(1 + r)]$$

including the probabilities appropriate to each term. This can then be solved for V:

$$V = (1 + r)[A_r/(A_r + r)]\bar{w}_r$$

Depending upon the reservation wage chosen by the searcher, $\bar{w}_r$ and A_r will differ, a rise in w_r raising $\bar{w}_r$ but lowering the probability of success A_r. The searcher chooses w_r to balance these two factors in maximising V, his gain from search.

The choice of a reservation wage to maximise V is easiest to see in the case where there are only two possible wage-offers, w_1 and w_2, with probabilities a_1 and a_2. The searcher can choose w_r to be either w_1, so he accepts all offers, or w_2, so he accepts only high wage offers. The resulting V values are:

$$V_1 = a_1 w_1 + a_2 w_2$$
$$V_2 = (1 + r)[a_2/(a_2 + r)]w_2$$

The searcher observes the wage and probability values, calculates V_1 and V_2 and sets the reservation wage appropriate to the larger value.

Now that we know how an individual searcher behaves, we can examine the nature of equilibrium in this model. To complete the model, we suppose that there is a fixed workforce in the economy of size L, with a number N currently employed and $S = (L - N)$ unemployed. Of the N workers, a certain proportion n are taken to retire each period. In an equilibrium there must be nN new hires to maintain employment at N. The unemployment pool is maintained by new entrants into the labour force in numbers nN, keeping the labour force at the size L.

We will examine the equilibrium with reference to our two wage example. Suppose that after calculating V_1 and V_2 the searchers decide on the reservation wage w_1, so that they accept the first job on offer. Then all S are hired directly, to replace the retiring workers, and equilibrium requires that $S = nN$. Substituting $N = L - S$, we have $S/L = n/(1 + n)$ as the resulting unemployment rate. If, on the other hand, searchers have the reservation wage w_2, then only the proportion a_2 of the searchers are hired in the current application period, and equilibrium requires that $a_2 S = nN$. This leads to the unemployment rate $n/(a_2 + n)$, which is larger than when searchers accepted all jobs, as is intuitive.

The equilibrium unemployment rate then depends upon the searchers' choice of reservation wage. Returning to the calculations of V_1 and V_2, it is apparent why workers might choose the higher reservation wage: if r is small, if a_2 is large, or if w_2 is quite large relative to w_1. Changes in these factors are likely to affect the equilibrium unemployment rate. Another change that is pertinent is a change in the length of time θ needed for an application; a fall in this means that the interest rate is operating over a shorter time period, and is equivalent in that sense to a fall in the interest rate, raising the reservation wage. However, it also requires a change in our specification of the number of new hirings needed in the application period, since during a shorter period fewer retirements can be expected. Except for the role of the interest rate, which was absent in Chapter 6, these effects are all the same as in our search model there. The difference is that here we have a partial-equilibrium problem that limits our analysis. Where does the wage distribution come from? Why do some firms offer w_1 and others

w_2? To examine this, we will need to 'endogenise' the wage-setting.

8.2   EQUILIBRIUM SEARCH AND INEFFICIENCY

To examine a search equilibrium with endogenous wage-setting, we return to the environment of Chapter 6. There were two possible output prices that *ex ante* identical firms might face; we modify the analysis to allow for f firms with (after prices are learned) half facing p^+ and half facing p^-. Each firm has a production function $q(N_f)$ with the usual shape. An application by a searcher will take θ of the total period as before, and the first application is made before workers learn the output prices associated with the different firms. The second application is made with that information (otherwise the searcher may be unfortunate and continue to apply to low-price firms). We drop the assumption in section 8.1 that a searcher discounts future wages, and assume a well-organised search market in the sense that if a number of searchers are indifferent between applying at a number of firms, they are sent in equal numbers to each firm by some central employment agency.

Since the economic environment is essentially identical to that in Chapter 6, the efficient outcome remains more or less the same. The rule for efficient allocation, where the condition for any movement is met, is that S applicants (at time 0) to low-price firms should move (at time θ) to high-price firms, where S is such that:

$$(1 - \theta)p^+ MPL(N^+) = p^- MPL(N^-)$$

and we define N^+ and N^- to take account of the number of firms: $N^+ = L/f + (1 - \theta)S(2/f)$ and $N^- = L/f - S(2/f)$. The efficient unemployment can be written as before as S^*.

We now want to examine the S_s obtained as an equilibrium in the current search model, which differs from that in Chapter 6 in that we no longer have competitive sectoral labour markets determining wages. From the analysis in section 8.1, the wage distribution determines the behaviour of searchers, and the primary requirement for an equilibrium wage distribution is that no firm has an incentive to change its wage offer. Introduce the 'subjective' wage distribution, the expectations of workers about wage offers. An equilibrium is then defined by rational expectations, where the subjective wage distribution corresponds to the actual one that firms find it in their interest to offer.

Now add the additional assumption that searchers only apply at firms at times 0 and θ, and if they decline the job-offer at time θ they remain unemployed for the rest of the period. (This assumption can be dropped, allowing the unemployed to apply at 2θ, 3θ, and so on up to the end of the period, without any change in the conclusions.) Workers have some subjective wage distribution in mind composed of wages offered by firms in each sector at each time: w_0^+, w_0^-, w_θ^+, w_θ^-. In equilibrium, these must correspond with the actual wages on offer. But consider time θ; firms at that point know that any applicant, if he declines the offer, will remain unemployed and under our assumptions gain a zero leisure-value (from the fixed-labour-supply assumption); the applicant has a zero reservation-wage. The firm will then offer any applicant at that time the minimum wage he will accept, 0. Thus the only equilibrium values of w_θ^+, w_θ^- are zero. From this, however, a searcher's reservation wage at time 0 is also 0, and the wages paid by firms at that time are also 0. In this extreme case, the firms have total monopsony power (the threat to continue search is meaningless) and the wage falls to 0. What is interesting, however, is that as a result of this 0 wage, even the p^- firm, at time 0, should hire all applicants, and there is no further search θunemployment is at zero as the search market collapses.

This is of course an extreme case, and one can lessen the firm's monopsony power to gain a more reasonable solution by introducing discounting, leisure value, and other factors. The result remains, as in Diamond (1981; Apr. 1982), that any monopsony power causes unemployment S_s to be too low relative to S^*. The reason for this is that searchers at time θ do not gain the full marginal value product of their labour (as they did in the competitive market in Ch. 6), and therefore their incentive to search is too low.

While our extreme example may make the result of inefficiently low unemployment seem unrealistic, actual practices that have developed in markets highlight the problem. In labour markets, searchers for new jobs do not relinquish their current job first (as the search model assumes), not necessarily because it is more efficient to search on-the-job but because having a job increases one's bargaining power with potential employers. Firms advertising vacancies typically attach an expected wage rate to the job to encourage applications. We can understand this as a response by a closer examination of the monopsony outcome.

In our zero-wage equilibrium (or any monopsony equilibrium of similar characteristics), there is inadequate search because applicants know that firms where they apply will use monopsony power to offer the minimum wage, and knowing that this will happen, they have an inadequate incentive to search. Firms with the p^+ price would be willing to pay a higher-than-zero wage to gain additional applicants given the disparity between the marginal value product and the wage. If they can communicate this through a binding commitment, they will do so. Indeed, if such commitments are allowed, each p^+ firm will start bidding up the wage until it reaches the marginal value product, and therefore the competitive solution in Chapter 6 (if there are enough firms to approximate a competitive market). Search will then return to the efficient level. This requires, however, that binding commitments can be made. If the firm advertises in a non-binding way a high wage, no applicant will respond to this, knowing that the firm will later renege and set the monopsony wage. Wage commitments then enter the situation as an optimal response by firms to the monopsony environment, and restore the efficient outcome, insofar as such commitments are possible. This is seen in practice in labour markets, with vacancies advertised at certain wages, and in the similar housing market, where vendors list properties at an offer price. We will discuss further how this relates to the contracting of Chapter 7 in the following section.

First, however, we note that the strong result in this section arises from rational expectations. This is a useful point to introduce another concept of expectations (which, although it would seem to have major potential in macroeconomics, has not yet been used extensively)—consistent expectations. These are expectations that meet the criterion that no agent holding these expectations learns that they are wrong; that is, they are ratified by experience, even if they do not meet the full rationality of an entirely solved economic model. To examine this, we must change our assumptions slightly to allow the searcher declining a job at time θ to apply for jobs at time 2θ rather than be forced into continuing unemployment. Note that this does not change the rational expectations solution in that, at time 2θ, he would be unemployed if he declined the job offer, and therefore the reservation wage and the offer from a monopsonistic firm would be zero; then, recursively, his reservation wage at time θ is zero, and the monopsonistic firm would offer that, returning us to our original solution.

Suppose that, for whatever reason, the searcher believes that he would be paid some wage $w_{2\theta}$ if he applies to a firm at time 2θ. This then becomes his reservation wage for time θ, and if this is less than his marginal product, the firm will pay this at time θ, and therefore it is also the wage at time 0. So long as $w_{2\theta}$ is less than $(1 - \theta)p^+MPL[L/f + (1 - \theta)2S^*/f]$, there is a determinate outcome with full employment at time θ: if it just equals that value, the efficient solution is reached; if below, an inefficient solution with too little search. But within this range, there is no further search after time θ, and the expected wage $w_{2\theta}$ is never tested. The resulting equilibria all meet the notion of consistent expectations, but not of rational expectations. This multiplicity of equilibria suggests that maybe consistent expectations will be important in the development of a Keynesian macroeconomic theory, but work to date has been somewhat rudimentary, and we will return to using rational expectations for the rest of the book.

8.3 SEARCH AND CONTRACTING

Search markets where workers must negotiate with individual firms tend to collapse, following our example in section 8.2, due to monopsony power. A worker does not leave his current job and search for a new one because, having lost his bargaining power, he will not be rewarded for this search. The only way for a firm to recruit at time θ is to in some sense actively do so by offering currently employed workers a guaranteed wage when they move, or alternatively to commit itself by some form of advertising to offering applicants that wage. The zero-unemployment outcome in section 8.2 begins to unravel since firms drawing p^+ have an incentive to advertise jobs with a guaranteed wage (from the initial wage of zero, additional workers have a marginal product well in excess of that, and the firm thus would find it in its interest to actively recruit by offering a higher wage), and there is some reason to believe that they will bid up the wage to the marginal product in a competitive process.

Suppose we introduce this process into the section 8.2 model. At time 0, the workers are initially allocated in equal numbers, L/f, to each firm; firms then learn their output price. Firms with p^+ might then advertise wage rates to recruit new workers; firms with p^- would then have to offer the same wage to keep any workers. The bidding process stops when this wage, now uniform throughout the economy, is such that it equals the marginal product at the p^+ firms, when each such firm receives its share of the moving workers, $S/(f/2)$, or $2S/f$. Since these workers work for only $(1 - \theta)$ of the period, we have:

$$w = (1 - \theta)p^+MPL[(L/f) + (1 - \theta)(2S/f)]$$

and, since the p^- firms must meet that wage to retain any workers, they will set that wage but then have an employment level such that:

$$w = p^-MPL[(L/f) - (2S/f)]$$

Together these imply the restoration of the efficient employment level S^* since the marginal value product in the p^+ sector, as adjusted for search time, equals that in the p^- sector. Workers are still exploited in the sense that the workers fortunate enough to be in the p^+ sector from the beginning only receive w, which is less than their marginal value product $p^+MPL[(L/f) + (1 - \theta)(2S/f)]$, but the monopsony exploitation is no longer distorting.

However, if firms can actively recruit in the sense of advertising wages at time θ, why can't they do so at time 0 before knowing their output price? A worker obtained at time 0 has an average marginal product in excess of the w calculated above, so it would pay the firm to advertise wages from the beginning to raise its initial share of the applicants above L/f. Indeed, firms would bid for workers from the beginning until the advertised wage from time 0 equalled the average marginal product, taking account of the workers who would then leave if the firm learned it faced the output price p^-.

It is precisely in this sense that a search market naturally leads to a contracting market—it is in the interest of individual firms to make commitments to recruit applicants both at time 0 and at time θ, to increase their share of applicants beyond the levels the monopsonistic search market would give them. Contracting arises as an optimising response to the monopsony market failure. Further, the contracting would take precisely the form specified in Chapter 7, if that is possible, since firms at time 0 would find it in their interest to make employment as well as wage commitments. If only wage commitments are possible, a different sort of market failure, with excessive unemployment, will arise, as discussed in Chapter 9.

8.4 UNEMPLOYMENT BENEFITS

The introduction of the monopsony search process should now clarify completely the relationship of contracting to search— contracting is a natural institution to arise in a search framework as firms find it in their interest to commit themselves to not using monopsony power, in order to recruit workers. Further, it is in the social interest (as measured by economic efficiency) for governments to encourage contracting institutions. There is however another government policy that can also lead to efficient unemployment, starting from the monopsony outcome—unemployment benefits.

Returning to the environment in section 8.2, the search market collapsed because anyone unemployed at time θ had no bargaining power with the firm to which he applied since, if he did not accept the job, he would remain unemployed and gain a wage of zeroθas such, no one would voluntarily quit their job at time 0 to search for a new one. Suppose the government introduced an unemployment benefit scheme paying an amount c equal to $(1 - \theta)p^+MPL[(L/f) + (1 - \theta)(2S^*/f)]$ where S^* is the efficient unemployment level from Chapter 6, but only paying that to workers who remain unemployed after time θ. The worker's reservation wage for time θ will then equal c, and it is straightforward that we will return to the efficient allocation of labour. The unemployment scheme removes the monopsony distortion. Interestingly, the government never actually pays out any money since the unemployed worker accepts the job-offer.

We make this point here since many neoclassical economists have begun to emphasise the role of unemployment benefits in 'creating' unemployment without a careful consideration of the basis for such benefits. In the current model, with monopsony exploitation leading to too low a rate of mobility unemployment, an unemployment benefit scheme that lessens that exploitation also increases economic efficiency and, in our example, actually raises real GNP. One can thus support an unemployment benefit scheme on strict economic efficiency grounds and not just on social-welfare/income-distribution grounds. It is true that unemployment rises, but to an efficient level. A similar efficiency argument is made in the risk-aversion contracting context, when there is not the possibility of contractual compensation payments (see section 7.2), by Baily (1977) who argues that a government unemployment insurance scheme can lead to greater efficiency.

Of course the neoclassical argument against benefits is somewhat different, based upon the notion that workers with a leisure value will, if benefits become too great, choose leisure over search or employment. If benefits get so large that the combination of benefits and leisure value exceeds the marginal product of labour, this leads to voluntary unemployment (the labour supply curve shifts to the left). If one wants to argue for benefits that lead to unemployment in excess of the efficient rate, one would have to rely upon an income distribution argument. Whether such high benefits currently exist in either the US or the UK is a matter of empirical dispute; certainly no sensible economist would argue that increases in such benefits are the precipitating factor behind observed economic fluctuations.

8.5   CONCLUSIONS

The primary argument in this chapter is that search markets tend to be inefficient due to monopsony power, and that forms of contracting arise as agents in the economy, in their own interest, begin to offer commitments to increase their recruitment ability. Estate agents, when they list property, list sales prices; firms, when they advertise vacancies, advertise a wage rate. If the recruitment is done under uncertainty, firms make commitments about how they will treat the worker under the different possible eventualities. If contracts of the form in Chapter 7 are possible, these contracts arise naturally as recruiting offers. Even if those full contracts are not possible, it is still in the interest of firms to make what commitments they can. In Chapter 9 we will consider why the efficient contracts of Chapter 7 are not plausible, what sort of contracts we might actually expect to see in the economy, and the implications for the labour market. The major result is that excessive unemployment will occur.

9 Contracts and Inefficiency

The results in Chapter 8 suggest that contracts arise naturally in a 'thin' search market as firms seeking additional workers find it necessary to make commitments in order to induce those workers to join the firm. A firm knowing it was facing the high output-price would commit itself to a wage rate when advertising a vacancy. More generally, if a firm had to advertise before knowing its output price, we would return to an environment very similar to that in Chapter 7, and to contracts with both wage and employment commitments. Such contracts, however, following the arguments in Chapter 7, tend to lead either to efficient unemployment or, in the case of risk-aversion without contractual compensation payments, to inefficiently low unemployment. This feature of contracting, that it actually tends towards efficiency in the labour market, has been viewed as unfortunate by those seeking to use contracting as a basis for a Keynesian model of unemployment. A fairly large literature has arisen under the rubric of 'asymmetric information contracting' that seeks to demonstrate the possibility of excessively high unemployment in the contracting environment.

This literature, originated by Calvo and Phelps (1977) and developed by Grossman and Hart (1981), Hart (1983), and articles in the *Quarterly Journal of Economics* symposium in 1983, accepts that contracting is a device that can lead to greater efficiency, but that there is an enforceability problem that limits the use of contracting. We have earlier argued that contracts are '*ex post* suboptimal' in the sense that a firm will always wish to renege on its agreed contract and set the minimum (monopsony) wage necessary to retain its workforce (in general, less than the contracted fixed wage). It is taken not to do so due to the loss of reputation that will follow, and a resulting difficulty in recruiting workers in the future. Possibly, however, enforcement difficulties might explain why actual explicit contracts in the economy do not take on the complicated forms suggested by the literature, including employment commitments and lay-off compensation payments from the firm.

The asymmetric information literature attempts to model the notion of enforceability limitations on optimal contracting. It does this by making the following assumption: contracts are unenforceable if and only if one party lacks the information to ascertain whether the contract is being followed. The models then assume that firms (generally) have information that workers cannot observe, and therefore a contract cannot be written as contingent upon this information (since it would be unenforceable and therefore meaningless). The resulting second-best optimal contracts can then be examined. These are referred to as second-best optimal, since they are the best contracts available (for the firm to set) subject to the information structure. Surprisingly, perhaps, the firm suffers from this asymmetry in information and could do better, moving to the first-best contract, if the information became publicly available. What is particularly interesting about the second-best optimal contracts is that the divergence from the first-best, efficient solution is in some circumstances on the side of excessive unemployment.

To gain some intuition about the process, consider a related situation where a firm goes to a union and asks for a wage reduction because of severe financial problems. If the union knew that the firm would in fact be bankrupt in the absence of wage concessions, it would presumably agree. The problem is that the union will in general be sceptical, knowing that the firm always has an incentive to claim that 'times are hard' in order to lower wages. This is the dilemma at the centre of the asymmetric information approach: how does the firm convince the union (or individual workers in the contracting environment we have constructed) that in fact the situation is truly bad?

In this chapter we will examine the asymmetric information contracting model, and its primary implication—the underemployment result. A heuristic way of viewing the model is that the firm continues to adopt relatively rigid real wages but now is limited in its employment commitments; therefore, the outcome tends more to the sort of underemployment case that we saw in the monopoly trade-union model of Chapter 7. The argument can be taken to its limit with the simpler assumption that the contract can only specify wage rates, with no employment commitments. This leads us to the 'staggered contracts' models that are often viewed as the 'state-of-the-art' in founding Keynesian phenomena upon optimal labour-market behaviour. These models have been criticised for containing suboptimal contracts in that both the workers and the firm could do better if employment commitments were made. The asymmetric information contracting literature can therefore be viewed as supporting these models. More interestingly, as discussed in the following chapter, the underemployment result can be a basis for constructing equilibrium recessions in response to aggregate demand falls.

9.1 THE TRUTH-TELLING PROBLEM AND THE UNDEREMPLOYMENT RESULT

To examine the asymmetric information problem, we return to the simple contracting framework of section 7.1. Firms and workers are, for the time being, assumed to be risk-neutral expected-real-income maximisers, but there is uncertainty about the output price that will occur (p^+ or p^-). Before signing a contract and attaching to the firm, workers have an opportunity cost of G (the value gained by going to another firm), but after signing, should the worker be laid off, he only gains the leisure value $d < G$. The new assumption is that the output price facing the firm in a period is unobservable to attached workers. Thus, by the assumption that an unverifiable contract is unenforceable, contracts cannot be written in the form: 'if p^+ eventuates, then the wage is w^+ and the employment level N^+. Contingent (upon output price) wage rates and employment levels are no longer possible.

If contingent contracts are not feasible, what commitments are possible? The firm could commit itself to a fixed wage rate and employment level, irrespective of the output price. There is however, a more general possibility—the contract could list a number of acceptable combinations of w and N, with the stipulation that the firm can (after learning its output price) choose among these, but only these, combinations. We will define asym metric information contracts in precisely this way—combinations (w_1,N_1), (w_2,N_2), ..., along with the number of attached workers N_0, from which the firm can choose after it but not the workers learns the output price. The fixed wage and employment contract is contained within this formulation as a contract with only one allowable combination of w and N.

Now recall our original fixed-wage contract. This optimal contract followed the rules: attach workers to the point where the average marginal value product equals G, lay off workers when their marginal value product falls below d, and set a fixed wage w such that the average income of workers equals G (with, because of the unemployment, $w > G$). The contract generally contained two wage and employment combinations: (w,N^+) and (w,N^-). We can examine whether, if the output price is unobservable to workers, they will still accept a contract with these wage/employment combinations. They will do so if they are confident that in fact the firm will choose the combination (w,N^+) when p^+ occurs, and (w,N^-) when p^- occurs. Technically, the contract must be 'incentive-compatible with truth-telling'—the firm must choose the appropriate combination even though it knows that the workers cannot otherwise enforce the choice.

The major results are clearest in the case where $d = 0$, and we will adopt this as an introductory example, and indeed use it as the base for our macroeconomic analysis later in this chapter and in Chapter 10. In this case (assuming that marginal value products are always positive) the optimal contract has full employment $N^- = N^+ = N_0$, and therefore can contain a fixed wage $w = G$ (since there is no unemployment, a worker's expected income is then G). In the asymmetric information form, the contact could contain the single choice for the firm (w,N_0), and of course there is no truth-telling problem. To have such a problem, there must be an additional complication. This is usually provided by an assumption that firms are risk-averse. The contract with the firm always having w and N_0 leaves the firm suffering very great variability in its profits, these falling in the bad outcome by the full fall in revenues: $(p^+ - p^-)q(N_0)$. Due to bankruptcy problems or other factors (in particular, if the bad outcome is not firm-specific but represents a general recession, finance theory would justify firm risk-aversion), the firm might be willing to accept a lower expected profit to lessen its variability. In the absence of the truth-telling problem, the assumption of firm risk-aversion would create no difficulties. While the fixed-wage contract is *an* optimal contract in the risk-neutrality case, there are other contracts that are just as good with varying wages but full employment; these would now be preferable. The risk-averse firm could raise w^+ and lower w^-, maintaining their expected value at G so that workers will still accept the contract, and in this way transfer profits from the good outcome to the bad outcome. But here the truth-telling problem arises. If the contract is written with the two possibilities (w^+, N_0), (w^-, N_0), the firm will always choose the low-wage option—there is no contract with varying wages but the same employment level that is incentive-compatible with truth-telling. If the firm wants workers to accept wage cuts in the bad outcome, this can only be sustained if the firm can convince workers that the bad outcome has occurred; this in turn will require, as we shall see below, that employment falls in the bad outcome to an inefficient level $N^- < N_0$. Even when there is no opportunity cost to labour, $d = 0$, unemployment still occurs.

To show this underemployment result, we return to the general case with $d \geq 0$. The risk-aversion of firms is modelled by means of a concave utility function on current profits $V(\Pi)$; when profits are low, an additional pound of profits is 'worth more' to the firm than when profits are high. This is an analogous construction to our risk-averse workers in Chapter 7, and firms will maximise the expected utility of profits. For simplicity, we retain the assumption of risk-neutral workers. We do add the slight complication (to be more in accord with the literature; it will not affect the results) that lay-off compensation payments c^+, c^- are allowed as in section 7.2.

We want to examine the nature of the optimal contract (maximising the expected utility of the firm subject to potential workers accepting the offer) under asymmetric information. The contract must be of the form $(w^+, c^+, N^+), (w^-, c^-, N^-), N_0$, listing the combinations of w, c, N available to the firm *ex post*. The multiple wage and employment combinations allowed are only of interest if the firm actually chooses the appropriate combination when the relevant output-price occurs, and therefore we will restrict our interest to 'incentive-compatible with truth-telling' combinations (Note that a contract with two combinations where the firm only chooses one is equivalent to a contract with just the one combina tion, and a contract where the firm chooses the combination labelled with $+$ whenever p^- occurs, and *vice versa*, is equivalent to a relabelled contract replacing the $+$ with $-$, and *vice versa*.)

For the two combinations to be incentive-compatible with truth-telling, we have two conditions in that, whenever p^+ occurs, it must be more profitable *ex post* for the firm to choose the N^+ combination, and whenever p^- occurs, the N^- combination:

$$p^+q(N^+) - w^+N^+ - c^+(N_0 - N^+) \geqslant$$
$$p^+q(N^-) - w^-N^- - c^-(N_0 - N^-)$$

$$p^-q(N^-) - w^-N^- - c^-(N_0 - N^-) \geqslant$$
$$p^-q(N^+) - w^+N^+ - c^+(N_0 - N^+)$$

Denote the total labour costs (both wages and compensation payments) in each eventuality as C^+ and C^-, and observe that we can rewrite the truth-telling conditions as:

$$p^+[q(N^+) - q(N^-)] \geqslant C^+ - C^- \geqslant p^-[q(N^+) - q(N^-)]$$

requiring that the difference in total labour costs in the combinations be limited. If labour costs C^+ were higher than this, relative to C^-, the firm would always choose the N^- combination; if lower, the N^+ combination. In fact, given our assumptions, it is always the first inequality that is relevant in the truth-telling conditions, and not the second. Consider any employment levels $N^+ > N^-$. These define a range for $C^+ - C^-$ that is consistent with the truth-telling conditions. But observe that it must be the case, from the first inequality, that:

$$p^+q(N^+) - C^+ \geqslant p^+q(N^-) - C^- > p^-q(N^-) - C^-$$

and therefore profits are higher in the p^+ outcome. But from the firm's concave utility on period profits $V(\Pi)$, it prefers to equalise profits over the outcomes; for any N^+, N^- this requires raising C^+ relative to C^- to the extent possible, where this is limited by the first inequality in the truth-telling condition. The second inequality becomes irrelevant since it is automatically met when the first condition is met with equality.

As in Chapter 7, we approach the problem by considering the cost-minimising wage-setting, conditional upon arbitrary values of N^+, N^-, N_0, and then examine the profit-maximising choice of the employment values. The firm transfers labour costs to C^+ to the extent possible by the condition:

$$C^+ - C^- = p^+[q(N^+) - q(N^-)]$$

Further, the contract offer must meet the feasibility condition that workers are wiling to sign the contract. Because of the truth-telling condition, they know that they will receive a total compensation C^+ when p^+ occurs, and C^- when p^- occurs. (Recall that we suppose that each event has equal probability, 1/2.) The workers are concerned that their expected income, including the opportunity cost from lay-off d, exceeds the opportunity cost to signing the contract G:

$$[w^+N^+ + w^-N^- + (c^+ + d)(N_0 - N^+)$$
$$+ (c^- + d)(N_0 - N^-)]/2 \geq GN_0$$

This can be rewritten with the C values as:

$$[C^+ + C^- + d(N_0 - N^+) + d(N_0 - N^-)]/2 \geq GN_0$$

This will be met with equality since the firm wants to minimise total labour costs, and using the condition above on $C^+ - C^-$ we can solve explicitly for:

$$C^+ = GN_0 + 1/2\{-d(N_0 - N^+) - d(N_0 - N^-)$$
$$+ p^+[q(N^+) - q(N^-)]\}$$
$$C^- = GN_0 + 1/2\{-d(N_0 - N^+) - d(N_0 - N^-)$$
$$-p^+[q(N^+) - q(N^-)]\}$$

Note that both the firm and workers care only about the total magnitude of the labour compensation bills C^+, C^-, and not how this is divided up between wages and lay-off compensation. One possibility is to set $w^i = c^i + d$ for $i = {}^+, {}^-$ so that workers are indifferent to lay-off; alternatively, the contract might be set with $w^i > c^i + d$ with workers subject to involuntary lay-offs—both contracts are equally good for the problem with risk-neutral workers. A model with risk-averse workers as well as firms would lead to the result in section 7.2, with lay-off compensation set to bring indifference between lay-offs and continuing to work.

We now turn to the choice of the optimal contract. The firm will want to choose the contract values of the N's to maximise the expected utility of profits:

$$[V(\Pi^+) + V(\Pi^-)]/2,$$

or:

$$\{V[p^+q(N^+) - C^+] + V[p^-q(N^-) - C^-]\}/2$$

recalling that N_0 must exceed the actual employment levels N^+, N^-. It is immediate that N_0 will be chosen to equal the chosen value of N^+, since a higher N_0 raises both C^+ and C^- without any increase in revenues. Our interest, however, is in examining the rule for N^-; in particular, we will show that N^- does not meet the earlier 'efficient' rule that lay-offs occur to the point where $p^- MPL(N^-) = d$, but rather N^- is somewhat less than this, giving us the excessive unemployment result. To show this, we take an arbitrary N^+ and a smaller N^-, and argue that the N^- could only be optimal if in fact the marginal value product of the N^- is greater than d. (We will ignore the possibility of a no unemployment optimal contract $N_0 = N^+ = N^-$.)

For a given N^- to be optimal, it must not be possible to raise the firm's expected utility of profits by raising or lowering N^-. The impact of a rise in N^- is shown in Table 9.1, where the rise in N^- raises revenue in the p^- outcome only, but changes labour costs C^+ and C^-; C^+ must fall relative to C^- to meet the truth-telling condition since the increase in N^- would otherwise make a false choice (of the N^- combination when p^+ has occurred) more profitable. Multiplying each of the net changes in profits by the marginal utility to the firm of those changes, we find the net expected utility effect of the rise in N^-.

$$[MU^+/2]\{1/2[p^+MPL(N^-) - d]\}$$
$$+ [MU^-/2]\{p^-MPL(N^-) - 1/2[d + p^+MPL(N^-)]\}$$

Table 9.1: Calculations for the asymmetric information contracting model

	p^+ outcome	p^- outcome
revenue change	0	$p^-MPL(N^-)$
labour cost change	$1/2[d - p^+MPL(N^-)]$	$1/2[d + p^+MPL(N^-)]$
net change	$- 1/2[d - p^+MPL(N^-)]$	$p^-MPL(N^-) -$ $1/2[d + p^+MPL(N^-)]$

This must equal zero at the optimal choice since otherwise it would pay to raise (or lower) N^-. Rewriting:

$$[MU^-/2][p^- MPL(N^-) - d] +$$
$$[(MU^+ - MU^-)/2] \{1/2[p^+ MPL(N^-) - d]\} = 0$$

Recall that profits must be higher in the p^+ outcome than the p^-, and therefore given the shape of the firm's utility function, $MU^+ < MU^-$. But then, if the first term equals zero, $p^+ MPL(N^-) - d$ will exceed zero, and the second term will be negative, so this is not possible as an optimum. For an optimum, the first term must be positive, so that the negative second term will be offset. The marginal value product of labour in the p^- outcome must exceed d, implying underemployment.

The intuition of this result is that, by the efficient rule, a rise in N^- would just add to revenues what it adds to labour costs (the foregone leisure d). The problem is that it makes it more desirable to choose this combination if p^+ occurs, unless if labour costs fall in the N^+ combination and rise in the N^- combination in the contract. But this has precisely the wrong effect in terms of equalising profits, since it raises profits in the p^+ outcome and lowers them in the p^-. The optimal N^- takes account of this, and is somewhat less than the efficient amount.

We should at this point note that while we refer to the condition $p^- MPL(N^-) = d$ as the benchmark efficiency rule, the asymmetric information literature is very careful to avoid the inefficiency designation and instead refers to 'underemployment by Walrasian standards' and a 'second-best efficient outcome'. The reason has to do with varying assumptions about information structure in the models. To understand this, return to the Chapter 6 model, where there was an underlying information problem in that workers are initially allocated to sectors before the output price in each sector is known. As long as this information is not known to anyone in the economy before the initial allocation, there is an unavoidable cost in optimally reallocating labour relative to what could be achieved if the initial allocation could have occurred with the knowledge. We therefore referred to an efficient unemployment rate as the best reallocation once the information was learned. That 'second-best, subject to the information structure, efficient outcome' might not be achieved, as in Chapter 6, due to noise created by a random monetary policy and the Lucas information problem. This additional information problem, however, is in some sense avoidable since it was government policy that was creating the problem. In Chapter 8 an additional 'inefficiency' was added by monopsony power; again, however, this could be avoided by government policies in the allocation of labour (the government, having the same information as other parties in the economy, could impose a better allocation by dictation). Thus the information structure imposed a certain desirable level of unemployment, but market imperfections might cause a further, inefficient departure from this level. The asymmetric information problem adds another underlying information problem (and firm risk-aversion), and it is certainly the case that a better result would occur if this was absent. But consider a government which is only as well informed as workers in the model. Could it impose a better outcome than the asymmetric information, underemployment result, where 'better' is defined in the usual economic sense of Pareto efficiency, making everyone better off? If not, then the new unemployment is unfortunate, but still 'second-best efficient'.

This goes to the very important issue of how Keynesian the contracting models are. The asymmetric information version results in high unemployment relative to what might be characterised as Walrasian efficiency with marginal value products equal to opportunity costs, and in that sense government action might in principle be desirable, but in the absence of an *effective* policy, the government remains in a non-activist position. That sort of policy has not yet been shown in our discussion. To this point, then, all we have shown is that asymmetric information can lead to high average (over states) unemployment relative to the contracts of Chapter 7, this unemployment occurring in firms facing a low output-price. We have not shown, as in the Lucas model, that during some time periods the aggregate (over firms) unemployment rate will be high, and during others low, since to this point we are still in the Chapter 7 framework where a low output-price must be interpreted as a relative price or real productivity decline. Nor have we shown any role for macroeconomic fiscal or monetary aggregative policies. We will consider those issues after first considering how the model in this section might be simplified for more convenient analysis.

For embedding our contracting model into an aggregate demand framework, in Chapter 10, we will eventually simplify by returning to the initial set of assumptions in this section—we will suppose that $d = 0$, so full employment is the efficient level in any outcome (provided that the marginal product of labour remains positive); the inefficiencies of the second-best contract are then reflected in any resulting unemployment. Rather than adopting a general concave utility function over profits, however, it will be easier to use a simpler formulation where there is a minimum profit level, denoted by ϕ, that the firm must achieve in any outcome. The magnitude of ϕ essentially represents the degree of risk-aversion of the firm, and can be viewed as the cash-flow necessary to avoid bankruptcy. Further it will be useful to reintroduce the idea of probabilities over the outcomes, π^- and π^+, differing from 1/2. While we are developing this model mainly for later use, it may clarify the results of the more general risk-aversion model presented earlier in this section.

As we have already observed, the contract with the efficient employment rule $N^- = N^+ = N_0$ and a fixed wage $w = G$ is consistent with asymmetric information (since the contract is non-contingent, there is no truth-telling problem) but leads to a wide variance in the profits of the firm over the two outcomes. Denoting the profit levels as Π^+ and Π^-, even for a generally highly profitable firm Π^- might be very low or negative since revenues (at full employment) would fall in proportion to the fall in output prices, but labour costs would remain unchanged. For this reason the firm might turn to a contract with w^- and N^- differing from the full-employment levels, and in that way meet the minimum profit level ϕ requirement. As before, it does this by lowering N^- from N_0, lowering wage costs in the bad outcome and raising them in the good outcome.

With $d = 0$, but with general probabilities over outcomes $\pi^+ + \pi^- = 1$, the algebra now solves for labour costs in each outcome as:

$$C^+ = GN_0 + \pi^- p^+[q(N^+) - q(N^-)]$$
$$C^- = GN_0 - \pi^+ p^+[q(N^+) - q(N^-)]$$

and observe that, as before, expected wage bills equal GN_0 as is required for workers to be willing to sign the contract. The new minimum profit constraint can be written:

$$p^- q(N^-) - C^- \geqslant \phi$$

and we will in the following assume that this is binding (at the optimal full employment contract, the firm would not make this minimal level of profits).

Now consider how the optimal contract is chosen. We know, for the usual reasons, that the firm will never attach more workers N_0 than are ever employed, so N^+ will equal N_0. For the moment, suppose that $N_0 = N^+$ has already been chosen, and consider the choice of N^- as shown in Figure 9.1. As N^- is lowered from the full employment level, C^- can fall, lowering w^- as shown by the $w^-(N^-)$ curve in the figure, where this curve shows the wage rates that maintain the truth-telling condition as derived in the algebra above. The firm moves along this curve until w^- has fallen

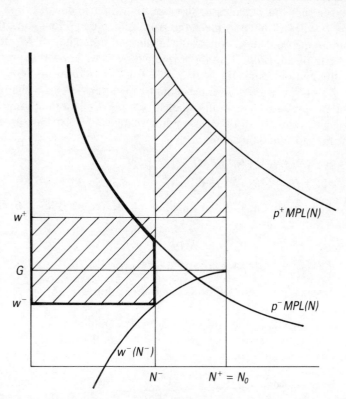

Figure 9.1: *The asymmetric information optimal contract where truth-telling occurs since the two marked areas are equal and the minimum profit condition is met since the bold-bordered area $\Pi^- = \phi$*

sufficiently to restore profitability to the level ϕ. Observe in Figure 9.1 that the firm would not do better to lie, in the $+$ outcome, since the additional profits gained are zero, the savings in wages just balanced by the loss in revenues.

While the choice of N^-, for given N_0, is therefore simpler than in the general risk-aversion case (being determined entirely by the binding profit constraint), the choice of $N^+ = N_0$ (as before, there is no point in raising N_0 unless if those workers will in some outcome actually be employed) is also straightforward and takes on the form we have seen in the other contracting models: $\pi^+ p^+ MPL(N^+) = G$. (Recall that in the current case $d = 0$, so this is equivalent to the rule in Ch. 7 for the efficient contracting.) To see that this is the case, suppose that the firm decides to raise N_0. It will still have to meet the truth-telling conditions, and the minimum profit level constraint in the bad outcome, so N^- may have to be adjusted. With the formula for C^-, we know that profits in the bad outcome, $\Pi^- = p^- q(N^-) - C^- = p^- q(N^-) - GN_0 + \pi^+ p^+ [q(N^+) - q(N^-)]$, must remain at ϕ after $N^+ = N_0$ changes and N^- perhaps changes in response, writing dN^+ for the change in $N^+ = N_0$ and dN^- for the responding change in N^-, we have profits in the bad outcome changing as:

$$[p^- MPL(N^-) + \pi^+ p^+ MPL(N^-)] \, dN^-$$
$$+ \, [\pi^+ p^+ MPL(N^+) - G] \, dN^+$$

To keep profits in the bad outcome at the required level ϕ, this must sum to zero, or:

$$\frac{dN^-}{dN^+} = \frac{[G - \pi^+ MPL(N^+)]}{[p^- MPL(N^-) + \pi^+ p^+ MPL(N^-)]}$$

represents the ratio of how much N^- adjusts as $N^+ = N_0$ increases.

Since profits in the bad outcome will remain at ϕ, the point in increasing N_0 is to raise profits in the good outcome, thereby raising expected profits. Profits in the good outcome are written:

$$\Pi^+ = p^+ q(N^+) - C^+ = p^+ q(N^+) - GN_0$$
$$- \, \pi^- p^+ [q(N^+) - q(N^-)]$$

Now as $N^+ = N_0$ and N^- change, Π^+ changes as:

$$[(1 - \pi^-) p^+ MPL(N^+) - G] \, dN^+ + \pi^- p^+ MPL(N^-) \, dN^-$$

or, since the change in N^- is in response to the change in N^+, we write the change in profits to a change in $N^+ = N_0$ as:

$$[(1 - \pi^-)p^+ MPL(N^+) - G]$$

$$+ \frac{\pi^- p^+ MPL(N^-) [G - \pi^+ p^+ MPL(N^+)]}{[p^- MPL(N^-) + \pi^+ p^+ MPL(N^-)]}$$

Recalling that $(1 - \pi^-) = \pi^+$, observe that all this equals zero (and therefore profits in the good outcome are no longer increased) once $N^+ = N_0$ is such that $\pi^+ p^+ MPL(N^+) = G$. Interestingly, what happens is that, at that point, Π^- remains unchanged if N^- is not adjusted in response to a further increase in N_0; with N^- unchanging, we are left with the simple term for profit-changing in the good outcome $\pi^+ p^+ MPL(N^+) - G$.

We have thus fully characterised the optimal, second-best contract in this asymmetric-information, minimum-profit-constraint environment. The firm signs workers to the contract to the point where $\pi^+ p^+ MPL(N^+) = G$, and then lays off workers (and lowers real wages) in the bad outcome to the extent necessary to meet the minimum profit level ϕ, as however constrained by the $w^-(N^-)$ truth-telling condition. This simpler model of asymmetric information contracting will be used in Chapter 10 as the basis for our model of equlibrium recessions, and we present an algebraic derivation at the end of this section. In the next section, however, we will temporarily adopt an even more restricted approach where the firm cannot make any employment commitments as the basis for an examination of the staggered-contracts approach to deriving macroeconomic implications.

First, we note one final point about the asymmetric information contracting model. In an aggregate equilibrium with a number of firms, we have to specify not just the contracts they initially offer but something about the mobility possibilities within the economy. For this we could either adopt the assumption from Chapter 6 that workers can leave one sector and obtain a job in another, or we could adopt the assumption from parts of Chapter 7 that they imply remain unemployed, enjoying leisure (possibly, as we shall assume, at zero value). The asymetric information approach interestingly tends to justify the latter assumption. Consider an economy where there are a number of firms, each of which has entered into the sort of contract described in this section. Those contracts are incentive-compatible with truth-telling only because the firm, in order to lower the wage in the bad outcome, must also choose a low employment level to convince workers that the outcome is indeed bad. But that constraint becomes meaningless if the firm could go to the outside labour market and hire additional workers. With this rationale in mind, we will assume that in an economy with firms operating under asymmetric information contracts, there is essentially no mobility and laid-off workers remain unemployed even if there is no leisure value.

Algebraic Derivation of the Profit-Constraint Asymmetric Information Contract

The problem facing the firm is to maximise expected profits:

$$\pi^+[R^+(N^+)-C^+] + \pi^-[R^-(N^-) - C^-]$$

where we write $R^i(N) = p^i q(N)$ for ease of notation. This maximisation is subject to the constraints on number of signees:

(i) $N_0 \geqslant N^+$ $[\propto]$
(ii) $N_0 \geqslant N^-$ $[\beta]$

the truth-telling conditions:

(iii) $R^+(N^+)-C^+ \geqslant R^+(N^-)-C^-$ $[\gamma]$
(iv) $R^-(N^-)-C^- \geqslant R^-(N^+)-C^+$ $[\lambda]$

the feasibility condition for workers to sign contracts:

(v) $\pi^+C^+ + \pi^-C^- \geqslant GN_0$ $[\mu]$

and finally the minimum profit constraint:

(vi) $R^-(N^-)-C^- \geqslant \phi$ $[\eta]$

where we have written the symbol for the relevant Lagrangian multiplier by each constraint and write the usual Lagrangian function L.

In the case of interest where (i), (iii), (v), and (vi) are binding, taking the appropriate derivatives provides no additional information except for the determination of N_0 (N^+ will of course equal N_0 and N^- is then determined entirely by the constraints as in the text), and to examine this we need the derivatives with respect to N_0, C^+ and N^+.

(a) $\partial L/\partial N_0 = \propto + \beta - \mu G = 0$

(b) $\partial L/\partial N^+ = \pi^+R^{+\prime}(N^+) - \alpha + \gamma R^{+\prime}(N^+) - \lambda R^{-\prime}(N^+) = 0$

(c) $\partial L/\partial C^+ = -\pi^+ - \gamma + \lambda + \pi^+\mu = 0$

When (ii) and (iv) are non-binding, β and λ are zero. Substituting from (c) into (b): $\pi^+\mu R^{+\prime}(N^+) = \alpha$, and therefore (a) becomes $\pi^+R^{+\prime}(N^+) = G$, as claimed in the text.

9.2 STAGGERED CONTRACTS

The asymmetric information approach developed in the previous section derives from the inability of workers to observe the output price of the firm. As a result, even when the leisure value d is zero and therefore 'efficiency' (as in the section 7.1 contracts) requires full employment, there will be lay-offs in the low-output-price outcome. There are, as we have already observed, two ways of interpreting the different 'output price' outcomes: they may be due to relative price shifts, following the model in Chapter 6, or they may be due to real productivity changes. In this section we will assume that it is only the latter that causes changes in the marginal value product curve facing a firm. Thus a fall in real productivity, under asymmetric information contracting, leads to an inefficient fall in output. That output falls with such a productivity shock is not particularly interesting from a macroeconomic perspective since a similar result holds in the simple neoclassical labour market of Chapter 2. There a real productivity fall leads to lower employment and output as real competitive wages decline and workers with an opportunity cost below the market wage withdraw from the market. The only difference here is that there is in effect an overreaction creating inefficient unemployment. If this were the total story, we still would have unemployment only when real productivity fell and not due to monetary or aggregate demand effects. An independent literature, the 'staggered contracts' literature originated by Gray (1976) and Fischer (1977), has arisen that can be viewed as providing an interesting extension of the approach to showing how monetary shocks may have a similar effect. Examination of this approach is important since it has been viewed by many Keynesians as providing a suitable model upon which to base claims for an activist government policy.

It will first be helpful to recall why monetary phenomena had no particular place in the contracting model. This result arose since the contracting was in real terms; since both the firm and the workers were only concerned with real values, nominal values and any role of monetary policy in affecting nominal values were irrelevant. The staggered-contracts approach gets around this by introducing an information role for nominal indexation of contracts. As we have noted, the asymmetric information contract arose because workers could not observe the firm's pertinent marginal value product curve—they did not know whether the firm faced a favourable or unfavourable environment. But now suppose that by observing the aggregate price level in the economy, the worker can deduce information about the likelihood of the different outcomes. For example (for reasons that we will see shortly), a high aggregate nominal price level may indicate that a fall in productivity has probably occurred. But then this information might possibly be used in constructing a better contract than the best one where no such information, imperfect as it may be, is available. In fact, unless the 'signal' contains full information so that a proper contingent contract of the form in Chapter 7 is possible, it is not immediate how this information might be usefully applied in constructing a better contract. For this reason we will not attempt to show the argument generally for the environment discussed in section 9.1, but will instead follow the staggered-contracts literature which considers particularly limited contracting possibilities.

A basic assumption in this literature is that firms and workers contract only over wages and not employment levels; as in our discussion of the monopoly union model (see Ch. 7), this leads immediately to an underemployment result. Here, however, the contract will include a nominal wage rate and a rule for indexation with respect to the price level; this allows for a rigid real wage but does not require it should a different, partial indexation be better. Since there are no employment commitments by the firm, when the latter learns the real wage (using the indexation formula on the observed aggregate price level), it uses the marginal-productivity/real-wage comparison to then determine employment. We will take the contract form as given by assumption without attempting to justify it on the basis of firm risk-aversion and asymmetric information, as in the previous section; that analysis, however, suggests that limitations on contracts, if not the very strong limitation here assumed, are likely.

For our analysis we will largely follow the argument presented by Gray (1976). In this model there is an environment with aggregate monetary and real productivity shocks, but no sector-specific shocks. The f firms in the economy are taken to be fully identical (each can be viewed as facing a relative price of unity). Each has a production function: $Q(N)\epsilon$, where $Q(N)$ takes on the usual concave form and ϵ, the same for each firm, is a random 'shock' to productivity ($\epsilon > 0$) with an expected value of 1—this is the real productivity shock to the economy in the given period. We assume that the labour supply is fixed at L, with workers having no disutility of work. The monetary side of the economy is represented by the quantity equation for the demand for money, $M^d = kPQ$, and a money supply determined by the Central Bank, but subject to a random error. We assume that the Bank aims for a known money supply M, but the actual money supply turns out to be $M^s = Mv$, where $v > 0$ has a mean of 1. Both firms and workers are assumed to be risk-neutral.

For given values of ϵ and v, we can return to the neoclassical labour market of Chapter 2 to solve for the 'competitive' equilibrium. Since the labour supply is fixed at L, this is the equilibrium employment with aggregate production $fQ(L/f)\epsilon$. The real wage will equal the marginal product of labour $MPL(L/f)\epsilon$, where we continue to write $MPL(N)$ derived from $Q(N)$ alone and multiply by the value of the productivity shock to find actual marginal productivity. For the money market to clear, money supply must equal demand: $Mv = kPQ$—or substituting in the expression for Q and solving for P, $P = (1/k)Mv/fQ(L/f)\epsilon$. The nominal wage follows: $W = (1/k)MvMPL(L/f)/Q(L/f)$. Note that the competitive equilibrium nominal wage depends upon the monetary shock v but not the real shock ϵ; this will be the basis for the results below and arises since an increase in productivity would lower P and therefore, for a given W, raise $w = W/P$ by the appropriate factor ϵ. In the competitive model, output fluctuates with the real shock ϵ but not the monetary shock v (money is neutral). There is always full employment at L as is efficient since workers have a zero disutility of work but always have a positive productivity (and there is no sectoral basis for unemployment).

To provide a basis for contracting we follow the arguments in this part of the book that workers lose their mobility once they have been allocated to a given firm and therefore would become subject to monopsony power (the firm could lower the wage to zero) in the absence of a binding contract; firms therefore, in the initial recruitment process, commit themselves to a contract. We now consider what happens when the firm and workers agree a contract specifying the nominal wage as a function of the observed aggregate price level $W(P)$ or, equivalently, a real wage function $w(P)$. They will do this with knowledge about the possible values that ϵ and v might take on, but without knowing which value they are actually going to have. There are no employment commitments, so the firm, which is taken to be able to observe ϵ and v, then chooses employment N, subject to the contracted $W(P)$, to maximise its profits, following the usual rule that N is such that the marginal product of labour $MPL(N)\epsilon$ equals the real wage. The contract will imply a certain expected income to workers, and we will assume that firms bid for workers by their contract offers, with a market value G that in equilibrium leads each firm to sign $N_0 = L/f$ workers to contracts. Note the important sense in which this model is similar to the asymmetric information model of the previous section—we are not allowing contingent contracts to be written in the form that the real or nominal wage is contingent upon observed values of ϵ and v. These are assumed to be unobservable by workers, who are however allowed to observe the aggregate nominal price level P.

We will analyse the outcomes with this sort of contract by considering the form of the optimal contract if only one type of shock existed, and show that for each type of shock (in isolation) there is a contract that achieves efficiency, with full employment; we then note that the two sorts of contracts are inconsistent. Note that if a full employment contract were available, it would be in the firm's interest to offer this, for the same reasons that the firm offers a contract with efficient employment in Chapter 7—for a given G, the contract that maximises the firm's expected profits subject to the feasibility conditions is the Chapter 7 contract. If the Chapter 7 contract cannot be sustained given the limited form of allowable contracts, the firm will have to offer a second-best contract.

Begin with the case of no real shocks (ϵ always equals 1) but with monetary shocks. The marginal product of labour curve at a firm is then fixed as $MPL(N)$. If the contract form of Chapter 7 was allowed, each firm could set a fixed real wage $w = G$, have full employment, and an N_0 such that $MPL(N_0) = w = G$. The labour market would then clear with a G such that each firm chooses $N_0 = L/f$. But this identical contract remains feasible in the current environment. When the firm sets a rigid real wage (full indexation in our nominal wage formula) at $w = G = MPL(L/f)$, and then performs the marginal-product/real-wage comparison to determine how many of the N_0 will actually be employed, it has no incentive to engage in lay-offs. To provide full indexation so that the real wage is unchanged with respect to monetary shocks that change P according to $P = (1/k)Mv/Q(L/f)$, W must rise in proportion to P: $W = PMPL(L/f)$. The monetary shock raises nominal P and W in proportion to the shock, with full employment maintained and output unchanging.

Now consider real shocks in isolation. Here the marginal product of labour curve is shifting about with ϵ. With the marginal-product/real-wage comparison determining lay-offs, full employment cannot be maintained by a rigid real wage as with the monetary shocks. The real wage w, for each value of ϵ, must be less than or equal to $MPL(N_0)\epsilon$ for full employment. This can be achieved if the nominal wage can be indexed such that the real wage, for each ϵ, takes on the requisite value $MPL(N_0)\epsilon$. The firm will then choose N_0 such that the expected marginal product, $MPL(N_0)$ (recalling that the expected value of ϵ is one) equals G. For the labour market to clear with each firm signing L/f workers to the contract, we have a G such that $MPL(L/f) = G$. We must now show that the real wage w can be indexed in an appropriate manner. For the real wage to be $MPL(L/f)\epsilon$ for each ϵ, the nominal wage must take on the form: $W = PMPL(L/f)\epsilon = (1/k)MvMPL(L/f)\epsilon/Q(L/f)\epsilon$, substituting for P from the quantity equation. But, recalling the absence of monetary shocks so that $v = 1$, we have $W = [(1/k)M]MPL(L/f)/Q(L/f)$; the nominal wage is fixed. The absence of indexation works in the following way: if productivity falls by a certain factor, full employment output would fall by that factor and by the quantity equation for money, the price level would rise by that factor; this lowers the real wage by that factor and provides the firm with an incentive to maintain full employment.

Thus for either type of shock in isolation, the full employment contract can be sustained, even when firms cannot make employment commitments or contingent contracts based upon the actual values of the shocks (as opposed to the observable P). This is done by, in the case of monetary shocks, fully indexing the nominal wage and maintaining the value of the real wage; since productivity is unchanging, the firm will choose full employment by the real-wage/marginal-productivity comparison. In the case of real aggregate shocks, zero indexation (a constant nominal wage) causes, with the higher price level due to a fall in productivity, a fall in the real wage in accord with lowered productivity—again full employment is chosen by the firm. In the terminology of the last section, the indexation rules lead to 'incentive-compatible' full employment contracts.

But now suppose that both types of shocks occur. The contract cannot neutralise both, since real shocks are avoided (in terms of employment changes) by zero indexation, and monetary shocks by full indexation. The optimal contract would have to balance the two types of shocks by a partial indexation (between 0 and 1), which will lead to falls in employment below L for some shock values. If ϵ is low, the fall in productivity causes a rise in prices, but, because of the partial indexation, the fall in real wages is insufficient to maintain full employment; if v is low, the fall in aggregate demand causes a fall in prices, but a smaller fall in wages, raising the real wage and causing a fall in employment. The actual degree of indexation depends upon the relative monetary uncertainty and real uncertainty, but the fundamental implication is clear—the nature of the partial indexation means that the firm will respond to both real and monetary shocks by changes in employment. Money is no longer neutral. This is in many ways a reiteration of the point in Chapter 5 about the sustainability of the Phillips curve if there is only partial indexation. Here, however, the partial indexation is shown to be desirable in the sense that it balances the losses to the firm from real and monetary shocks.

It is important to understand precisely the phenomenon that is operating here. Workers are unable to observe the actual shock values of ϵ and v, so a contract cannot be written contingent upon these. They can observe P, and from this can infer something about the shock values, and therefore the ability to write a contract with a wage indexed on P is useful. Given that the firm will use the marginal-productivity/real-wage comparison to determine employment, the useful information is about changes in productivity that would lead to a lowered real wage to induce the firm to maintain employment. In the absence of monetary shocks, P conveys complete information about productivity since P rises when (and only when) productivity falls. With monetary shocks, the rise in P may be due to a productivity shock or it may be due to an increase in the nominal money supply. This then leads to the partial indexation rule.

This argument should appear very reminiscent of the Lucas information problem in Chapter 6, and it is indeed very similar. There workers could not distinguish between sectoral real productivity effects and general inflation—an increase (or decrease) in their wage could be due to either, and this confusion could lead them to undesirably remain in or leave their current sector to move to the other sector where they anticipate higher wages. Here the confusion is between aggregate productivity shocks and monetary shocks, but this is not a fundamental difference. Indeed, the policy conclusions of this model are largely the same. The government could remove the excessive unemployment by limiting money supply uncertainty; firms would then adopt the zero-indexation contract that maintains full employment under real shocks. Any anticipated changes in monetary policy similarly have no effect—they raise the expected money supply and therefore the base nominal wage, but do not change the degree of indexation and unemployment for a given uncertainty.

The Keynesian interest in the approach derives from a different implication: that the government can, after observing the real shock ϵ, adopt a mitigating monetary policy to stabilise the economy. There is a 'discretionary' government policy $M(\epsilon)$ that does better than the 'fixed rule' policy of a constant target M. To see why the discretionary monetary policy where M varies with ϵ can be effective and desirable, consider what happens when a low ϵ occurs in the partially indexed contract. If the nominal wage remained the same, employment would stay at L since P rises by the factor ϵ and therefore the real wage falls by that factor. But partial indexation entails that the nominal wage rises to some extent with P and the real wage falls by less than ϵ, an insufficient fall to induce the firm to maintain employment. Suppose, however, that the government, upon observing the low ϵ, raised the money supply target. Then P would rise further (on average since the imperfect control expressed in v is assumed to continue) and

W, because of the partial indexation, would follow to a lesser degree leaving a net further decrease in the real wage *w*, tending towards a restoration of full employument. This argument relies upon the government using an 'information advantage' to stabilise the economy—it can observe and act upon ϵ, yet private agents, for whatever reason, cannot draft contracts contingent upon ϵ. Yet even this argument can be made in the context of the Lucas model. Recall that we observed in Chapter 6 that a rise in the price level might be due to a shift in the *LM* curve due to monetary effects or a shift in the *IS* curve due to 'aggregate demand' effects, and that insofar as the government had an information advantage in observing *IS* shifts, it could adopt a stabilising monetary policy to lower monetary uncertainty and inefficient levels of unemployment. The current argument is just a variant of that.

The staggered-contracts model does have some advantages over the Lucas model in the area of plausibility. Here the economy reacts incorrectly to shocks not because of confusion *per se* but because firms have contracted to behave in a certain way. The staggered-contracts approach allows workers to observe *P* (which they were implausibly not allowed to observe in the Lucas model); on the other hand, it doesn't allow them to observe real shocks or the money supply figures. Further, because of the nature of the contracting, unemployment occurs through the mechanism of lay-offs rather than voluntary quits.

Despite this improvement in the area of plausibility, there are severe reservations about adopting this model as the basis for the Keynesian approach. The first problem is the reliance upon aggregate productivity shocks. These shocks provide the basis for the current mechanism; without them there would be no real response to monetary shocks and no unemployment. In the context of the 1970s, with the two major oil price shocks, this might seem the basis for a macroeconomic theory, but more generally one is loath to adopt this as the fundamental cause of economic fluctuations. The second problem is the mechanism by which the model operates. A restrictive monetary shock is taken to operate by a fall in the nominal price level (relative to expectations) and from that to a rise in the real wage; firms respond to this by lowering employment. This is not the Keynesian mechanism. In that, the restrictive monetary policy leads to a fall in aggregate demand and in individual firm's demand; for whatever reason, they respond to this not by lowering prices and wages, in nominal terms, but rather by cutting employment and output. This whole process, the role of aggregate demand and firm's optimal responses to it, is missing. In a sense, the staggered-contracts model is not fundamental nor general enough. We need a model with a role for aggregate demand as well as productivity effects, and one that works through optimising decisions by a firm with price-setting and wage-setting power.

9.3 CONCLUSIONS

Over this part of the book we have examined labour markets, and possible imperfections in those markets, in some depth. The search model in Chapter 6 gave us a well-defined natural, efficient rate of unemployment in response to shifting productivities between sectors in the economy; that efficient rate was sustained by competitive sectoral labour markets, where wage rates provided appropriate signals for workers to voluntarily quit their jobs to seek employment in another sector where their productivity would be higher. That process, however, required that the searcher receive the full benefits to his search, gaining a wage in his new employment equal to his marginal product. While that condition holds in competitive markets, search markets (as we saw in Ch. 8) are more likely to contain monopsonistic market failures; as a result, workers would have an insufficient incentive to search and *GNP* would fall due to inadequate mobility. That might be mitigated by a government unemployment benefits scheme that would, admittedly, raise unemployment, but would raise it to the efficient level.

In Chapter 7 we presented an alternative model of the organisation of labour markets: the contracting model. In that model, firms would commit themselves to maintaining a rigid wage, and would then adjust their workforce by involuntary lay-offs. Relative to efficient competitive labour markets, the contracting markets replicate the same solution, changing only the mechanism by which labour is efficiently transferred across sectors. In that sense, contracting shows that explaining involuntary unemployment is not the same thing as explaining Keynesian excessive unemployment. That is part of the answer about the relation between contracting and search models—both approaches, in one variant, lead to the same outcome, the same allocation of labour. The rest of the answer comes about from our analysis in Chapter 8—search is likely, in actual markets, to be subject to monopsonistic market failure, and contracting naturally and voluntarily (on the part of firms and workers) arises in response. We observe implicit and explicit contracting behaviour in labour markets because it is in the interests of the participants in the markets. (With respect to implicit contracting, we mean that firms do not operate in their short-term interest with respect to employment practices but maintain their reputation in this sphere by protecting wage rates and employment in response to adverse economic conditions.) Firms compete to recruit workers, and do so by their commitments about future treatment. Contracting thus not only meets the neoclassical view that voluntary arrangements have a sort of *prima facie* claim to desirability, but should be actively encouraged by governments seeking to achieve efficient, mobility-preserving labour markets. Further, as we observed in Chapter 7, trade unions can be seen as a part of this process with the same possibility of efficient contracting.

The limitation on this efficiency arises as perfect, complete contracts might not be sustainable. The asymmetric information contracting arguments in this chapter are an example of why this might be the case—if workers cannot observe whether a contract (or implicit commitments) is in fact being followed, the contract is not pertinent. This led to the notion of incentive-compatible with truth-telling contracts where the contract is designed to be self-enforcing. The problem is that, under certain circumstances, the truth-telling constraint means that the best possible contract is not feasible, and the firm instead sets the optimal second-best contract. These contracts can be viewed as having only limited employment commitments; in particular, the firm might use excessive (relative to the first-best, or 'efficient', contract) lay-offs in adverse outcomes. The reason is that by adopting a low employment level in the adverse outcome, the firm has no incentive to cheat and claim that the economic environment facing the firm is worse than it actually is. The importance of this result will become clear in the next chapter where it is suggested that firms overreact to adverse environments, and thus sustain those environments; we will suggest that this maintains a recession initiated by an aggregate demand fall.

The main conclusions to this point are largely microeconomic in nature—labour markets are very likely to be imperfect, although institutions (contracting) naturally arise to mitigate the market failures. Government policies should be to correct any weaknesses in this respect. Interestingly, this can involve a government unemployment benefits system to lessen monopsonistic market failures, and support for contracting by trade-union protection laws. An example of the latter possibility is that the asymmetric information truth-telling problem of this chapter might be less likely in an environment where the firm has had ongoing relations with an organised trade union than where it deals with individual workers—the union might be in a better position to monitor the carrying-out of a contingent contract.

But for macroeconomic implications, we are left with only the Lucas information problem of Chapter 6 and its variant, the staggered-contracts approach of this chapter. In Chapter 6 workers might become confused as to whether a wage rise in their sector was due to a relative improvement in that sector or due to a general inflation, and therefore efficient unemployment might not be achieved. A short-run Phillips curve would appear in the aggregate data, although there was no effective policy trade-off and certainly no long-run Phillips curve. Desirable government policies are either to improve monetary control, lessening the uncertainty of inflation, or (where the government has an information advantage) to adopt a stabilising monetary policy. The staggered-contracting model reinterprets this in a contracting setting, retaining the same basic results, but adding a greater plausibility in that unemployment occurs through the contracting mechanism of involuntary lay-offs, and further, agents are allowed to observe the aggregate price level, although not the money supply figures.

Our effort in Chapter 10 will be to follow the notion of contracting as limiting firms' responses to changes in their environment, but we will reinterpret these as true aggregate demand and supply shocks and not the confusion process of the Lucas model. The resulting model will be much more reminiscent of the *General Theory* approach, although it contains important differences from the aggregate demand-Phillips curve synthesis of the Keynesian school in Chapter 5.

10 Equilibrium Recessions

Over the course of the book to this point, we have covered a large amount of territory in an attempt to clarify a number of issues: the fundamental differences in the nature of neoclassical and Keynesian equilibrium in properly formulated aggregative microeconomically-based models; the problems in the post-war, neo-Keynesian synthesis aggregate-demand Phillips curve model and in the traditional Keynesian model with respect to providing full microeconomic foundations, particularly in the labour market; the ability of search and contracting, in the literature, to address the special nature of the labour market, and how in particular these two approaches relate; and finally the drawbacks of the Lucas information approach, and its variant, the staggered-contracts approach, to developing macroeconomic implications. We have also, however, been following a particular line of argument that we want to conclude in this chapter with the claim that 'contracting theory performs as advertised' in providing an explanation not only for involuntary unemployment but also for Keynesian macroeconomic effects. The steps in the argument are:

1. Search markets tend to collapse due to monopsony power, and it becomes in the interest of agents to make commitments—contracts, implicit or explicit, naturally appear in the labour market (Ch. 8).
2. First-best contracts, achieving the 'efficient' employment levels, are unlikely to be sustainable due to enforcement problems which can be formalised by the asymmetric information approach and lead to underemployment in bad outcomes (Ch. 9).

3. The underemployment that results from the contractual commitments can be used in a model to explain why a fall in aggregate demand becomes consistent with microeconomic behaviour since firms do not seek to increase production and sales and therefore have no incentive to change nominal prices and set in motion the neoclassical 'real-balance' adjustment process (Ch. 10).
4. Further, contracting provides an argument as to why there are involuntary lay-offs rather than voluntary quits (Ch. 7), and the asymmetric information approach suggests why those laid-off in a recession are unlikely to obtain jobs at other firms (Chs. 9 and 10).

We observed in our initial discussion of contracting that there was disappointment with regard to developing contracting into a macroeconomic model, in two respects: the contracting model was in real terms rather than the nominal wage rigidities felt necessary to sustain Keynesian equilibria, and further the employment decision was divorced from the wage rigidity; that is, one could not say that the rigid wages implied that under adverse circumstances employment would fall, since there were independent employment commitments. The asymmetric information contracting approach begins to address the second problem by limiting those employment commitments. In this chapter we want to show how that approach can be placed into an aggregate model that displays Keynesian properties, in particular with reference to the primary role of aggregate demand in determining the level of aggregate economic activity. Interestingly, the analysis can be done entirely in real terms, so the supposed limitation of contracting (the absence of nominal rigidities) proves to be unimportant.

The fundamental feature of the current analysis relative to our earlier discussions of contracting is that we want to interpret the uncertainty facing a firm not as relative price (as in Chs. 6 and 7), or as aggregate productivity (the staggered-contracts approach in Ch. 9) changes, but rather as aggregate demand changes. As before, the firm may face either a favourable or unfavourable marginal value product of labour curve, but now this arises due to aggregate demand effects, where the state of aggregate demand limits the extent of the market for each particular product. This clearly requires a monopolistic competitive view of the economy, following suggestions in Hart (1982). In a low state of aggregate demand, for the firm to maintain its sales, it must lower its relative price—this gives us a marginal value product curve for labour that has shifted inwards relative to that in a high state of aggregate demand. The firm can either lower its price to maintain sales, or cut employment or production.

The introduction of the monopolistically competitive formulation incorporates firm price-setting into the model. The firm, in choosing its production level, is also choosing the price it will set for its product. We can therefore directly address the neoclassical problem with claimed Keynesian equilibria: why don't firms lower prices to gain greater sales, and in that way set in motion the neoclassical real-balance adjustment process? The fundamental answer in our analysis is that the asymmetric information contracting limits firms to a real wage and employment point where they do not desire either to change the real wage or to increase their production and sales. The low-output point is truly an equilibrium where, subject to the level of aggregate demand, firms do not want to increase production beyond the point consistent with that level of aggregate demand. It is important to keep in mind why this cannot in general happen in a neoclassical economy. If aggregate demand and output in the economy were below the full-employment level, one of two things would happen: individual firms would decide, based upon the current real wage rate, to increase production by lowering prices, and in that way the low-output level would not be an equilibrium; or unemployed workers would lower their wage demands, increasing the incentive on the part of firms to increase employment and output, again lowering prices and restoring the full-employment equilibrium. The neoclassical adjustment process has these attempts to lower wages and prices operating through real-balance effects to restore aggregate demand to the point where it is consistent with the full-employment level of output. It is this adjustment process that must be attenuated to sustain a Keynesian low-output equilibrium.

Monopolistic competition, of itself, will not provide the answer; its only purpose in the current analysis is to endogenise the price-setting so that we can directly address the neoclassical contention. What does provide the answer is the notion that contracting, voluntary and optimal on the part of firms, limits their responses to an aggregate demand fall in such a way as to ratify it

Firms enter into (largely implicit) contracts with workers, intended to last over an extended period of time. The contract offer, at the level necessary to attract new workers, is based upon the firm's expectations of the likelihood of various eventual environments—in this context, upon the likely states of aggregate demand and thus demand for its individual product. We formalise this by opening our economy with an *ex ante* equilibrium in the labour market, essentially a market for contracts, where the market clears at a contract-offer value (*G*, in our earlier notation) that causes firms to want to attach workers (offer them contracts) in the same number as the size of the labour supply. These contracts then specify how the firm will behave in each of the possible outcomes. The only relevant outcomes are those that might actually occur in the economy, equilibrium outcomes *ex post*. Each of the anticipated possible aggregate demand levels becomes an *ex post* equilibrium if, when the postulated level of aggregate demand occurs, each firm responds in such a way that, when aggregated over firms, leads national income to be at the level that leads to that level of aggregate demand. With rational expectations (as we shall of course assume) only these aggregate demand levels that represent *ex post* equilibria will be specified in the contract. What makes a low-output-level equilibrium a possibility *ex post* (it can only occur if it has some probability less than unity) is the nature of the optimal asymmetric information contract. In a bad outcome these contracts contain underemployment relative to neoclassical norms; this underemployment tendency can then sustain the low-output level as an aggregate equilibrium. We refer to these low-output equilibria as equilibrium recessions since there is no adjustment process that automatically brings them to an end. An important feature is that they are effected through, from the nature of the employment contracts, involuntary unemployment; further, from our discussion of asymmetric information contracting, there is likely to be little opportunity for obtaining a new job in a different firm.

The process we will examine bears a common logic, to some extent, with the 'trade coordination problem' discussed in Diamond (Oct. 1982; 1984) and Weitzman (1982); where it primarily differs is that we incorporate contracting to provide a proper labour-market closure to the model. We will begin this chapter with a discussion of the Diamond parable, show how monopolistic competition without contracting cannot solve the problem, and then introduce the asymmetric information contracts to provide equilibrium recessions subject to both aggregate demand and supply-side effects.

10.1   THE TRADE COORDINATION PARABLE

The major feature of trade coordination problems can be understood from a very simple 'parable' by Diamond. Consider an economy where there are only two individuals: individual A produces a good a in quantity q_a, while individual B produces a good b in quantity q_b. Unfortunately, A gains utility only from the consumption of good b, and B gains utility only from good a. Hence they must trade in order to gain any utility from their production. Each individual suffers a constant utility cost per unit of production, d, and gains utility from consuming the other's good in the amount $U(q)$. From $U(q)$ we can construct the marginal utility schedule $MU(q)$, with $MU(1) > d$ so that some production and trade is optimal, but with a diminishing marginal utility—denote by q^* the level of consumption such that $MU(q^*) = d$. One efficient solution is for A to produce $q_a = q^*$ and for B to produce $q_b = q^*$, and then for the two to trade their production. (There are in fact many other efficient production levels, with differing distributions of income-utility at the end, but we need not consider this.) On the other hand, if both agents are producing less than q^*, we clearly have an inefficient, underproduction, outcome. Consider any production outcome (q_a, q_b) with both $q_a, q_b < q^*$. When the agents trade their production (if they don't trade there is immediate inefficiency since the production is wasted), individual B has a marginal utility for further consumption of a in the amount $MU(q_a) > MU(q^*) = d$, and A has an $MU(q_b) > MU(q^*) = d$. B could therefore offer to produce another unit of b and trade it to A for an additional unit of a and both would benefit.

The outcome $q_a = q^*$, $q_b = q^*$ is sustainable as a competitive equilibrium where the market sets the price ratio for trading the two goods of unity (a one-for-one trade). Person A would maximise $U(q) - dq$, as does B, and the result is production at the point where $MU(q) = d$; that is, at q^*. The coordination problem arises if one of the agents begins to doubt the competitive assumption that he can sell all that he wants at the competitive price of 1. Suppose that both A and B become pessimistic and expect the other to produce only the amount $q_0 < q^*$. If A continues to produce at q^*, he expects to be able to trade for only the q_0 units that B produces, and therefore his optimal strategy is to produce only q_0. B follows the same reasoning, and the expectations are self-fulfilling. The problem is a coordination one, since both A and B would prefer to produce and trade q^* units and, if they could get together and coordinate, they would agree to do so. Importantly, however, there is a low-level equilibrium with each producing q_0, depending upon expectations of 'aggregate demand' or, more strictly, availability of trading opportunities.

In fact, this simple story (while extremely interesting as an approach) has a number of weaknesses. The first is that there is little role for price-setting behaviour on the part of agents—if there were many producers and traders in the economy, could not a small agent produce more than he expected others on average to produce, and then sell his output by lowering its price below the ratio of unity assumed above. This is of course just the old neoclassical argument that a Keynesian 'equilibrium' fails because it leaves agents with an incentive to do something differently. It might be argued, following Diamond, that in a search process as in Chapter 8, that sort of price-setting is impossible as agents meet randomly without information or commitments to engage in trades, with an agent having no way of advertising his lowered price and gaining additional trades from it; but that is not particularly convincing as a description of actual market structures. As we have already argued in Chapter 8, search markets naturally lead to some form of advertising commitments and contracting. Therefore any realistic application must be in a world where agents can set and advertise prices, and indeed enter into contractual commitments. Further problems with the simple parable lie in developing the labour market into the model and generalising the assumptions about the technology of production. For all these reasons, we will base our approach upon the contracting models developed earlier in the book, beginning in the next section with an examination of monopolistic competition as suggested in the trade-coordination context by Weitzman (1982).

10.2   MONOPOLISTIC COMPETITION EQUILIBRIUM

A model of equilibrium recessions will have to explain why firms, seeking to gain greater output sales, do not lower their output price and in that way, in the aggregate, lower the nominal price level and through real-balance effects restore aggregate demand to full-employment levels. To examine that, one needs to model the price-setting power of firms; this can be done by adopting a monopolistically competitive view of the economy. Each firm will produce a good that is an imperfect substitute for other goods, and therefore each firm will face its own demand curve; as it lowers its relative price, it can gain additional sales. Recall that the nominal price adjustment in the neoclassical model is taken to come about as firms try to lower their relative prices by changing their nominal price; although they may not succeed in changing their relative price, the ensuing nominal price adjustments restore aggregate demand and sales to the point where the firm no longer desires to change its price to gain further sales. The monopolistic competitive approach, by incorporating price-setting into the model, will allow us to examine whether this adjustment process will actually occur.

We will consider an economy with F firms that are identical in production technology $q(N_f)$, where the form of this function will be specified later, although they do produce different goods q (where f takes on the values $1, 2, ..., F$). Each firm produces a good which is an imperfect substitute for other goods as reflected in the demand curve for its product. The demand curve for each product is identical. Finally, there is a labour force of L in the economy with each worker having no utility of leisure. We will want to examine the nature of equilibrium in this economy.

Since each firm's demand curve is part of an aggregate market for goods, it will be helpful to construct an underlying model of goods demands to derive individual firm demand curves. Further, it will be much easier to work in the context of an example, taking care that the specification we choose is sufficiently general to retain the interesting features of the problem. We will use the notion of composite goods: each firm produces a unique and distinct good, but these are combined by a production process into a 'composite good' which is then the sole consumption and investment good in the economy, being used interchangeably for either purpose. Writing q_f for the amount of the product of the fth firm ($f = 1, 2, ..., F$), we have: $Q(q_1, q_2, ..., q_F)$, where Q is the amount of the composite good producible. We will assume that each of the individual goods enters symmetrically into this composite goods production process (otherwise, our firms would no longer be functionally identical)—that is, we could relabel each of the goods in the composite good production function with no change in production. In addition, we assume that composite good production is subject to constant returns to scale (if each of the q_f's rises in proportion, Q rises by that proportion) and that Q is increasing in each of the q_f's, but at a decreasing rate. These are the important general specifications of the composite good production process; it will however be easiest to work with a specific form of $Q(q_1, q_2, ..., q_F)$ that meets these properties. We will adopt a constant returns-to-scale, constant-elasticity-of-substitution (CES) production function of the form:

$$Q = [q_1{}^a + q_2{}^a + ... + q_F{}^a]^{1/a}$$

where the elasticity of substitution equals $1/(1 - a)$ and we restrict our attention to functions with $a < 1$ (so there is a well-defined positive elasticity of substitution). Confirm that the Q function is indeed constant returns to scale in that, if each of the q_f's rises by the same proportion, Q rises by that proportion. In fact, it will be desirable to 'normalise' the functional form to:

$$Q = F^{1-1/a}[q_1{}^a + q_2{}^a + ... + q_F{}^a]^{1/a}$$

This normalisation gives us the additional property that, if each firm produces the same amount q (as will happen in an equilibrium with the identical firms), Q will then equal F_q. We will interpret Q both as a measure of GNP (aggregate production) and as a measure of aggregate demand. The reason for this is our observation in Chapter 2 that, in either a Keynesian or a neoclassical equilibrium, the goods market must clear requiring that aggregate supply equals aggregate demand.

To gain individual firm demand curves we need to specify the market for the inputs into Q. We suppose that Q is produced in a competitive market by a number of other firms $f = F + 1, F + 2, ...$ Given our constant returns assumption, the production process is the same for each composite-good-producing firm and takes on the form given above. The demand from these composite-goods-producing firms for the various inputs (the individual goods q_f) can be examined in the same way as we examined a firm's demand for labour in Chapter 2—the demand curves are the marginal product curves measured in production of Q. As the availability of an individual product (input into production of Q) q_f changes, its marginal product measured in units of Q changes, and this determines its relative (to units of Q) price; this is the real value that firms and workers are interested in since Q is both the consumption and investment good in the economy. To find the marginal product of a good q_f in the production of Q, we take the derivative of the Q production function:

$$\partial Q/\partial q_f = F^{1-1/a}[q_1{}^a + q_2{}^a + \ldots + q_F{}^a]^{1/a-1}q_f{}^{a-1}$$

With substitution using the original Q function, this can be rewritten as:

$$= [q_f/(Q/F)]^{a-1}$$

recalling that $a - 1$ is negative. From the derivation, this represents the price p_f at which the given quantity of q_f can be sold when aggregate demand is at the given Q: if the firm produces just its share of aggregate demand, $q_f = Q/F$, the price p_f equals unity; as the firm seeks to expand its sales beyond this, from $a < 1$ (note the importance of this assumption), p_f falls; alternatively, if aggregate demand Q/F rises but the firm maintains its production q_f, its output price p_f rises. That p_f, at $q_f = Q/F$, equals unity follows from our normalisation of the Q function. In an equilibrium where all the identical firms end up producing the same quantity q, we have $Q = Fq$ and with $p_f = 1$ for each individual good—total composite good production equals the revenues of firms (which is then distributed in wages and profits, and comes back in demand for Q). Even outside of equilibrium, however, with firms possibly producing different quantities, the same effect holds because of our assumption of constant returns to scale. In a CRS world, there is a result that total factor payments (in this case, the factors of production being the individual goods) equal total revenues from (composite good) output: $\Sigma_f p_f q_f = Q$, $f = 1, \ldots, F$. Q is then aggregate real income in the economy as well as production, and in any equilibrium it will equal aggregate demand as well.

As a first step towards examining equilibrium, we must consider individual firms' optimal behaviour in response to the above demand function. Given the stipulated form of the demand curve, the firm f can calculate its total revenue at each level of production, subject to aggregate demand Q:

$$p_f(q_f, Q)q_f = [q_f/(Q/F)]^{a-1}q_f$$

Given the firm's price-setting monopolistic power, we find its optimal production level using its marginal revenue curve showing how revenue increases with production. This follows as the derivative of the total revenue curve:

$$MR(q_f, Q) = a[q_f/(Q/F)]^{a-1}$$

Note that we have taken Q (aggregate demand) to be fixed in taking the derivative with respect to q_f; in fact, an increase in q_f will have a small effect in increasing Q (by producing more, a given firm can raise aggregate demand but gets only a very small proportion back in increased demand for its own product) that we will ignore. The role of aggregate demand is that an increase will shift the individual firms' demand curves to the right, and with them the marginal revenue curves. From this expression for MR we see that it will be useful to impose another constraint on a in addition to $a < 1$, that a is strictly positive implying from our earlier definition that the elasticity of substitution is greater than unity. When $a = 0$, so the elasticity is exactly unity, we have the Cobb–Douglas case where the firm's revenues are independent of production; if a were to be negative, we would have revenues failing with production, which would not be a useful case to examine.

To find actual production by the firm, we need to specify the cost structure and then, following the usual rule, equate marginal revenue to marginal cost to find the profit-maximising output. The cost structure depends in turn upon the production technology facing the firm. The simplest case is to suppose that the firm has a constant-returns-to-scale production function in employment: $q_f = q(N_f) = bN_f$. Each additional unit of quantity produced then requires $1/b$ units of labour. If labour is hired in a competitive market at a real wage w (measured in units of the composite good Q), we have a constant marginal cost of production of w/b. As a monopolist, the firm would produce to the point where marginal revenue equals marginal costs:

$$a[q_f/(Q/F)]^{a-1} = w/b$$

An increase in Q, or a fall in w, would both lead to increased production (recall that $a - 1$ is negative), as is intuitive.

We now want to examine equilibrium in this economy. Since our F firms are identical, they would (following the $MR = MC$ rule) produce the same amount q, giving an aggregate production level $Q = Fq$. Further, since each firm produces just the average amount, $p_f = 1$ for each firm. Then the $MR = MC$ rule becomes:

$$w = ab$$

Of course, this is not a total specification of equilibrium since we have not yet explicitly solved for the labour-market equilibrium. Observe that, for $w = ab$, any Q could be (from our discussion to this point) an equilibrium in the sense that if each firm expects the aggregate demand level Q, it will produce at $q_f = Q/F$ and sustain Q as an equilibrium. But for each aggregate demand level, there is also a demand for labour given by Q/b. The labour market only clears at the wage $w = ab$ if the demand for labour at that wage, Q/b, equals the supply L (given the vertical labour supply curve). The labour market then establishes full-employment output as the only complete equilibrium.

While the monopolistically competitive economy still leads to full employment in this case, it does display one difference from the pure competitive economy. The wage here is $ab < b$. But b is the marginal physical product of labour, and the price of each firm's output in equilibrium is unity. The competitive economy would then, since workers are paid their marginal products, lead to a wage of b, but here the wage is less than that. This is the only difference between the two sorts of equilibria, however, reflecting the monopoly power of the firms. If we examined an economy where the labour supply curve took on the non-vertical form in Chapter 2, $L_s(w)$, then the monopoly power would be reflected in a lower wage than in a competitive economy; but further, the lower wage would move the economy down the labour supply curve, and the monopoly power would lead to lowered employment and output, although there would be no involuntary unemployment and still no role for aggregate demand expectations in leading to equilibrium recessions.

This rightly suggests that monopolistic competition on its own, or even with the constant-returns-to-scale production process for individual goods, cannot lead to equilibrium recessions. Some form of labour-market imperfection will be necessary as well. In the following section, we construct interim models with an arbitrary real wage rigidity and then, in section 10.4, use the asymmetric information contracting model to provide a proper basis for the equilibrium recession phenomenon.

10.3 REAL WAGE RIGIDITY: AN INTERIM MODEL

In the previous section, we observed that monopolistic competition is insufficient to establish equilibrium recessions in the absence of some other imperfection; rather there is a well-defined full-employment equilibrium. We now want to use a set of somewhat artificial assumptions about the labour market to construct an interim model that allows for equilibrium recessions; this interim model will be useful in clarifying our more fundamental approach in the following section. In particular, we assume that firms acquire labour in a competitive labour market of the form in the previous section, anticipating a full employment output result. Thus the real wage takes on the value ab (in the linear production function case $q_f = bN_f$). However, there is an imperfection in the labour market in that real wages will be taken to remain rigid at ab, even if a recession and unemployment occurs. We want to ask whether that real wage rigidity is sufficient to establish an equilibrium recession, where the equilibrium is relative to that restriction on lowering real wages. The reason we refer to these as artificial assumptions is that we have not derived this wage rigidity as part of optimal contracting; since this is merely an interim model, however, we will not worry about the strict legitimacy of the assumptions.

We therefore start out with the monopolistically competitive full-employment equilibrium of the previous section, denoting the equilibrium values of the variables by *. Each of the F firms produces an amount $q_f^* = bL/F$ at a price of unity at the equilibrium real wage of $w^* = ab$. Firms are induced to produce at the given level by following the $MR = MC$ rule:

$$a[q_f^*/(Q^*/F)]^{a-1} = w^*/b = a$$

implying that $q_f^* = (Q^*/F)$. Q^* represents both aggregate demand and aggregate supply, which must of course be equal in an equilibrium. We want to ask what happens if firms expect aggregate demand to fall from Q^* to some lower level Q_0. If, with the rigid real wage at w^*, firms cut their desired production to $q_{f0} = Q_0/F$, then this will represent an equilibrium recession as aggregate supply has fallen to equate with aggregate demand. In particular, firms will have no incentive to attempt to lower their prices to achieve greater sales, and therefore there will be no tendency for nominal prices to fall to set in motion the neoclassical real-balance adjustment process.

At w^* and the anticipated aggregate demand Q_0, each firm chooses its production by the $MR = MC$ rule:

$$a[q_{f0}/(Q_0/F)]^{a-1} = w^*/b = a$$

But this solves for $q_{f0} = Q_0/F$ as required to sustain the low aggregate demand level as a recession. Indeed, any anticipated level of aggregate demand Q less than Q^*, if real wages remain rigid at w^*, calls forth an aggregate supply response equal to Q, and the aggregate demand level Q is sustained as an equilibrium. The real wage rigidity is then sufficient to establish equilibrium recessions, and further, the recession can be of any arbitrary magnitude.

Does this differ at all from the *General Theory* labour market in Chapter 2, where Keynes supposed that real wages in the economy adjusted to leave firms satisfied with producing at a low (relative to full employment) level of aggregate demand? To make the comparison clearer, introduce constant marginal productivity of labour, at b, into our original labour-market model (without the monopolistically competitive firms). The marginal product curve, the labour demand curve, is then horizontal at (in the notation of the previous section), the unit productivity of labour b. If $w = b$, the firm is quite happy to produce at any employment and output level since in any case it gains the same amount of profits, zero (the area between the marginal product curve and the wage being zero)—it will quite happily accommodate any level of aggregate demand. Thus real wage rigidity would have been sufficient in the *General Theory* labour market, if there was a constant-returns-to-scale, or constant-real-marginal-product, production technology.

The one difference here derives of course from our introduction of monopolistically competitive firms. At each aggregate demand level Q, the firm has a downward-sloping MR curve that it uses, by assumption, to choose its labour force size. This can be transformed into the labour-market diagram as a marginal revenue product curve, $MRP(N)$, by multiplying the $MR(q_f)$, conditional upon Q, curve by the unit productivity of labour, b. This $MRP(N)$ curve differs from the $MPL(N)$ curve, used in the traditional labour market of Chapter 2, by taking account of the price of the good at different production levels, and how the price changes as production is increased. Even in an equilibrium when all firms produce the same amount and therefore the price of each good equals unity, the marginal revenue product of labour is ab (rather than $pMPL = b$) due to the fall in p as another b units are produced. It is this that leads to the equilibrium real wage at full employment of $ab < b$, where b is the value in the competitive labour market. What allows for equilibrium recessions, however, is that when the $MRP(N)$ curve shifts downwards due to a fall in aggregate demand, it continues to take on the value ab at that level of employment N_f such that $q_f = bN_f = Q/F$, where Q is the new low level of aggregate demand. For each level of aggregate demand Q, if real wages remain rigid at ab, the firm will uniquely choose to produce at Q/F because of the downward-sloping marginal revenue product curve for labour (that remains even though the marginal physical product curve is horizontal). This differs from our Keynesian labour market with a fixed real wage at b (for the constant marginal real productivity b), where the firm is simply indifferent to producing at Q/F—here it is the unique profit-maximising outcome. This is important, since in choosing q_f the firm is also making its (now modelled) pricing decision. Since the firm optimally chooses to produce $q_f = Q/F$, the quantity it can just sell at the relative price of unity (the price it had at the full employment level as well), it has no incentive to attempt to lower its output price to gain further sales. The model is in that sense more complete than our Chapter 2 labour-market models, endogenising the firm's pricing decisions through its output choice, but it does not represent a significant improvement until we can add a story justifying the wage rigidity. To some extent, real wage rigidity is provided by the contracting models, and it is important that real wage rigidity (rather than the nominal rigidities of the Phillips curve Keynesian models) may be sufficient for our purposes. Nominal prices do not adjust, not because they are rigid but because the real wage rigidity leaves firms with no incentive to adjust their nominal prices.

There is however a serious problem with the above story of real wage rigidities leading to equilibrium recessions: the model does not generalise to other production technologies. If we return to our original assumption of diminishing marginal physical productivity, we can rewrite the marginal-revenue/marginal-cost optimisation rule for the firm as:

$$a[q_f/(Q/F)]^{a-1} = w^*/MPL(N_f)$$

where $w^* = aMPL(L/F)$ as a straightforward generalisation of the earlier equilibrium and the general form $MPL(N_f)$ with MPL diminishing with N_f replaces the constant $MPL(N) = b$. But now consider what happens for any $Q < Q^*$ when real wages are rigid at w^*. If this is to be an equilibrium, we must have the firm following the $MR = MC$ rule to produce $q_f = Q/F$. But when the firm produces this amount, the left-hand side (MR) equals a; however, since q_f has fallen from q^*, N_f must have fallen from L/F, and under diminishing marginal productivity $MPL(N_f) > MPL(L/F)$, and therefore the right-hand side no longer equals a, but something less. Then the firm's optimal response q_f, for any aggregate demand level Q less than the full employment level Q^*, cannot be Q/F but in fact (under real wage rigidity) is somewhat more. There are no equilibrium recessions. Rather, when aggregate demand falls, each firm seeks to produce more than its share of aggregate demand, presumably causing prices to fall and, through the real-balance adjustment process, restoring aggregate demand to the full employment level. Real wage rigidity is sufficient for establishing equilibrium recessions only for the special case of the linear production function $q_f = bN_f$. This is not surprising as can be seen by a further comparison with the *General Theory* model. There, under decreasing marginal productivity, the real wage actually has to rise to sustain a recession, the increased real wage inducing firms to cut their production in accord with their share of aggregate demand. While real-wage downward rigidity in the face of a recession perhaps can be justified (although our model in the next section has real wages falling with the recession), it is very hard to comprehend why real wages should actually rise; indeed, it was this 'shortcoming' of the *General*

Theory labour-market model that, according to Barro and Grossman (1971), made the fixed-price models with their assumed nominal price rigidities and possibly pro-cyclical real wage patterns preferable as a theoretical construct. Yet we would not want our model to depend entirely upon an arbitrary specification of the production process; indeed, one of the nice features about a monopolistically competitive formulation is that it allows for both decreasing and increasing marginal products to gain a proper market equilibrium. We will therefore need to seek out an approach that does not depend upon an assumption of linearity. This is provided in the following section by integrating into the monopolistically competitive economy the asymmetric information contracting approach.

10.4   EQUILIBRIUM RECESSIONS

We now have the various pieces necessary to establish our model of equilibrium recessions. In particular, we will adopt the model of monopolistic competition from section 10.2, as generalised to include diminishing marginal physical productivity, in conjunction with the asymmetric information contracting model of Chapter 9. It will be easiest to use the simplified form of that model where the risk-aversion of the firm is represented by a minimum 'profit' level ϕ that must be achieved in the bad outcome. We will find that the asymmetric information contracting result of underemployment in the bad outcome, with the extent of underemployment depending upon the risk-aversion of firms, will allow us to sustain equilibrium recessions.

In order to integrate the contracting model into the monopolistically competitive economy, minor modifications must be made to both approaches. In contrast to our model in section 10.2, the contracting model relies upon the notion that contracting takes place under uncertainty, where there are a number of possible environmental outcomes, each of which has an *ex ante* probability of occurrence. Following our discussion to this point in this chapter, and examining the two-outcome case as we did in earlier chapters for simplicity, we will view the outcomes as two possible levels of aggregate demand $Q^+ > Q^-$, where in fact Q^+ will be the full employment level where each of our F firms produces at

$q_f = q(L/F)$ and Q^- will represent the equilibrium recession. Agents in the economy will have (identical) expectations that Q^+ will occur with probability π^+ and Q^- with probability $\pi^- = 1 - \pi^+$; these expectations are important in that, as we shall see later, there cannot be an equilibrium recession if $\pi^- = 1$; that is, if agents are certain before contracting that the recession will occur. The second modification to our section 10.2 model is that, for the asymmetric information contract to lead to the underemployment that can sustain an equilibrium recession, the firm must be risk-averse (as shown in Ch. 9); we model this by the idea of a minimum real profit level ϕ that the firm must attain in any outcome (possibly to avoid bankruptcy). The larger the value of ϕ (in particular, as it approaches profits in the full-employment outcome), the more risk-averse the firm. While we thus add uncertainty and firm risk-aversion to the discussion to this point in this chapter, we must also modify the asymmetric information contracting model to account for the monopolistically competitive nature of firms. Recall that we earlier supposed that an essentially competitive price-taking firm would either face a high relative price for its output p^+ or a low price p^-, giving it a high or low marginal value product curve. Here the uncertainty in environment is common to all firms (the level of aggregate demand), but on the firm level this still presents two curves that are the equivalent of the earlier high and low marginal value product curves—a high and low marginal revenue product curve. If aggregate demand is high, the firm can sell a high output at a high price, but if aggregate demand falls, to gain the same output-price, it must cut production in proportion to the fall in aggregate demand. The marginal revenue product curves are downward-sloping, as the earlier marginal value product curves, and can be used in exactly the same way, representing the additional real contribution of another unit of labour. We write $R^i(N)$ for the total revenue curve, with aggregate demand level i, and $MRP^i(N)$ for the marginal revenue product.

We will in this section use the results from Chapter 9 with some but not complete, repetition of the arguments there. Recall that in the asymmetric information contracting model with two possible environments facing the firm, the firm will offer potential workers a contract stipulating the real wage and employment in each outcome: (w^-, N^-) and (w^+, N^+), where these may be the same, as well as the number of workers N_0 signed to the contract. Since workers are taken not to observe the environment facing the firm, this contract actually operates in the following way: the firm is allowed, after learning the outcome, to choose between the two wage and employment combinations stipulated in the contract. Workers cannot directly observe whether the good environment Q^+ has occurred and therefore whether the firm is choosing the high wage and employment combination (w^+, N^+) when appropriate (and, less pertinently, since it does not prove to be a binding constraint, whether the firm chooses $[w^-, N^-]$ when the bad environment Q^- occurs), so the contract is only meaningful if it is 'incentive-compatible with truth-telling'. The problem is that the risk-averse firm will want to lower wages in the bad outcome in order to maintain profits. Yet if the contract allows w^- to be very low, the firm will have an incentive to choose that low wage combination even in the good outcome. This can only be avoided if the contracted N^- is low as well, so that the firm would lose in revenues what it saved in wages. This requires that the truth-telling condition:

$$R^+(N^+) - w^+ N^+ \geq R^+(N^-) - w^- N^-$$

is met, so that the revenues net of wages in the + outcome, when the appropriate wage and employment combination is chosen, are as high as if the firm inappropriately chooses the − outcome wage and employment combination.

The contract must also, in addition to the truth-telling constraint, meet the condition that potential workers, who have an opportunity cost to signing the contract of G, are willing to sign; that is, the expected income (for our risk-neutral workers) from the contract must be:

$$\pi^+ w^+ N^+ + \pi^- w^- N^- \geq GN_0$$

and the number of signed workers N_0 is the maximum value for N^+ or N^-. Finally, the risk-averse firm must meet the minimum profit condition in the bad outcome:

$$R^-(N^-) - w^- N^- \geq \phi$$

and seeks to maximise expected profits subject to this constraint. To do this, it needs to transfer labour costs from the − outcome to the + outcome, but the truth-telling condition limits, for given N^+ and N^-, the extent to which labour costs can be transferred.

The solution to this problem, the determination of the optimal second-best contract, contained two major rules. The first was that the firm would sign to contracts the maximum number it would ever employ: $N_0 = N^+$. Further, this would be determined by the rule:

$$\pi^+ MRP^+(N^+) = G$$

so that, usefully, only π^+ and G are needed to determine N_0 (i.e. it can be determined before considering the ultimate choice of N^-, which will usefully simplify the later arguments). N^- is then chosen to meet the minimum profit constraint. First use the expected-income-for-workers constraint and the truth-telling condition, both of which will be met with equality, to solve for the total wage bill in each outcome, for arbitrary N^+ and N^-:

$$C^+ = w^+ N^+ = GN_0 + \pi^-[R^+(N^+) - R^+(N^-)]$$
$$C^- = w^- N^- = GN_0 - \pi^+(R^+(N^+) - R^+(N^-))$$

For a given N^+, the firm determines by its choice of N^- the extent of the labour cost transfer with, as N^- is lowered, an increased C^+ and decreased C^-. In fact, it is not guaranteed that a fall in N^- will raise profits in the bad outcome, although it will certainly lower the wage costs—to raise profits, the fall in C^-, $\pi^+ MRP^+(N^-)$, must exceed in value the decline in revenues in the bad outcome, $MRP^-(N^-)$. This second-order condition, similar to conditions we have had in both the search and contracting approaches for demonstrating unemployment, is met as long as π^+ is sufficiently large and the $MRP(N)$ curves sufficiently apart for the two aggregate demand outcomes. Provided that the condition is met, the firm then keeps lowering N^- until profits in the − outcome rise to ϕ.

We will in due course want to examine how the precise solution differs depending upon the assumed risk-aversion for firms. First however, we must clarify precisely what is needed in results to sustain the model of equilibrium recessions. This is primarily an issue of considering how the individual firm's optimal contract aggregates into the market equilibrium. In the current analysis, for the two-outcome case, we will have an equilibrium *ex ante* and *ex post* if we have two aggregate demand states Q^+ and Q^- with associatied probabilities π^+ and $\pi^- = 1 - \pi^+$, such that the labour market (the market for signing workers to contracts) clears *ex ante* before the aggregate demand level is learned and further the optimal contracts (from the F identical firms) are such that we have an equilibrium in the output markets *ex post* with N^+ and N^- such that $Fq(N^+) = Q^+$ and $Fq(N^-) = Q^-$. The *ex post* condition is the one for sustaining the two output levels since each firm is choosing to produce just its share of the aggregate demand. We can make two immediate observations. Q^+ must be at the full employment level with $N^+ = L/F$. The reason for this is that firms sign to contracts only a number $N_0 = N^+$, so for the initial labour market to clear, G must have adjusted to provide contracts for all L potential workers, who then all work in the high aggregate demand outcome. The second observation, following from this, is that π^+ must be positive and therefore the probability of a recession less than unity; otherwise the supposed recession would end up with full employment as G adjusts to cause the firm to sign L/F workers to the contract and employ them in the supposedly low-output outcome.

What remains to be shown to establish the notion of equilibrium recessions is that the N^- in the optimal contract leads to an output level at the firm $q(N^-) = Q^-/F$ for the given Q^-. It may not be obvious why this is not immediate. We know from the nature of the asymmetric information contract that, for *a* $Q^- < Q^+$, the risk-averse firm will respond with an $N^- < N^+$ due to the fall in the aggregate demand leading to a fall in the marginal revenue product curve. What we don't know is whether this fall is sufficient for the firm to be cutting back its output exactly in proportion to the fall in aggregate demand; in particular, if the cutback in output in response is less than the fall in aggregate demand, we will not have an equilibrium recession since each firm will be attempting to lower prices to sell its excess output relative to its share of the reduced market. The equilibrium recession requires that there be a Q^-, for given values of F, π^+ and ϕ, that is exactly sustained by the optimal contract.

It will be helpful to keep in mind the particular revenue function from section 10.2, where total revenues at each firm take on the form $R(N) = [q_f/(Q/F)]^{a-1}q(N)$ and the marginal revenue product

$MRP(N) = a[q_f/(Q/F)]^{a-1}MPL(N)$ since this shows clearly the nature of the environment facing a particular firm. As before, an increase in aggregate demand Q, for our case of $0 < a < 1$, leads to a shift outwards in the revenue and marginal revenue product curves at the firm, and pictorially in the labour market looks precisely as in the earlier search and contracting diagrams, Figures 6.1 and 7.1b. We will begin our analysis by considering the risk-neutral firm to provide a benchmark for the discussion. The risk-neutral firm does not face a binding minimum profit level constraint, and will choose as its optimal contract (to maximise expected profits) the full employment contract with a rigid real wage $w = G$ and employment $N^+ = N^- = N_0$. Examination of the earlier conditions on C^+ and C^- shows that this meets (trivially) the truth-telling condition and the expected income of workers condition. Since the firm is risk-neutral, it adopts in effect the efficient contract of Chapter 7, for the case where there is no leisure value to unemployment and the marginal revenue product is always positive, bearing the high variance in profits occasioned by a fall in revenues (when aggregate demand falls) with no compensating fall in labour costs. But then, for any possible $Q^- < Q^+$, irrespective of the values of π^+ and F, each firm continues to produce at Q^+/F and aggregate production exceeds the anticipated aggregate demand.

To establish the possibility of equilibrium recessions, we must consider risk-averse firms and the nature of their reaction functions in terms of their own production level for each level of anticipated aggregate demand. To do this we consider the situation when there is a fixed perceived probability π^+ of the full-employment outcome Q^+. Then with the fixed number of firms F, the rule that the firm signs workers to contracts to the point where $\pi^+MRP^+(N_0) = G$ leads to a G equal to $\pi^+MRP^+(L/F)$ in the labour market equilibrium. We now consider possible levels of Q^- and ask, if the stipulated Q^- was the only perceived other possible aggregate demand level (and therefore had the probability $\pi^- = 1 - \pi^+$), what level of production would the firm produce. This will be graphed in Figure 10.1a where it must be understood that the vertical axis shows the firm's reaction to different possible levels of Q^-, assuming that Q^- takes on the probability of $1 - \pi^+$. As we have already observed, the risk-neutral firm always would have the full-employment contract

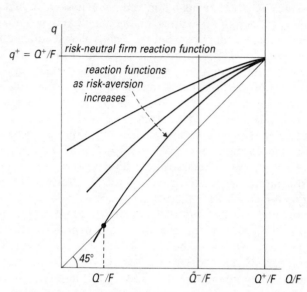

Figure 10.1a: *Reaction functions of firms of differing risk-aversion showing firm production at different levels of aggregate demand— Q^- represents an equilbrium recession*

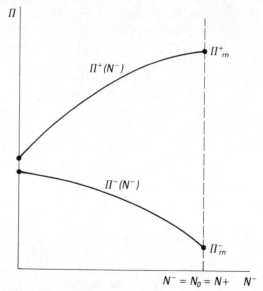

Figure 10.1b: *Profit levels, in good and bad óutcomes, for given levels of aggregate demand Q^+ and Q^-, as N^- is changed in the contract from 0 to N_0*

Figure 10.1: *Derivation of the equilibrium recession model*

and produce at Q^+/F, giving a horizontal reaction curve as shown in the diagram. Risk-averse firms, on the other hand, will not have horizontal reaction functions, but their particular features remain to be derived. The way we proceed is to take an arbitrary Q^- level, shown as $\tilde{Q}^-$ in the diagram, and show that depending upon the risk-aversion of the firm, its offered contract to workers includes an $\tilde{N}^-$ that can take on any value from N^+ to 0, and a resulting $q(\tilde{N}^-)$ that takes on any value from Q^+/F to 0.

Return first to the benchmark risk-neutrality case where we have full employment $N^- = N^+ = N_0 = L/F$ at both aggregate demand levels, the full-employment level Q^+ and our hypothesised low-output aggregate demand level $\tilde{Q}^-$; further, from the equations for C^+ and C^- there is a fixed wage $w = G$. The firm gains profits in the high aggregate demand outcome of $R^+(N_0) - GN_0$ and in the low aggregate demand outcome of $R^-(N_0) - GN_0$, which will be considerably less, with the relevant revenue curves being those at the respective levels of aggregate demand. We denote these profit levels by Π_{rn}^+ and Π_{rn}^-, as shown in Figure 10.1b at the point on the horizontal axis where $N^- = N_0$. We will use this diagram to show how firms of different degrees of risk-aversion, modelled by a minimum profit level in the bad outcome, choose their N^- level; this will obviously be a binding condition only if the requisite profit level ϕ exceeds the amount obtainable by the full-employment, expected-profit-maximising contract: Π_{rn}^-.

We will consider what happens as the firm's risk-aversion, measured by the size of ϕ increases from $\phi = \Pi_{rn}^-$ and becomes a binding constraint on the firm's contract offer. It is important to remember that, since π^+, F, Q^+ are fixed throughout the exercise, the condition on choosing $N_0 = N^+$ ensures that G will remain the same over the various contracts obtained by considering more and more risk-averse firms; all that will differ will be the $\tilde{N}^-$ chosen in response to $\tilde{Q}^-$. The point is that, within the asymmetric information contract and its conditions for wage bills in the two outcomes:

$$C^+ = GN_0 + \pi^-[R^+(N^+) - R^+(N^-)]$$
$$C^- = GN_0 - \pi^+[R^+(N^+) - R^+(N^-)]$$

a risk-averse firm can transfer labour costs from the $-$ outcome to the $+$ outcome according to the truth-telling conditions by lowering N^- from $N_0 = N^+$. As N^- is lowered, this raises C^+ but lowers C^-. Profits in the $+$ outcome, Π^+, must fall since N^- does not change revenues but only labour costs in that outcome. Consider the profits in the $-$ outcome, Π^-: as discussed earlier, a fall in N^- lowers revenues by $MRP^-(N^-)$ and lowers costs by $\pi^+ MRP^+(n^-)$. Thus Π^- rises, as N^- is lowered, if $\pi^+ MRP^+(N^+) > MRP^-(N^-)$; this condition is met provided that π^+ and the difference in demand for the two outcomes are great enough. Assuming that this condition is met, we graph the profit levels in the two outcomes, for the various levels of N^- possible, in Figure 10.1b. As N^- falls, Π^- rises and Π^+ falls, although of course the expected level of profits falls as we diverge from the efficient full-employment contract (since that contract was designed to maximise expected profits, and here we are sacrificing expected profits in favour of lessening their variance). It is important to note for further analysis that Π^- can never exceed Π^+ in the graph, even as N^- approaches zero. The reason for this is straightforward. Suppose we had a contract with a w^-,N^-,w^+,N^+ such that $R^-(N^-) - w^-N^- > R^+(N^+) - w^+N^+$. We know that $R^-(N^-) - w^-N^- > R^-(N^-) - w^-N^-$ since demand for the firm's product and therefore its revenue must be higher in the high aggregate demand case. But then it follows that $R^+(N^-) - w^-N^-$ must exceed $R^+(N^+) - w^+N^+$, violating the truth-telling conditions.

We can now use Figure 10.1b to determine the reaction of firms, of varying degrees of risk-aversion, to a particular aggregate demand level. We model risk-aversion by the notion of a minimum profit level ϕ. If the firm is risk-neutral and therefore there is no constraint on profits in the $\bar{Q}^-$ aggregate demand outcome, the optimal contract for the firm has $\tilde{N}^- = N^+ = N_0$ as we have already observed. But now suppose that, for the postulated level of aggregate demand, $\phi > \Pi^-(N_0) = \Pi^-_{rn}$ where the latter is shown in the graph. Then N^- must be lowered to the point where $\Pi^-(N^-) = \phi$. Increasing risk-aversion can be examined by increasing ϕ and as this is raised the necessary N^- continues to fall to 0; eventually of course there is a maximum ϕ sustainable, at $\phi = \Pi^-(0)$. The important point is that, for a given level of aggregate demand $\bar{Q}^-$, provided that the condition $\pi^+ MRP^+(N^-) > MRP^-(N^-)$ is met, there are degrees of risk-aversion on the part of firms that lead to employment levels anywhere between N_0 (full-employment) and 0. While for a given aggregate demand level $\tilde{Q}^-$, the degree of risk-aversion on the part of the firm determines $\tilde{N}^-$, it is also the case that, for a given degree of risk-aversion, each different level of Q^- will lead to a different N^-. To see this, observe that in Figure 10.1b a further fall in aggregate demand Q^- would lower the $\Pi^-(N^-)$ curve and therefore the requisite N^- to sustain the minimum profit level ϕ.

We can now use the information developed here to return to Figure 10.1a and draw in reaction curves, for firms of varying degrees of risk-aversion, for different potential levels of aggregate demand $Q^- < Q^+$. As shown, for each level of aggregate demand, firms of greater risk-aversion respond with a lower N^- mapping into a lower $q^- = q(N^-)$; further, for a firm of given risk-aversion, it displays a lower q^- in response to a lower Q^-—the reaction curve of a firm of given risk-aversion bends downwards from the full-employment horizontal line of the risk-neutral firm. Our interest is in the following point—there is some degree of risk-aversion on the part of firms such that their reaction curve intersects the 45-degree line from the origin. Recall that for any Q^- there is some degree of risk-aversion that leads firms to produce 0 at that level of aggregate demand. This means that we can get the reaction curves to bend downwards to the extent that they intersect the horizontal axis, at some positive Q^-, and therefore they must intersect the 45-degree line. The significance of this is that the 45-degree line shows those points that are self-sustaining equilibria in that each firm is producing just its share of aggregate demand: $q^- = Q^-/F$. We have therefore achieved our desired end, of showing the possibility of equilibrium recessions.

The nature of this result must be carefully understood. It says that in an economy with sufficiently risk-averse firms, the degree of their risk-aversion measured by ϕ, in conjunction with the expectations that they hold of the probability of a recession occurring ($\pi^- < 1$) and the other parameters of the economy (the number of firms F, the size of the labour force L, the composite goods production process determining the elasticity of demand for each individual product and the technological production function facing each firm), determines the existence of an equilibrium recession as well as its magnitude. In contrast to the interim model with constant returns to scale production and real wage rigidity, there is not a continuum of possible equilibrium recessions where each potential level of aggregate demand becomes self-fulfilling as firms find it in their interest to cut down their own production and sales in accord with the fall in the size of the aggregate market, therefore having no reason to attempt to lower their prices and set the neoclassical real-balance adjustment process into motion. Rather, there is a discrete [we will not address the issue of whether there might be several rather than one] equilibrium recession level. The reader might note that changing the parameters of the economy changes the 'depth' of the recession; for example, if firms are more risk-averse, the shifting downward of the reaction curve in Figure 10.2a means that the intersection with the 45-degree line will actually be at a higher Q^-, a somewhat paradoxical result. This rightly suggests that adopting a model of this sort as a basis for establishing a Keynesian model on firm microeconomic foundations, lends additional features to the macroeconomic model. We will discuss the macroeconomic implications of the approach in section 10.5, but first let us construct a numerical example that should clarify the analysis.

An Example of an Equilibrium Recession

The analysis in this section might be clarified by a numerical example; we will deliberately choose a rather extreme case where output in the recession falls to a quarter of the full-employment output. A number of specifications must be made. We adopt the CES composite-good function of section 10.3, so that for each of the F identical firms:

$$R(N) = p_f q_f(N) = [q_f(N)/(Q/F)]^{a-1} q_f(N)$$
$$MRP(N) = a[q_f(N)/(Q/F)]^{a-1} MPL(N) = a p_f MPL(N)$$

where $R(N)$ is total revenue at the firm, $MRP(N)$ the marginal revenue product and $MPL(N)$ the marginal physical product of labour. We need a numerical figure for a, and adopt $a = 1/2$; note that then total revenue can be written as $q_f^{1/2}(Q/F)^{1/2}$ and rises as the square root of either individual firm production or aggregate demand. We specify the $MPL(N)$ as being derived from the quadratic production function $q(N) = 20N - N^2$, so that $MPL(N) = 20 - 2N$. Thus the MRP is positive for all $N < 10$; we will choose a labour supply and number of firms consistent with this, $L = 20$ and $F = 10$, so in equilibrium each firm signs 2 workers to contracts.

From the nature of the truth-telling asymmetric information contracts, we know that firms sign workers N_0 to the point where:

$$\pi^+ MRP(N_0) = G$$

and of course employ in the good outcome $N^+ = N_0$ workers. In the labour-market equilibrium ('the market for contracts') G adjusts so that total demand for 'signees' FN_0 must equal 20, thus:

$$\pi^+ MRP^+(2) = G$$

We will adopt numerical values $\pi^+ = 9$ and $\pi^- = 1$, so that the recession is viewed as unlikely. We can now calculate G, recalling that in the full-employment equilibrium Q^+ (and, indeed, in the equilibrium recession Q^-) each firm produces the same amount $q_f = Q/F$ and therefore has a product price of unity:

$$MRP^+(2) = 1/2 MPL(2) = 10 - 2 = 8$$

G is therefore $\pi^+ = .9$ times 8, or 7.2.

Full-employment output q^+ at each firm is then $q(2) = 20 \cdot 2 - 2^2 = 36$, and multiplying by the 10 firms, we have $Q^+ = 360$. It will be easiest numerically to construct an example where $Q^- = 90$, with $q^- = 9$ and N^- being somewhat less than 1/2 (employment falls by more than output due to the decreasing marginal productivity of labour, so average productivity rises as N^- falls), although we do not need to calculate its exact amount for constructing the example. With $a = 1/2$, these figures of production in full employment and in the recession mean that a firm, anticipating an aggregate demand Q^+ but producing at q^- would face a product price of 2, and anticipating Q^- but producing q^+, 1/2.

Now consider what would happen if the firm, having the probabilities π^+ and π^- over the two aggregate demand levels, nonetheless offered the workers the full employment contract $N^- = N^+ = N_0 = 2$. To do this, because of the truth-telling problem, the contract would have to consist of a constant wage $w = G = 7.2$. In each outcome, the wage bill is then 7.2 for each of the 2 workers, or a total $GN_0 = 14.4$. Revenues in the $+$ outcome are, at a price of unity, the output of 36; profits are then $36 - 14.4 = 21.6$. As observed, in the $-$ outcome, if the firm continues to produce 36, its output price falls to 1/2 and therefore revenues to 18, giving a profit level of 3.6. Profits fall dramatically, and if the firm is sufficiently risk-averse, it would not offer this contract.

We have modelled the risk-aversion by supposing that there is a minimum profit level ϕ that the firm must achieve in even the bad outcome. Rather than stipulating this level now, we instead show how to calculate what it must be to cause the Q^- of 90 to actually be an equilibrium recession. Recall that the firm can shift labour costs between the two outcomes, and yet meet the truth-telling conditions, by the formulae:

$$C^+ = GN_0 + \pi^-[R^+(N^+) - R^+(N^-)]$$
$$C^- = GN_0 - \pi^+[R^+(N^+) - R^+(N^-)]$$

(giving of course an expected wage bill $\pi^+C^+ + \pi^-C^- = GN_0$, required to get workers to sign the contract). We already know the value of $R^+(N^+) = 36$; $R^+(N^-)$ is the price of 2 gained by cutting production to one-quarter, multiplied by the new output of 9—18. Thus, for our stipulated values of q^+ and q^-, costs would be shifted to give:

$$C^+ = 14.4 + .1[36 - 18] = 14.4 + 1.8 = 16.2$$
$$C^- = 14.4 - .9[36 - 18] = 14.4 - 16.8 = -2.4$$

Indeed, the stipulated recession is so severe that it is sustained only with a negative wage bill. (Other examples can of course be constructed with positive wage bills, but this is not important for our analysis.)

The resulting profits in each outcome are:

$$\Pi^+ = R^-(N^-) - C^+ = 36 - 16.2 = 19.8$$
$$\Pi^- = R^-(N^-) - C^- = 9 + 2.4 = 11.4$$

What this means is that our example is pertinent if the firm's minimum profit level ϕ was equal to 11.4. Meeting this profit level, if aggregate demand were to be at $Q^- = 90$, would require an N^- (allowing costs to be shifted sufficiently) that leads to $q^- = 9$, thereby sustaining the recession as an equilibrium. Note as claimed in the analysis of this section that Π^- remains below Π^+, and further that expected profits under the optimal second-best (with risk-aversion and asymmetric information) contract are less than with the full-employment contract, being 18.96 rather than 19.8 (where the small fall occurs due to the low probability of Q^-).

10.5   POLICY IMPLICATIONS

The analysis in the previous section establishes the possibility of multiple aggregate demand and income levels, with associated probabilities of occurrence, that are sustainable as equilibria. The probabilities are important in that the resulting contracts achieve an equilibrium *ex ante* in the labour market—the low output level Q^- can only be an equilibrium *ex post* if $\pi^- < 1$, if there is only a possibility and not a certainty of recession. The optimal contract then constrains firms' behaviour *ex post* and allows a recession at the low output level to be such an *ex post* equilibrium. It is an equilibrium (along with the full-employment outcome Q^+) since, when firms anticipate an aggregate demand of Q^- and operate subject to the optimal *ex ante* contract, they choose to produce that level of output q^- such that $Fq^- = Q^-$; they have no incentive to seek to gain market share by lowering their nominal price, and the low-output anticipations are self-fulfilling.

The mechanism by which Q^- is sustained can be stated in a somewhat more heuristic manner. First, consider the outward appearance of the scenario described. For whatever reason, a fall in investment or a contractionary fiscal or monetary policy, aggregate demand falls. Firms respond to this with a fall in employment and output to cut costs and restore profitability, this real contraction further allowing a downward pressure on real wages, ultimately restoring (at the low output level) profitability to at least minimum levels. Unlike the Lucas and staggered-contracts approach, firms do not respond in a subtle manner to anticipations of prices and inflation, but actually respond to a fall in aggregate demand reflected through their individual product demand curves. Behind this outward appearance, our model suggests that the fundamental driving factor is the need for firms to maintain their profitability at minimum levels in the face of what might be a prolonged recession. The only way they can do this is to lower real wages, and to convince workers to accept that they must convince them of the legitimacy of the need for wage cutbacks—this is done, according to the asymmetric information approach, by shutting factories and laying off workers. The workers losing their jobs at one firm do not gain employment elsewhere because the asymmetric information contracts become meaningless if the firm can hire workers from outside, thereby in effect negating the contract; if all firms have similar contracts, and face a similar environment (from the level of aggregate demand), there will be very little mobility. If one accepts the logic of the asymmetric information approach (and, indeed, there are some weaknesses in the model that we will discuss later), and the monopolistically competitive nature of product markets, the resulting equilibrium recessions seem well founded.

These equilibrium recessions are in some ways very Keynesian in nature. The first observation is that, because of the nature of the optimal contracts, unemployment occurs through lay-offs and is involuntary (in our case of risk-neutral workers who do not gain lay-off compensation payments as described in Ch. 7). Second, economic welfare is clearly less at Q^- than at Q^+, and all agents suffer—firms have lower profits and workers have lower wages or are laid off. If there is a macroeconomic policy that can return the economy to full employment, that would clearly be desirable. This is an issue that we will now turn to, first considering just how the model of equilibrium recessions relates to traditional Keynesian analysis.

Recall the basic *IS–LM* apparatus in the absence of inflation. The *IS* curve shows those combinations of the real interest rate and national output-income that lead to clearing in the loanable funds market, a necessary condition for a general equilibrium in the economy. The *LM* curve, dependent upon the real money supply, shows the combinations of r and Q that lead, through portfolio-balance conditions for example, to clearing of the asset markets in the economy, again a necessary condition for a general equilibrium. The intersection of the *IS* and *LM* curves marks the point where these markets clear. In the neoclassical context, however, the absence of labour-market clearing at any output level other than Q^* leads to a disequilibrium situation, and the claim is that at low output levels nominal prices and wages fall to raise the real money supply (for a given nominal money supply), shifting the *LM* curve to the right and restoring the intersection to the Q^* level of output. Our counter-argument was that, at an equilibrium recession, firms are satisfied with their level of output (subject to the low aggregate demand) and have no incentive to increase production and attempt to gain market share by lowering their relative prices, a process which would be effected by a lowering of the nominal price—there is no mechanism for nominal prices to fall and restore aggregate demand.

However, we have not solved for a continuum of aggregate demand equilibrium recessions, but have shown the two equilibrium case—in the model, there is a certain probability *ex ante* that full employment will occur at Q^+ (which can, with due care for the switch to a monopolistically competitive economy, be associated with the earlier neoclassical equilibrium Q^*) and a certain probability that equilibrium will occur at the recession level Q^-. The possible level of Q^- (and any possibility that there may be more than one such equilibrium recession level) depends, following our analysis, upon all the factors entering into firm optimisation decisions—the degree of risk-aversion, the elasticity of demand for the various products, and so on. Importantly, however, only a certain number of Qs (again, we have only shown two) are possible as equilibria and, further, they are possible only because *ex ante* they have probabilities other than unity. This means that the *IS–LM* apparatus must be used with care. It is still the case that the analysis behind that approach is valid, and an equilibrium output level must occur at the intersection of the *IS* and *LM* curves. But while that intersection need not be at the unique neoclassical output equilibrium, it cannot be at any arbitrary level as in the traditional Keynesian analysis.

This is an important change from standard Keynesianism, and emphasises expectations and transition paths. Nothing in the analysis suggests that it is correct to say that a fall in the nominal money supply will lead to the recession at Q^- rather than a fall in the price level; a similar statement can be made about a fall in intended investment or a 'contractionary' fiscal policy. Rather, statements must be predicated in the form: 'if firms expect P to remain constant, then a fall in the nominal money supply can lead to a recession'. This is made clear by considering what happens when M falls such that, if P remains constant, the intersection of the *IS* and *LM* curves occurs to the left of Q^+ but to the right of Q^-. Some other factor must cause the curves to shift further. There are several possibilities: P could adjust to move the *LM* curve to the left or right to cause an intersection at either Q^+ or Q^-; investment might shift depending upon expectations of the future (as in our discussion in Ch. 3); or any of the other factors underlying the *IS* and *LM* curves. Expectations in this sense become paramount in the model. Further, the transition paths, the intermediate dynamics such as discussed in Chapter 3 for the notion of interest-rate rigidity due to unintended investment, achieve a major importance, although we will not attempt to further develop this in the book. What happens in the short run very much determines the eventually obtained equilibrium. This enhanced role for expectations and transition paths is in fact much more reminiscent of the *General Theory* than later Keynesian analyses. Further, it incorporates what has been perhaps the major contribution of the new classical macroeconomics—the notion that expectations about nominal prices and inflation affect the outcomes of various shocks and policies. Interestingly, this is very neoclassical in the sense of the accelerationist arguments about the instability of the Phillips curve, that agents' expectations about inflation determine the outcome; where we have generalised from the neoclassical model is that we no longer have a natural rate outcome, but rather there are effects on equilibrium real national output and upon unemployment.

With the important proviso about expectations, however, government policies can still have a major effect on the real economy. A suitable increase in the real money supply, or an increase in government expenditure that is not expected to be inflationary (so that the *IS* curve shifts but not the *LM*), will cause the intersection of the *IS* and *LM* curves to shift from Q^- to Q^+, and thereby restore full employment to the economy. Further, the model stands up to the rational expectations critique. That is, if the government adopts a stabilisation policy of always expanding the economy through monetary or fiscal measures to maintain Q^+, all that happens is that agents change their *ex ante* probabilities of a recession to zero and of full employment to unity. But then the optimal contracts include only the one possibility, the full employment possibility.

This issue of expectations and transition paths represents the major area in which the current approach must be extended. We have modelled our contracts to specify the firm's behaviour in equilibrium positions only. Clearly, proper contracts, including transitional periods, must specify the firm's behaviour over the whole range of possible temporary outcomes. This might then, by constructing a reaction function over the whole range of possible aggregate demand levels, explain the dynamics as firms for certain aggregate demand levels seek to increase production and thereby are lowering prices, and for others are seeking to cut back production and thereby raising prices. Similarly, we have not discussed the basis for the expected probabilities of a recession of full-employment, π^+ and π^-. These might, for example, be based upon observation of historical data, that recessions occur π^- of the time.

While these areas represent the direction in which the model should be extended, there is a weakness in the model that needs some further development. The asymmetric information approach as specified, where workers cannot observe an aggregate recession and therefore contracts cannot be written contingently upon the state of aggregate demand, is not entirely plausible. Why can't workers observe a recession and thereby accept the need to cut wages, without the firm itself cutting production? There are a number of possible answers to this. One is that firms are differentially affected by the fall in aggregate demand so that workers in a particular firm await evidence that their firm is actually in financial difficulties. Another possibility is that, taking account of contracts defined over all transitional levels of aggregate demand, the information problem gains additional plausibility; that is, workers may observe an aggregate recession but not know quite how bad it is and therefore how much they should accept real wage cuts. Related to this is the problem about the duration of a recession—the firm might more easily determine whether a recession is temporary and therefore can be ignored from its financial position or whether the downturn will continue for an extended period and require financial stringency including wage reductions. Nonetheless, this remains a weakness in the analysis that requires further work.

There are two additional points that we should note about the equilibrium-recession approach, suggested by recent neoclassical arguments. The first refers to arguments that high unemployment is caused by excessively high real-wage rates, workers 'pricing themselves out of jobs'. Interestingly, our model (unlike, for example, the staggered contracts approach in Ch. 9) has real wages falling in a recession not rising; the problem in the recession is not high real wages but rather a lack of aggregate demand. It might nonetheless be argued that our effects depend upon firms convincing workers to accept the fall in real wages (at least, relative to productivity) and that the recession might be avoided if the real wage cuts were encouraged by government. On the one hand, this raises the problem of how to effect such cuts; typically in the UK, those cuts have pertained predominantly to public rather than private sector employees and therefore had only an indirect (if any) effect on firms' desired production levels. But even if such cuts could be effected by mandatory laws, it is not clear that they are desirable in a longer-term context. From our discussion in Chapter 8 about the inefficiencies that arise in a search labour market (and, because of the heterogeneity of workers and jobs, among other reasons, the labour market really must be a search market of some sort), even limited contracting is desirable to affect proper labour mobility. Government intervention in effect provides further limitations on contracting (that the government may declare the contract void), and would therefore have deleterious longer-term effects.

The other recent neoclassical argument has been about 'supply-side' effects. One of the advantages of our approach is that it can readily incorporate such 'supply-side' effects as well as demand effects. That is, beyond the notion of expectations or government policy creating a recession, a downturn in economic activity might also be due to such factors as an oil price shock or an upturn to such phenomena as tax-incentive effects. In our modelling to this point, we have supposed that labour was the only factor of production, but we could easily add capital (and relevant interest charges) and raw materials, and incorporate the role of taxation. For example, suppose that oil is an input into the production process, and firms have *ex ante* expectations about the probabilities of different oil prices. This changes our earlier, Figure 10.1a diagram in that a firm of given risk-aversion will have differing reaction curves depending upon the *ex post* oil price. Even if there was no equilibrium recession at the lowest oil price (i.e. the reaction curve intersects the 45-degree line only at full employment), a large increase could shift down the reaction curve and in that way allow for an equilibrium recession. That such traditional neoclassical factors continue to have a role in the eventual equilibrium should not be surprising, since we have entirely based our model upon optimisation factors which must include all the neoclassical influences as well as the Keynesian one, aggregate demand anticipations.

10.6   CONCLUSIONS

This book has had three major aims: to clarify the distinctions between the Keynesian and the neoclassical models; to examine the search and contracting models and their macroeconomic implications; and to consider the nature of a more hopeful approach to developing a proper macroeconomic theory.

The generalisation of economic theory contained in the *General Theory* was to allow aggregate output to become a variable in the system. A change in 'entrepreneurial spirits' or 'business confidence', a change in monetary policy or a change in government fiscal policy might all have effects on aggregate output rather than just price effects. In the process, the change might well create involuntary unemployment where there are qualified unemployed, willing to work at the going real wage, who cannot locate jobs. Allowing for aggregate fluctuations requires two changes to the neoclassical model of the economy. Agents must take account of the possibility of aggregate output changes and how it affects their own optimal behaviour, in making their decisions. Thus the theory of investment must consider expectations of aggregate demand in determining whether a given machine will be profitable. But, more directly, a macroeconomic theory of business fluctuations requires a new method of solving for equilibrium, one where aggregate output as well as the price level is a variable. To some extent this was provided by the *IS–LM* apparatus and its adjunct, the Phillips curve. Depending upon the extent to which the nominal price level adjusts to a change in the economic environment, aggregate output might vary. Which will occur (price or quantity adjustment) in response to, for example, a monetary shock, is unclear from the static theory, and the study of dynamic transition paths, such as the Phillips curve, might provide the answer.

The traditional Keynesian theory, however, cannot avoid the fundamental neoclassical argument that any underproduction equilibrium fails a simple rationality test: if there are unsold goods, why don't prices fall and, through a real-balance mechanism, restore aggregate demand? This is a valid objection and should not be answered with such Keynesian claims as: 'but surely, in the short run, prices are sticky' or 'of course, nominal wages can't fall and that limits price falls'. The monetarists in the 1970s focused on a true problem with Keynesian analysis that became clear during that period when high inflation was coincident with high unemployment—the Phillips curve, or nominal price rigidities in general, no longer provided even an apparently adequate answer to the neoclassical objection to Keynesian theory. It is precisely this issue that we have tried to address in this last chapter of the book with our model of equilibrium recessions. Our answer is that contracting (and we can justify the use of contracting by reference to the imperfections of a search labour market) *ex ante* limits firms' optimal responses *ex post*, and in particular, a fall in aggregate demand can be sustained as firms cut back their production in proportion to the fall. Nominal prices don't fall because it is not in firms' interests to attempt to increase their share of the market by lowering prices. This is not the same as assuming a nominal wage or price rigidity; rather we observe from our modelling that the neoclassical adjustment process is *not*, in this specification of the economy, the result obtained from individual agents' optimisation processes.

It is important to understand how our approach derives from contracting, and in particular that it does not follow the original contracting models which did not incorporate Keynesian macroeconomic implications. We noted in Part I that the two major features of a Keynesian equilibrium—low output and involuntary unemployment—are separate and logically distinct. Even if there is a low-output Keynesian equilibrium, wages can fall and remove involuntary unemployment as workers voluntarily depart from the workforce. Of course, on usual economic welfare grounds, there is no reason to find the voluntary nature of low employment (sustained by low wages) particularly desirable—if the level of employment is fixed, and all potential workers are identical with the same disutility of work, it does not really matter on economic grounds whether low employment is sustained by involuntary redundancies or by lowering wages to the point where workers voluntarily quit. That is simply a distribution of income issue that is beyond the judgment power of economists. The efficient contracting models, of Chapter 7, simply carried this aggregate result to the level of an individual optimising firm. A firm can either lower wages or use involuntary redundancies to decrease its workforce in those outcomes where it faces low demand for its product. If it follows the former strategy, it will have to pay compensatingly higher wages in good times to recruit workers, and the average result over time is the same. In this sense the contracting story is successful in explaining involuntary lay-offs (although the later literature in this area argues that lay-off compensation payments may usefully be introduced so that a laid-off worker is just indifferent to that status) and in explaining real wage rigidity. What it doesn't explain is why the neoclassical adjustment process to a fall in aggregate demand doesn't occur. The problem in particular is that an efficient contract of the sort in Chapter 7 leads firms, if anything, to overemploy and overproduce, and the neoclassical adjustment process would be amplified, not eliminated. To see this, take the specification of labour supply that we adopted in this chapter, where there was a fixed labour supply with a zero disutility of work. In the efficient contract models, even if a monopolistically competitive firm anticipated a fall in aggregate demand and thus in the demand for its own product, but the marginal revenue product of labour remained positive (if small), the optimal contract would always contain full employment—in terms of our formalisation, the 'reaction curve' of such a firm would be the horizontal line at Q^+/F, and there could never be an equilibrium recession.

A later contracting approach, the asymmetric information contracting approach, is necessary for this. That approach argues that firms are risk-averse, perhaps because they need a certain level of cash-flow to avoid bankruptcy, and therefore in bad outcomes need to lower wages to maintain profitability at a minimum level. However, workers can only be convinced that times are truly bad, and therefore that they should occur to negotiate wage 'give-backs', if the firm demonstrates this to them convincingly; that is, if the firm meets the 'truth-telling conditions'. A firm therefore closes a number of factories and cuts production (inefficiently, relative to a full-information world or one in which the firm is risk-neutral) to make its case. From this, if the firm anticipates a recession, and the demand for its product falls, the resulting reaction curve can lead firms in the aggregate to in effect ratify the fall in aggregate demand by cutting their own production and income of their workers and shareholders. As an empirical story, this is not implausible. As a recession begins, due to supply-side, business confidence, or government policy measures, firm profits decline sharply and firms engage in production cutbacks to save cash-flow. Since labour costs are the major component of expenditures, profits recover only when wages fall or more usually grow at a slower rate (often falling in real terms; certainly falling relative to productivity).

The major difficulty in applying the model is that all evaluations of the effects of exogenous shocks or government policies depend upon the expectations of the agents in the economy. An 'expansionary' fiscal or monetary policy only operates positively upon real variables if it is expected to be non-inflationary. This again takes us to the issue of transition paths and the dynamics of the system, including the theory of inflation, all features of the economy that we have not really encompassed in our discussion in this book. If we have developed an optimisation-based model which uses contracting to explain the involuntary nature of redundancies and the possibility of excessive redundancies leading to sustained equilibrium recessions, this is merely the rudiment of a proper Keynesian generalisation of neoclassical theory. What it does give us is the basis for developing a fuller theory, founded on full optimisation including (through the monopolistic competitive nature of the modelled economy) endogenous price-setting. Developing this model, the transition paths consistent with it, and the full implications for inflation as well as unemployment, will be an extended task.

Throughout the book, we have accepted the fundamental Keynesian observation—recessions occur and last for an extended period of time, are driven by falls in aggregate demand and lead to involuntary unemployment. We have also, however, accepted the premises of neoclassical methodology—economic results are based upon optimising behaviour of individual agents, appropriately aggregated into equilibrium phenomena. This forces us to jettison some of the post-war Keynesian apparatus. We cannot, to be consistent with principles of optimisation behaviour, assume nominal rigidities or irrational expectations. The Phillips curve did shift about in the 1970s, for precisely the reasons of inflationary expectations argued by the monetarists. Our argument is that the nominal rigidities, and the Phillips curve, were never a necessary part of the Keynesian model, but that such a model could be based entirely on real behaviour. We have in effect accepted the Keynesian model without the adjunct Phillips curve and the nominal price aggregate supply curve favoured by textbooks. While we cannot claim to have provided a full theory of Keynesian behaviour, the approach in this chapter should hopefully convince the reader that such a model is possible and suggest the directions for its further development.

Besides the equilibrium recession model of Keynesian behaviour, we have covered a number of important issues that we shall now summarise in concluding the book. The unifying principle of Part II has been the theory of unemployment, in both neoclassical and Keynesian formats, as developed over the last twenty years. The first point is that unemployment is not necessarily undesirable or economically inefficient. As discussed in Chapter 6, unemployment can be useful if it is part of an efficient process in which workers are temporarily unemployed while moving from one job to another with a higher productivity. In an economy with job opportunities shifting from one sector to another in response to demand and supply changes, workers efficiently move between the sectors. This mobility may take time, either due to the time necessary to move from one location to another or due to the need to gather information or training for alternative job opportunities. This is one basis for defining an efficient rate of unemployment for an economy, and economists have an interest in examining whether the economy actually achieves this level and what policies, microeconomic or macroeconomic, might facilitate its attainment.

There is another sort of unemployment that is efficient, but in a sense it is less interesting since it is not clear that it should be characterised as unemployment at all. In the simple neoclassical labour market not all the potential workforce will be employed, since the actual labour supply comes about as potential workers compare their disutility of work (utility of leisure) to the market real wage in deciding whether to become a participant in the labour force and supply their labour. If the leisure value gained by not working exceeds the marginal product of the worker, it is efficient that he should not be employed. Generally, we have ignored this sort of 'unemployment' since it does not correspond to standard measures of unemployment (these individuals are not seeking jobs) and is not the unemployment of interest in macroeconomic discussions. Where it perhaps becomes relevant is in discussions of fiscal policy issues as the 'poverty trap', where at low wages there is an incentive for individuals not to work due to a 'distortionary' government tax-and-benefits system. Where we have examined it in this book is in the context of contracting models, but there it achieves a greater importance due to assumptions of immobility that we will discuss below.

Given a mobility basis for efficient unemployment, we next ask whether the market achieves this level. One way of formulating the market system is the search model, either the competitive search model in Chapter 6 or the monopsonistic search of Chapter 8. Here firms make wage offers to the unemployed applicants, who then either accept the job-offer or continue to search, remaining temporarily unemployed. The monopsonistic search model makes the interesting point that the labour market might well suffer a microeconomic market failure due to this monopoly power, a market failure that is reflected in inefficiently low unemployment as workers do not gain the full return to shifting jobs, and therefore display an inefficiently low level of mobility across sectors. That sort of microeconomic inefficiency is subject to the usual microeconomic policy tools of fiscal incentives; for example, an unemployment compensation scheme would encourage unemployment (job mobility) to raise it to the efficient rate. This result is important in that unemployment compensation tends to be viewed, incorrectly, as always being a method for redistributing income at the cost of economic efficiency, when in fact it may lead to greater economic efficiency.

More interesting for our purposes, however, are the possibilities of 'macroeconomic market failures' creating inefficiently high unemployment. One approach to this was the Lucas expectational-errors model in Chapter 6. Workers were unable to distinguish perfectly between monetary shocks creating a general inflation and sectoral productivity or demand shocks—given that efficient unemployment arises due to mobility to higher productivity jobs, unemployment due to a general inflation would be inefficient, while that due to sectoral shocks would be desirable. If workers are unable to distinguish whether their relative wage has gone down or whether it is just their nominal wage falling (relative to expectations) in a period of generally low inflation, they may incorrectly quit their current job and be temporarily unemployed in excess numbers. That the inflation must be 'unexpectedly' low is important and underlies the 'policy ineffectiveness' result of this rational-expectations literature. There is no long-run Phillips curve trade-off, but a variance in the money supply can lead to periods with unexpectedly high or low inflation and thus unemployment. Indeed, one can extend the model somewhat beyond this to provide a potential role for government stabilisation policies. If the unexpectedly low inflation is due, for example, to a leftward shift in the *IS* curve leading to a fall in *P* to restore aggregate demand, this would nonetheless lead to excess temporary unemployment. But if the government has an 'informational advantage' and observes the shift in the *IS* curve and expands the money supply to compensate, *P* does not change and therefore the high unemployment does not occur. The Lucas model is interesting in that it goes some way towards explaining differential observed unemployment rates over time, and even in providing a mechanism for an activist stabilisation policy. The major difficulty lies in the plausibility of the mechanism. The whole process depends on workers being unable to observe the price level in the economy, and therefore their real (or relative, rather than nominal) wage before deciding whether to voluntarily quit their current job and accept temporary unemployment while looking for a, hopefully, better-paid job.

This raises a further problem with the whole search approach— the unemployment is all voluntary as workers, disappointed with their current wage, voluntarily quit to seek a better job. Simple observation indicates that most job separations into unemployment, rather than into a job already arranged by on-the-job search, occur through involuntary redundancies. It is here that contracting theory, as discussed in Chapter 7, begins to make its first contribution to our analysis. The contracting models in that chapter, referred to as the efficient contracting models, basically replicate the results of the Chapter 6 search story, but change the mechanism. The argument is that a risk-neutral firm, hiring risk-neutral workers before it knows the actual state of demand or productivity in its sector, will pay the same total wages on average (and thereby gain the same expected profits) whether it fixes its real wage over the various environments it might face or whether it adopts a varying wage strategy. If it fixes the real wage, any reduction in the workforce is effected through involuntary lay-offs. However, and it is a vital point, unemployment remains at the efficient level discussed in Chapter 6. This then shows that the issues of the involuntary nature of unemployment, and the Keynesian macro-model, are not inextricably linked—the efficient contracting model explains involuntary unemployment, but it remains at the efficient rate. Finally in this context, we examined the role of trade unions and saw that there was no particular reason to expect employment to differ whether the contracting was of an implicit or explicit nature with individuals, or whether it was with trade unions—there is no particular reason to think that trade unions create inefficient unemployment.

To this point in the analysis, we had two models—search and contracting—that gave the same results, but differed in mechanism, in whether the unemployment generated occurred through voluntary quits or involuntary redundancies. This is of course one reason that the contracting analysis has greater plausibility. But in Chapter 8 we had a constructive argument as to why contracting arises in the labour market, as search markets tend to collapse into monopsonistic outcomes where firms have an excess demand for labour that can be recruited only when they make commitments. If the efficient contracts of Chapter 7 are available to firms, these are ideal; if they are not, for reasons we have discussed in Chapter 9, the best available contracts still arise as firms find it in their interest to make those commitments to recruit workers.

Why might the fully-efficient contracts of Chapter 7 be untenable? The predominant answer in the literature is the asymmetric information problem: a contract is unenforceable if it is written as being conditional upon events that are unobservable to one of the parties; that is, if one of the parties cannot ascertain whether or not the contract is being carried out. Now suppose that the actual environment faced by the firm *ex post* is unobservable to workers and therefore contingent (upon the environment) contracts are not feasible. The firm can then only vary wages and employment in response to a change in environment if it meets the truth-telling conditions, that workers know from the construction of the contract that the firm will always choose the condition appropriate to the particular environmental outcome. When the firm is risk-averse, but workers risk-neutral, this leads to a contract where there is full employment in the good outcome but inefficiently high unemployment in the bad outcome. Of course, this is not necessarily a Keynesian result, since it is in the first instance a partial equilibrium result that merely describes unemployment at a particular firm facing a bad environment. It can be turned into a general equilibrium result in the sense in Chapter 6, that if the environmental uncertainty represents relative sectoral price changes, the asymmetric information contract economy leads to a higher average unemployment rate than is efficient (although one must be careful about the second-best optimal nature of these contracts—even though the unemployment rate differs from the full information solution, it is not immediate that there is a government policy that increases economic welfare if the government does not have an information advantage). But again this is not a Keynesian result but a microeconomic implication.

The first attempt to turn this type of model into a macroeconomic model was the staggered-contracts approach. Take an extreme version of the asymmetric information argument, where we assume that in fact contracts with employment commitments of any sort are infeasible, so the firm can only make commitments about wage rates, real or nominal. We will have a world with two types of aggregate shocks, real productivity (that affect each firm equally) and monetary (that in the first instance affect only the nominal price level). If firms commit themselves to a fixed real wage over the outcomes, it will generally be the case that a sufficient fall in real productivity will cause lay-offs in the absence of employment commitments, and we are not allowing such commitments. This can be avoided, for a subtle reason deriving from the specification of the model, by a contract specified in nominal wage terms. If real productivity falls in the aggregate, but the nominal money supply is unchanged, the nominal price level rises; if the nominal wage rate is unchanging, this lowers the real wage in accord with the fall in productivity, maintaining the firm's desired employment level. The problem with such a nominal contract is that the monetary shocks dictate, to maintain employment, a contract specified in real terms—if the real wage is fixed, monetary shocks will change only nominal values as in the original neoclassical neutrality results. In general in this environment, the optimal contract is a partial-indexation contract that causes employment to fall with a negative real productivity shock or a negative monetary shock. Through a very clever argument, nominal values are introduced into the optimal (restricted) contracting, and have the 'Keynesian' results common to nominal rigidities.

Yet we ultimately rejected this approach to Keynesian economics. The first problem we observed was that the model exactly replicated the implications of the Lucas expectational-errors process; that is, unemployment varied only with unexpected changes in inflation, thus maintaining the rational-expectations policy-ineffectiveness result. For the same reasons as in the Lucas approach, however, if the government had an information advantage, it could use this in a 'discretionary' monetary policy to offset real shocks and stabilise the economy. Where the model was improved over the Lucas approach was in two ways: the model has somewhat greater plausibility since agents are allowed to observe the rate of inflation in the economy (although they cannot tell whether a particular rate derives from productivity falls or from a monetary expansion); second, job losses occur through lay-offs rather than voluntary quits, due to the partial rigidity of the real wage. The major problem with the model, however, is the following. All the employment effects arise due to the real wage being too high for the particular environment, and nowhere in the model is there a major role for aggregate demand. The driving force of the approach is the real productivity shocks; to mitigate the impact of these, contracts are written that allow money to have non-neutral properties. But for a proper Keynesian model, we want to restore the impact of aggregate demand, to have firms cut employment and output when they feel a decline in the demand for their product due to a fall in aggregate demand. It is this Keynesian mechanism that is missing from the staggered-contracts approach and that we have attempted to restore in our equilibrium-recession model.

We have already in this section evaluated that model and its attempted contributions. The primary emphasis of that approach is to return to the real analysis of the *General Theory*, where a fall in real aggregate demand causes a decline in employment and output in the economy. That outcome is an equilibrium *ex post* and thereby avoids the neoclassical real-balance adjustment process; at the low level of aggregate output, income and demand, firms have no incentive to increase their production and sales—they have no incentive to lower prices and the real-balance effects are never set in motion. The economy remains in the equilibrium recession. As in the *General Theory*, the recession can be caused by numerous factors: a decline in business or consumer confidence ('animal spirits'); by a decline in investment opportunities; by a restrictive fiscal or monetary policy; or by real declines in productivity. And as the recession occurs, it can be cured by government fiscal and monetary policy. It is important to note, however, that the occurrence of the recession depends not just upon the driving event as listed above, but upon expectations that the recession will continue; if firms expect that a fall in aggregate demand is only temporary, they will instead lower their prices and the neoclassical adjustment will occur. Similarly, a government expansionary policy will only cure the recession if it is expected to be effective; otherwise, firms may expect the policy only to increase inflation, and will raise their prices rather than output. The answer to the question about price *versus* quantity adjustment that we raised in Chapter 5, at this stage in our analysis, is simple yet perhaps disturbing—the adjustment that occurs depends upon expectations about which adjustment will occur.

If our approach is very traditional Keynesian theory in respect to the role for expectations and animal spirits, it is also very traditional in giving up some of the later Keynesian adjuncts. We have largely accepted the neoclassical arguments against nominal rigidities and the accelerationist argument against the Phillips curve—there is no clear basis in the current approach for an inflation–unemployment trade-off. Inflation, although we have not examined it concretely, would seem to depend largely upon expectations, as in the accelerationist approach. Then, depending upon monetary growth and the expected rate of inflation, monetary policy is expansionary or contractionary. Incomes policies and price controls seem to have their place in changing inflationary expectations. The whole notion of a pragmatic and careful government policy, taking full account of expectations, seems to be validated in preference to the strict determinism of the post-war Keynesian analysis.

We began this book by rejecting the neoclassical macroeconomic model for its empirically absurd insistence that recessions could not occur and that government macroeconomic policy largely did not matter, and by rejecting the post-war Keynesian synthesis of aggregate demand and the Phillips curve based upon some notion of nominal price and wage rigidity. We do not claim to have provided a complete alternative model, but rather have intended to show the progress that can be made by remaining within the traditional methodology of economics and yet accepting the empirical realities as the objects for explanation.

Further Reading

2. THE LABOUR MARKET

Keynes (1936) and Pigou (1933) present the two fundamental, alternative models of unemployment.

3. THE LOANABLE FUNDS MARKET

Post-Keynesian theories of consumption appear in Farrell (1959) and Samuelson (1958), while Barro (1974) discusses the Ricardian equivalence proposition. Eisner and Strotz (1963) and Gould (1968) develop the adjustment-cost model of investment. Hicks (1937) introduces the *IS–LM* apparatus, while the notion of the Wicksellian process due to an excessively high interest rate is in Wicksell (1946).

4. THE MONEY MARKET

The new theory of money was developed in Hicks (1935) and Keynes (1936), with further examination of the transactions demand for cash in Baumol (1952) and Tobin (1956); the speculative demand for money was formalised in Tobin (1958). Friedman (1958) integrates the new theory of money into the quantity equation model, while Friedman (1970) and Tobin (Sept./Oct. 1972) clarify the fundamental differences in Keynesian and monetarist views. Real-balance effects are discussed in Patinkin (1965) and Gurley and Shaw (1960), where the distinction between inside and outside money is made. The role of inflation in the theory of money is introduced in Mundell (1963) and Tobin (1965).

5. PRICE AND QUANTITY ADJUSTMENT

The fixed-price model was introduced by Barro and Grossman (1971), following suggestions by Clower (1965) and Leijonhufvud (1968). A related approach is Solow and Stiglitz (1968). The Phillips curve is presented in Phillips (1958), and Lipsey (1960), with a general survey of inflation theory in Bronfenbrenner and Holtzman (1968). The UV curve was developed from Beveridge (1944) in Dow and Dicks-Mireaux (1958), Hansen (1970), Holt and David (1966), with related later discussion in Barron (1975), Frank (1982), Iwai (1974), Pissarides (1978), and Seater (1979). Friedman (1968) and Tobin (Mar. 1972) present contrasting views on inflation and natural rate of unemployment models, Friedman introducing the 'expectational errors' approach to the Phillips curve and Tobin the sectoral wage-floors model, further analysed in Ratner and Frank (1982).

6. SEARCH EQUILIBRIUM

The basic source for search models is Phelps *et al.* (1970). The competitive search model, and its properties, is discussed in Lucas and Prescott (1974), with further discussion in Prescott (1974). Rational expectations was introduced by Muth (1961) and is used by Lucas in his critique (1972) and in the equilibrium business cycle (1975). The policy-ineffectiveness result is discussed as well in Barro (1976; Mar. 1977) and Sargent and Wallace (1975). Taylor (1975) discusses transition paths in a rational-expectations environment, while Buiter (1980) argues that the policy-ineffectiveness result depends upon the model of the economy. For a further discussion of the various efficiency results in this and following chapters, see Frank (1985).

7. THE CONTRACTING MODEL

The model was introduced by Azariadis (1975) and Baily (1974), with Baily (1977) considering the case of risk-neutrality. Oi (1962) provided an early argument about treating labour as a non-variable factor of production. Feldstein (1976) argues that temporary lay-offs are an important feature of the economy. Further discussion of basic contracting models appears in Grossman and Hart (1981) and Holmstrom (1981). For a general discussion of trade unions, see Oswald (1982; 1983) and McDonald and Solow (1981); Minford (1983) emphasises the role of trade unions in creating unemployment. Frank (forthcoming) considers the issue of union membership size and how trade unions might actually lead to overemployment in an industry.

8. SEARCH AND INEFFICIENCY

The basic model here is the dynamic monopsony search model as in Mortensen (1970). Inefficiency within this model was noted by Diamond (1981; Apr. 1982) and Pissarides (1984). A model which adds firm-specific information to the search process is Salop (1973).

9. CONTRACTS AND INEFFICIENCY

The asymmetric information idea originated with Calvo and Phelps (1977), and was developed in Grossman and Hart (1981), Hart (1983), and in the *Quarterly Journal of Economics* supplement introduced by Azariadis and Stiglitz (1983). Hall and Lilien (1979) discuss a case where the problem is solvable without inefficiency. The staggered-contracts approach derives from Fischer (1977) and Gray (1976); Barro (July 1977) argues against these models on the grounds that they represent suboptimal contracting.

10. EQUILIBRIUM RECESSIONS

The market coordination problem is discussed in Diamond (Oct. 1982; 1984). Hart (1982) examines whether Keynesian results can be derived from a monopolistically competitive framework, while Weitzman (1982) explores the role of increasing returns. Cooper and John (1985) provide an excellent discussion of the trade coordination literature. Additional efforts to gain macroeconomic results in the asymmetric information framework include Farmer (1984) and Grossman, Hart, and Maskin (1983).

Bibliography

Akerlof, G. and H. Miyazaki, 'The implicit Contract Theory of Unemployment Meets the Wage Bill Argument', *Review of Economic Studies*, 47 (Feb. 1980), 321–38

Azariadis, C., 'Implicit Contracts and Underemployment Equilibria', *Journal of Political Economy*, 83 (Dec. 1975), 1183–262

—— and J. Stiglitz, 'Implicit Contracts and Fixed-Price Equilibria', Introduction to the supplement to the *Quarterly Journal of Economics*, 98 (1983), 1–22

Baily, M.N., 'Wages and Employment under Uncertain Demand', *Review of Economic Studies*, 41 (Jan. 1974), 37–50

—— 'On the Theory of Layoffs and Unemployment', *Econometrica*, 45 (Sept. 1977), 1043–63

Barro, R.J., 'Are Government Bonds Net Wealth?', *Journal of Political Economy*, 82 (Nov./Dec. 1974), 1095–118

—— 'Rational Expectations and the Role of Monetary Policy', *Journal of Monetary Economics*, 2 (Jan. 1976), 1095–117

—— 'Unanticipated Money Growth and Unemployment in the United States', *American Economic Review*, 67 (Mar. 1977), 101–15

—— 'Long-Term Contracting, Sticky Prices and Monetary Policy', *Journal of Monetary Economics*, 3 (July 1977), 305–16

—— 'Unanticipated Money, Output and the Price Level in the United States', *Journal of Political Economy*, 86 (Aug. 1978), 549–80

—— and H. Grossman, 'A General Disequilibrium Model of Income and Employment', *American Economic Review*, 61 (Mar. 1971), 82–93

Barron, J., 'Search in the Labor Market and the Duration of Unemployment', *American Economic Review*, 65 (Dec. 1975), 934–42

273

Baumol, W.J., 'The Transactions Demand for Cash: An Inventory Theoretic Approach', *Quarterly Journal of Economics*, 66 (Nov. 1952), 545–56

Beveridge, W., *Full Employment in a Free Society*, London, Allen and Unwin, 1944

Bronfenbrenner, M. and F.D. Holtzman, 'A Survey of Inflation Theory', *American Economic Review*, 58 (Sept. 1968), 593–661

Buiter, W.H. 'The Macroeconomics of Dr Pangloss: A Critical Survey of the New Classical Macroeconomics', *The Economic Journal*, 90 (Mar. 1980), 34–50

Calvo, G. and E. Phelps, 'Employment Contingent Wage Contracts', in K. Brunner and A. Meltzer, eds., *Stabilization of the Domestic and International Economy*, supplement to the *Journal of Monetary Economics*, 1977, 160–8

Clower, R.W., 'The Keynesian Counter-Revolution: A Theoretical Appraisal', in F. Hahn and F. Brechling, eds., *The Theory of Interest Rates*, London, St Martin's Press, 1965

Cooper, R. and A. John, 'Coordinating Coordination Failures in Keynesian Models', *Cowles Foundation Discussion Paper* #745, April 1985

Diamond, P., 'National Debt in a Neoclassical Growth Model', *American Economic Review*, 55 (Dec. 1965), 1127–56

—— 'Mobility Costs, Frictional Unemployment and Efficiency', *Journal of Political Economy*, 89 (Aug. 1981), 798–812

—— 'Wage Determination and Efficiency in Search Equilibrium', *Review of Economic Studies*, 49 (April 1982), 217–27

—— 'Aggregate Demand Management in Search Equilibrium', *Journal of Political Economy*, 90 (Oct. 1982), 881–94

—— 'Money in Search Equilibrium', *Econometrica*, 52 (Jan. 1984), 1–20

Dornbusch, R., 'Expectations and Exchange Rate Dynamics', *Journal of Political Economy*, 84 (Dec. 1976), 1161–76

Dow, J. and L. Dicks-Mireaux, 'The Excess Demand for Labour', *Oxford Economic Papers*, NS 10 (Feb. 1958), 1–33

Eisner, R. and R.H. Strotz, 'Determinants of Business Investment', in Commission on Money and Credit, *Impacts of Monetary Policy*, London, Prentice-Hall, 1963

Farmer, R.E.A., 'A New Theory of Aggregate Supply', *American Economic Review*, 74 (Dec. 1984), 920–30

Farrell, M.J., 'The New Theories of the Consumption Function', *The Economic Journal*, 69 (Dec. 1959), 678–96

Feldstein, M., 'Temporary Layoffs in the Theory of Unemployment', *Journal of Political Economy*, 84 (Oct. 1976), 937–58

Fischer, S., 'Long-Term Contracts, Rational Expectations and the Optimal Money Growth Rule', *Journal of Political Economy*, 85 (Feb. 1977), 191–205

Fisher, I., *The Purchasing Power of Money*, New York, Macmillan, 1920

Frank, J., 'Heterogeneous Labor and Implicit Contracts', *Economics Letters*, 6 (1980), 185–90

—— 'A Keynesian Model of Search and Labor Market Disequilibrium', *Journal of Macroeconomics*, 4 (Summer 1982), 293–308

—— 'Uncertain Vacancies and Unemployment Equilibria', *Journal of Economic Theory*, 30 (June 1983), 115–38

—— 'Search and Contracting—Efficiency and Inefficiency', *Oxford Economic Papers*, 37 (Mar. 1985), 72–82

—— 'Trade Union Efficiency and Overemployment under Seniority Wage Scales', *The Economic Journal*, forthcoming

Friedman, M., 'The Quantity Theory of Money: A Restatement', in *Studies in the Quantity Theory of Money*, Chicago, University of Chicago Press, 1958

—— 'The Role of Monetary Policy', *American Economic Review*, 58 (Mar. 1968), 1–17

—— 'A Theoretical Framework for Monetary Analysis', *Journal of Political Economy*, 78 (Mar./Apr. 1970), 193–238

Galbraith, J.K., 'Market Structure and Stabilisation Policy', *Review of Economics and Statistics*, 39 (May 1957), 124–33

Gould, J.P., 'Adjustment Costs in the Theory of Investment of the Firm', *Review of Economic Studies*, 35 (Jan. 1968), 47–66

Gurley, J. and E.S. Shaw, *Money in a Theory of Finance*, Washington, Brookings, 1960

Gray, J., 'Wage Indexation: A Macroeconomic Approach', *Journal of Monetary Economics*, 2 (Apr. 1976), 221–35

Grossman, S. and O. Hart, 'Implicit Contracts, Moral Hazard and Unemployment', *American Economic Review*, 71 (May 1981), 301–7

—— and E. Maskin, 'Unemployment with Observable Aggregate Shocks', *Journal of Political Economy*, 91 (Dec. 1983), 907–28

Hansen, B., 'Excess Demand, Unemployment, Vacancies and Wages', *Quarterly Journal of Economics*, 84 (Feb. 1970), 1–23

Hall, R. and D. Lilien, 'Efficient Contracts under Uncertain Supply and Demand', *American Economic Review*, 69 (Dec. 1979), 868–79

Hart, O., 'A Model of Imperfect Competition with Keynesian Features', *Quarterly Journal of Economics*, 97 (Feb. 1982), 109–38

—— 'Optimal Labour Contracts under Asymmetric Information: An Introduction', *Review of Economic Studies*, 50 (Jan. 1983), 3–36

Hicks, J.R., 'A Suggestion for Simplifying the Theory of Money', *Economica*, 2 (Feb. 1935), 1–19

—— 'Mr Keynes and the Classics', *Econometrica*, 5 (Apr. 1937), 147–59

—— *Critical Essays in Monetary Theory*, Oxford, Clarendon Press, 1967

Holt, C. and M. David, 'The Concept of Job Vacancies in a Dynamic Theory of the Labor Market', in *The Measurement and Interpretation of Job Vacancies*, New York, The National Bureau of Economic Research, Columbia University Press, 1966

Holmstrom, B., 'Contractual Models of the Labor Market', *American Economic Review*, 71 (May 1981), 308–13

Holzman, F.D., 'Income Determination in Open Inflation', *Review of Economics and Statistics*, 32 (May 1950), 150–8

Iwai, K., 'The Firm in Uncertain Markets and its Price, Wage and Employment Adjustments', *Review of Economic Studies*, 41 (Apr. 1974), 257–76

Keynes, J.M., *The General Theory of Employment, Interest and Money*, London, Macmillan, 1936

Leijonhufvud, A., *On Keynesian Economics and the Economics of Keynes*, London, Oxford University Press, 1968

Lipsey, R.G., 'The Relation Between Unemployment and the Rate of Change of Money Wage Rates in the United Kingdom 1862–1957: A Further Analysis', *Economica*, 27 (Feb. 1960), 1–31

Lucas, R.E., 'Econometric Testing of the Natural Rate Hypothesis', in *The Econometrics of Price Determination*, Federal Reserve Board, 1972

—— 'Some International Evidence on Output-Inflation Tradeoffs', *American Economic Review*, 63 (June 1973), 326–34

—— 'An Equilibrium Model of the Business Cycle', *Journal of Political Economy*, 83 (Dec. 1975), 1113–44

—— and E. Prescott, 'Equilibrium Search and Unemployment', *Journal of Economic Theory*, 7 (Feb. 1974), 1113–44

—— and L. Rapping, 'Real Wages, Employment, and Inflation', *Journal of Political Economy*, 77 (Sept./Oct. 1969), 721–54

McDonald, I.M. and R.M. Solow, 'Wage Bargaining and Employment', *American Economic Review*, 71 (Dec. 1981), 896–908

Minford, P., 'Labour Market Equilibrium in an Open Economy', *Oxford Economic Papers*, supplement to vol. 35 (Nov. 1983), 207–44

Mortensen, D., 'A Theory of Wage and Employment Dynamics', in E. Phelps *et al.*

Mundell, R.A., 'Inflation and the Real Rate of Interest', *Journal of Political Economy*, 71 (June 1963), 280–3

Muth, J.F., 'Rational Expectations and the Theory of Price Movements', *Econometrica*, 29 (July 1961), 315–35

Oi, W., 'Labor as a Quasi-Fixed Factor of Production', *Journal of Political Economy*, 70 (Dec. 1962), 538–55

Oswald, A.J., 'The Microeconomic Theory of the Trade Union', *The Economic Journal*, 92 (Sept. 1982), 576–95

—— , 'The Economic Theory of Trade Unions: An Introductory Survey', Institute of Economics and Statistics, Oxford, July 1983

Patinkin, D., *Money, Interest and Prices*, 2nd edn, New York, Harper and Row, 1965

Phelps, E., 'Money-Wage Dynamics and Labor-Market Equilibrium', in Phelps *et al.*

—— *et al.*, eds., *Microeconomic Foundations of Employment and Inflation Theory*, New York, Norton, 1970

Phillips, A.W., 'The Relation Between Unemployment and the Rate of Change of Money Wage Rates in the United Kingdom 1862–1957', *Economica*, 25 (Nov. 1958), 283–99

Pigou, A., *The Theory of Unemployment*, London, Macmillan, 1933

Pissarides, C., 'The Role of Relative Wages and Excess Demand in the Sectoral Flow of Labour', *Review of Economic Studies*, 45 (Oct. 1978), 453–67

—— 'Efficient Job Rejection', *The Economic Journal*, supplement to Volume 94 (1984), 97–108

Prescott, E., 'Efficiency of the Natural Rate', *Journal of Political Economy*, 83 (Dec. 1974), 1229–36

Ratner, J. and J. Frank, 'Sectoral Labor Markets, The Long-Run Phillips Curve, and Implicit Contracts', *Eastern Economic Journal*, 8 (Apr. 1982), 127–36

Salop, S., 'Systematic Job Search and Unemployment', *Review of Economic Studies*, 40 (Apr. 1973), 191–201

Samuelson, P.A., 'An Exact Consumption-Loan Model of Interest with or without the Social Contrivance of Money', *Journal of Political Economy*, 66 (Dec. 1958), 467–82

Sargent, T.J. and N. Wallace, 'Rational Expectations, the

Optimal Monetary Instrument and the Optimal Money Supply Rule', *Journal of Political Economy*, 83 (Apr. 1975), 241–54

Seater, J., 'Job Search and Vacancy Contracts', *American Economic Review*, 69 (June 1979), 411–19

Solow, R. and J. Stiglitz, 'Output, Employment and Wages in the Short Run', *Quarterly Journal of Economics*, 82 (Nov. 1968), 537–60

Taylor, J.B., 'Monetary Policy During a Transition to Rational Expectations', *Journal of Political Economy*, 83 (Oct. 1975), 1009–21

Tobin, J., 'A Dynamic Aggregative Model', *Journal of Political Economy*, 63 (Apr. 1955), 103–15

—— 'The Interest Elasticity of Transactions Demand for Cash', *Review of Economics and Statistics*, 38 (Aug. 1956), 241–7

—— 'Liquidity Preference as Behaviour Towards Risk', *Review of Economic Studies*, 25 (Feb. 1958), 65–86

—— 'Money and Economic Growth', *Econometrica*, 33 (Oct. 1965), 671–84

—— 'A General Equilibrium Approach to Monetary Theory', *Journal of Money, Credit and Banking*, 1 (1969), 15–29

—— 'Inflation and Unemployment', *American Economic Review*, 62 (Mar. 1972), 1–18

—— 'Friedman's Theoretical Framework', *Journal of Political Economy*, 80 (Sept./Oct. 1972), 852–63

Weitzman, M., 'Increasing Returns and the Foundations of Unemployment Theory', *The Economic Journal*, 92 (Dec. 1982), 787–804

Wicksell, K., *Lectures on Political Economy*, London, Routledge, 1946

Index